Management Accounting
in the
Public Sector

Published in association
with the Chartered
Institute of Management
Accountants

Management Accounting
in the
Public Sector

Edited by
MAURICE W. PENDLEBURY

Heinemann Professional Publishing

Heinemann Professional Publishing Ltd
Halley Court, Jordan Hill, Oxford OX2 8EJ

OXFORD LONDON MELBOURNE AUCKLAND SINGAPORE
IBADAN NAIROBI GABORONE KINGSTON

First published 1989
Reprinted 1990

British Library Cataloguing in Publication Data
Pendlebury, M. W. (Maurice W.)
Management accounting in the public sector.
1. Great Britain. Public bodies.
Management accounting
I. Title
354.410072'31

ISBN 0 434 91542 4

Photoset by Deltatype Ltd, Ellesmere Port, Cheshire
Printed and bound in Great Britain by
Redwood Burn Limited, Trowbridge, Wiltshire

Contents

Topic 2

TOPIC 2

Contributors

David Allen, is British Rail's Director of Management Accounting, with responsibility for all control systems, both business and production, within the railways. He is a CIMA member and since 1983 his main task has been the development of a radical approach to management information to support the new business (sector) management philosophy adopted by the board.

Philip Andrew is Deputy Director (Administration) of the South Yorkshire Area of British Coal. He read mathematics at Oriel College, Oxford, and spent a postgraduate year studying statistics. He joined British Coal in 1966 and has worked in operational research, opencast executive, audit department and, until recently, was chief accountant for the South Yorkshire Area.

Michael Bourn has been Professor of Accounting at the University of Southampton since 1980, having held chairs previously at the Universities of Liverpool and Canterbury (NZ). He was appointed Deputy Vice-Chancellor in 1986, and foundation Chairman of the Conference of Professors of Accounting in 1987. He is the author or editor of three books, and papers and reviews in many academic and professional journals. His current research interests are in financial and managerial control in health and in education, and in professional education. He is a member of the editorial boards of *Financial Accountability and Management* and *Accounting and Business Research*.

Anthony Cook is lecturer in financial management at the Health Services Management Centre at Birmingham University. He is a CIMA member and has extensive experience of capital investment appraisal in the steel and chemicals industries. He spent 2 years as research officer at the University of Bath, investigating the problems of capital expenditure planning and control in the NHS, and submitted his PhD thesis on the subject.

Desmond Farry is management accountant for Greater Manchester Police, and is responsible for budget preparation and development of costing throughout the force. He is a CIMA member and has previously worked for the Manpower Services Commission. He is a part-time lecturer at Manchester Polytechnic.

Tony Hope is Professor of Accounting at the University of Manchester. His current research interests are in the application of private sector profit measurements to public sector organizations, and in the recruitment procedures of auditing firms. He has published four books on different aspects of introductory accounting.

Rowan Jones is Professor of Public Sector Accounting at the University of Birmingham. He has previously worked in the public sector and his main research interests have been in public sector accounting topics. He obtained his doctorate from the University of Lancaster for a thesis on the financial control function of local government accounting.

Graham Keenleside is currently Bursar of the University of Manchester Institute of Science and Technology (1977 to date). He was formerly management accountant of the University of Liverpool and the University of Salford, with earlier experience in local government and the hospital service. He is a member of CIMA and has a close interest in the development and improvement of university management-accounting practices. He has visited overseas universities in Europe, the USA, Canada and Australia.

Tony Killikelly has spent most of his working life in Customs and Excise. He ran a local VAT office in Manchester for 5 years before moving to London to lead the department's FMI project team from 1983 to 1986. Customs and Excise is acknowledged to be one of the leading exponents of financial management in the civil service.

Linda Kirkham is a chartered accountant and is a lecturer in accounting and finance at the University of Manchester. Her major current research interest is the application of private sector profit measurements to public sector organizations.

David Otley is Professor of Accounting and Finance at the University of Lancaster and chairman of the Management Control Association. He began his working career in the operational research executive of the (then) National Coal Board, but then joined the doctoral programme of the Manchester Business School, where he developed his interest in the behavioural consequences of accounting control systems. The author of two books and numerous articles, he has been at the University of Lancaster since 1972.

Maurice Pendlebury is senior lecturer in accounting and finance at Cardiff Business School, UWIST. He has previously worked in the public sector and his main research interests have been in public sector accounting topics. He obtained his doctorate from the University of Wales for a thesis on management accounting in local government.

Preface

Many definitions of management accounting exist, and although these lack complete agreement, it is possible to detect frequent references to the part management accounting plays in the managerial tasks of planning, decision-making and control. All organizations need to make decisions and need to plan and control their activities, and all organizations, whether they be in the public or the private sector, ought therefore to be able to benefit from the use of management accounting. However, the management accounting literature and the development of the techniques of management accounting are almost exclusively concerned with a private sector environment.

In reality many public services are characterized by a lack of readily measurable outputs, and this has resulted in very little attention being given to the contribution that management accounting might have to offer. In such cases management accounting tends mainly to be restricted to budget preparation and budgetary control, but as the traditional approach to budgeting is to record inputs only and to ignore outputs, this means that very little information is given to managers and decision-makers on the quality and quantity of services provided. Nevertheless, changes are taking place. Examples can now be found of interesting and innovative developments in the use of management accounting, and the main purpose of this book is to provide the opportunity for a selection of these to be discussed and analysed. The intention is not to produce a conventional management accounting text but to give some indication of the important and active role that management accounting currently has to play in public sector management.

My thanks are due to the individual contributors who took the time and effort to put together the chapters that have made this book possible. I must also acknowledge the support of the Chartered Institute of Management Accountants, which not only came up with the idea for a book of this nature but also provided much helpful advice on the content and structure of each chapter.

Maurice W. Pendlebury
Cardiff Business School
UWIST

Introduction

An obvious difficulty facing any discussion of public sector accounting is that of deciding just what it is that distinguishes the public sector from the private sector. Since 1979 the boundary between the two sectors has not only changed significantly but has also become increasingly blurred. However, it is not at the boundary that most of the accounting differences occur. Nationalized industries, for example, do have outputs which are readily measurable in both physical and monetary terms and, although market failure suggests that performance ought to be measured on wider issues than simply the monetary position, the existence of these outputs does mean that a whole range of management accounting techniques are available to assist in decision-making and management control. It is when we move away from the boundary towards the services which are at the very heart of the public sector that the accounting differences become most evident.

The characteristic features of these services are that objectives are often ambiguous, outputs are difficult to measure, market prices are inappropriate, ability to pay should not affect consumption, and a substantial element of social control is necessary. Services exhibiting these features are likely to remain firmly entrenched in the public sector, and yet even here there have been pressures to supplement, wherever possible, the traditional, political and social control procedures with control through market forces. The philosophy which underpins the government's privatization programme, and its determination to expose the public sector to the disciplines of competition and market forces is all part of a belief that what is good for the private sector ought to be good for the public sector. This belief has led to many attempts to introduce private sector practices into public sector management and it could be argued that the increased attention that is being paid to management accounting is just one further example of this trend. This is not to say that management accounting does not already have a role to play in the public sector. It clearly does and yet its role has never been very prominent. Much of the management accounting emphasis has traditionally been associated with the requirements of budget preparation and budgetary control and, important though these requirements are, they have not given rise to a very sophisticated use of management accounting.

Budgets, for example, are typically concerned with inputs only. They serve the purpose of allocating scarce public resources to a variety of different activities, and through the use of detailed expenditure headings it is possible to ensure that authorizations to spend are very specific. Budgetary control is then concerned with ensuring that these detailed authorizations are complied with. This has more to do with the needs of financial accountability and the proper stewardship of public money than with decision-making, planning and control. In a world in which outputs are not measurable it is clear that mainstream management accounting techniques, such as cost–volume–profit analysis or standard costing, are not applicable. Lack of measurable outputs has also led to the demise of such suggested public sector budgeting reforms as planning, programming budgeting systems (PPBS) and zero-base budgeting (ZBB).

However, management accounting still has much to offer. The search for better value for money from public sector services has resulted in several developments aimed at improvements in management that have, at the same time, introduced a requirement for more effective systems of management accounting. For example, the NHS Management Inquiry Report (Griffiths Report, 1983), which recommended the introduction of a 'general management' style of management for the health service, also placed great emphasis on the need for a budget structure which would identify the resources consumed by clinicians in the treatment of their patients, i.e. clinical management budgets. In local government the Local

Government Planning and Land Act, 1980, required the housing repair and construction and the highways maintenance and construction functions of local authorities (i.e. direct labour organizations) to earn a specified rate of return on capital employed. This requirement meant that many local authorities had to revise and improve their management accounting systems for direct labour organizations. For universities the Jarratt Report (1985), which investigated the management and efficiency of universities, made recommendations concerning delegated budget centre responsibility, the information needed from the management accounting system, and the performance indicators which might be used in evaluating efficiency.

In the chapters that follow specific examples of the use of management accounting in different public-sector services are discussed and analysed, and in the course of doing this attention is given to the developments mentioned above. However, before going on to introduce each of the chapters, it might be useful to consider a management accounting initiative that was originally developed for use in central government departments but is now beginning to pervade other areas of the public sector. This is the financial management initiative (FMI).

The original White Paper which contained the details of the FMI (*Efficiency and Effectiveness in the Civil Service*, Cmnd 8616) was published in 1982. The FMI identified the need to produce for each department a system in which managers at all levels have:

(a) a clear view of their objectives; and means to assess, and wherever possible measure, outputs or performance in relation to those objectives;
(b) well-defined responsibility for making the best use of their resources, including a critical scrutiny of output and value for money; and
(c) the information (particularly about costs), the training and the access to expert advice which they need to exercise their responsibilities effectively.

It can be seen from the above that the FMI is a very clear example of an attempt to apply mainstream management accounting practices to central government. All that is needed is to identify budget responsibility and provide information on inputs consumed and outputs achieved. In a private sector setting this would be a very unremarkable system. In central government it represents a very major step forward. It requires objectives to be defined in such a way that achievements against objectives can be measured, it requires budget responsibility to be devolved away from centralized treasury control, and it requires information on costs on a more timely basis than the traditional cash accounting system used in central government.

The initial emphasis concerning the implementation of FMI was on the management of administrative expenditure, and there is evidence that some success has been achieved in this direction. However, the bulk of public expenditure is not on administration but on the specific programmes intended to achieve the policy objectives of the government. This is a much more complex situation because it impinges on policy decisions and also because the responsibility for managing programmes rests not only with government departments but also with a range of other organizations, such as local authorities, public corporations, and other public or voluntary bodies. As the FMI is applied to the management of programme expenditure, so its impact is being felt on these other organizations.

In an attempt to review the progress of the implementation of FMI a study of six central government departments and one non-departmental public sector body was undertaken in 1985. This study resulted in a report (*Multi-Departmental Review of Budgeting: Executive Summary*) which was published by the Treasury in 1986. The report shows that although progress is being made, this is not uniform across all departments. Perhaps the most important aspect of the report, however, is that it demonstrates a continuing commitment to improving financial management, and this is reinforced by the foreword inserted by the Prime Minister which emphasizes the importance attached to the following principles:

1   The responsibility of line managers at all levels for setting and reviewing budgets.
2   The need for close links between budgets and the Public Expenditure Survey.
3   The importance of the measurement and evaluation of output and performance.

4 The involvement of senior management in the allocation of resources and the review of performance.

Whether the objectives of the FMI will ever be fully achieved remains to be seen. Its underlying requirements do suggest that there will be many difficulties along the way, and it is also possible to question whether the true purpose of the FMI is to improve the quality of public sector management or simply to provide a means for cutting costs. Gray and Jenkins (1986), for example, state that 'when considered carefully some of the applications of FMI appear to be mechanisms of financial restraint rather than elements in a programme of strategic management'. They go on to suggest:

> The division of departments into 'businesses' with 'costs' that must be minimised and accounted for by 'managers' reveals a particular view of the world that is input-dominated. It may not, however, greatly assist the design of policy, the assessment of outcomes and the appreciation of customer needs. In fact, amongst all of the official literature of the FMI, policy outcomes are almost never mentioned, while the customer gets at best a passing glance.

Nevertheless, whatever its real purposes might be, the FMI does represent a very important development in the use of management accounting. The traditional belief has always been that the special circumstances of large areas of public sector activity have meant that conventional mainstream management accounting techniques are of little relevance. The importance of the FMI is that it has, for the first time ever, subjected this traditional belief to a very direct and persistent challenge, and whatever the final outcome might be, it is clear that it has already had a significant impact on the control of central government departments and on those public sector organizations closely connected with them.

The contributions that have been included in this book provide examples of management accounting developments in a wide range of public sector bodies. A very broad view of the role and nature of management accounting has been taken, and a particular requirement for each chapter was for attention to be given to recent initiatives. The intention was that this volume should not consist entirely of contributions from academic researchers, on the one hand, or from practitioners, on the other, but should attempt to achieve some balance between the two. Therefore, of the chapters that follow, some are the work of 'insiders' writing about their own organization and some are based on the work of external researchers. The aim has not been to produce a conventional management accounting text but to provide, from the few examples selected, some indication of the broad range of management accounting applications and practices that are currently used in public sector management.

The first chapter, by Rowan Jones and Maurice W. Pendlebury, examines the education service of local government. This service currently faces the prospect of far-reaching changes, and Jones and Pendlebury contrast one of the proposals for change, i.e. the devolution of the financial management of schools to the headmaster and governors of each school, with the more traditional practice of centralized finance department/education department control of spending.

In Chapter 2 Desmond Farry considers the role of management accounting in the police service and provides examples drawn from Greater Manchester Police of budgetary-control systems and cost control and cost reduction initiatives.

The third chapter, by Tony Hope and Linda Kirkham, is also on local government, but on this occasion attention is turned to uses of management accounting in direct-labour organizations. In particular the chapter discusses the impact of different organizational structures on the types of management accounting systems used by particular direct-labour organizations.

In Chapter 4 David Allen outlines the organizational structure and the planning and control requirement of British Rail and then focuses attention on the controversial issue of accounting for common costs. British Rail consists of five separate business sectors, but infrastructure and other facilities are shared jointly by all sectors. The chapter discusses the five different methods that have been attempted over the years for attributing infrastructure costs to the different business sectors.

Chapter 5, by Philip Andrew and David Otley, examines the accountability and control arrangements used by a specific coal-producing Area of British Coal. The coal industry is characterized by inherent uncertainty and variability in mining activity. To some extent it operates as a monopoly supplier to a monopsonist buyer, and it needs to balance the achievement of current productive output with the work required to ensure future production. All this imposes specific requirements on the management accounting system, and this chapter concentrates on the management accounting information used by Area staff in managing colliery activities.

In Chapter 6 attention is turned to management accounting in universities. Graham Keenleside describes the special features of the university environment and the uses to which management accounting information is put. A case study based on the approach adopted by UMIST its presented to examine how the management requirements of policy formulation, decision-taking, implementation, control and review and remedial action might be undertaken.

Chapters 7 and 8 are both concerned with the National Health Service. Chapter 7, by Michael Bourn, considers the resource allocation and planning practices for health service recurrent expenditure. Some of the recent developments in health service financial management, such as clinical budgeting, management budgeting and the use of performance indicators are also discussed and evaluated. Chapter 8, by Anthony Cook, looks at capital accounting in the NHS and focuses attention on the three management accounting issues of investment appraisal in the NHS, the financial control of capital spending, and charging for the use of capital in the management accounts of a district health authority.

Finally, Chapter 9 considers the central government department of Customs and Excise. Tony Killikelly explains how, following on from the requirements of the FMI, Customs and Excise has developed a system of management control for the collection of VAT which sets measurable output targets and reports on actual performance against target.

Reference

Gray, A. and Jenkins, W. I. (1986). Accountable Management in British Central Government: Some Reflections on the Financial Management Initiative. *Financial Accountability and Management*, 2, No. 3, Autumn, 171–86.

1 Management accounting in local government – the education service

Rowan Jones and Maurice W. Pendlebury

Introduction

The precise role and nature of management accounting in local government is far from clear. The mainstream accounting literature would suggest that management accounting has an important contribution to make to what Anthony (1965) describes as 'Management Control', i.e. 'the process by which managers assure that resources are obtained and used effectively and efficiently in the accomplishment of the organisation's objectives', and 'operational control', i.e. 'the process of assuring that specific tasks were carried out effectively and efficiently'. The development of management accounting and its techniques has largely assumed a business environment in which objectives are determinable and achievements against objectives are measurable. However, in the case of local government the vast bulk of expenditure is on services for which objectives can only be agreed upon if they are framed in very broad and imprecise terms and in which accomplishments are difficult to measure. Attempts to go beyond trivial statements, such as that the basic objective of the education service is to 'provide education', quickly run into trouble.

More detailed objectives could be expressed in many ways: to enable individuals to pass exams, learn social life skills, lead full and happy lives, maximize their earning power, contribute to the needs of society and so on. These objectives might overlap or they might be contradictory and it is unlikely that complete agreement about the emphasis to be attached to each objective could ever be reached.

Even   , it is unlikely that the actual achievement of many of
these   could be measured in neutral, value-free terms.
Under   nstances the appropriate management model for
the contr   rmance and achievement is 'political', or at best
'judgemen

The cont ution of management accounting, at least in its
traditional form, has therefore been restricted to the control of
inputs. Thus the major accounting emphasis is directed at budget
preparation and budgetary control, with the purpose of ensuring
budgetary compliance. Budgets allocate scarce public resources to a
variety of different activities, and through the use of detailed
expenditure headings it is possible to ensure that authorizations to
spend are very specific. An important aspect of the financial
accountability model of local government has been for financial
accounts to show actual spending against the detailed authorizations contained in the budget, thereby drawing attention to
budgetary compliance. Although local authorities have in recent
years begun to produce financial reports which no longer emphasize
this link between budget and actual, the internal accounting records
still reflect the traditional relationship.

Budget preparation and budgetary control are therefore heavily
influenced by the requirements of financial accountability. Indeed
Pendlebury and Jones (1985) develop the argument that because of
(1) the requirement in UK local government for balanced budgets,
(2) the existence of revenue constraints, and (3) the tax-determin-
ation role of the budget, budgeting means primarily 'ex ante'
financial accounting. All this has meant that the local government
accounting literature is quite different from its mainstream counter-
part. There is no equivalent to the very many standard
management accounting texts which dominate the latter, and in fact
the use of the expression 'management accounting' occurs much less
frequently. Discussions of this particular aspect of accounting are
often found under such headings as 'financial administration',
'financial management', 'financial control' or simply 'management
control'.

This is not to say that examples of how the routine, mechanistic,
almost cybernetic control techniques of management accounting
might be used in local government cannot be found. Direct labour
organizations (DLOs) carry out activities with measurable outputs

and are now required to operate profitably and earn a specified rate of return or face closure (see Chapter 3). Even within the education service there are activities such as school meals, maintenance of playing fields and grounds, cleaning services, etc., for which objectives are clearer and performance is more easily measurable. Nevertheless, it is the 'soft' services and activities which dominate, and by far the most important of these is that of education. In 1984–5 expenditure on education amounted to over £13,000 million out of a total expenditure on rate fund services by English local authorities of £32,275 million.[2] Moreover, education is facing some of its most radical and far-reaching changes since the 1944 Education Act. The next section to this chapter provides a brief background to the education service and discusses the nature of some of the proposed changes. This is then followed by a section on the traditional approach to management control, and the final section considers the implications for management accounting of one of the proposed changes, i.e. the devolution of the financial management of schools to the schools themselves.

A brief background to the education service

It was not until the nineteenth century that the state's responsibility for the provision of education became significant. Before this time education was mainly in the hands of the church and voluntary bodies, and much of their effort was directed at elementary education. Although the Elementary Education Act, 1870, recognized the principle that elementary education was a state responsibility, there was still a substantial dependence on voluntary effort.

Local Education Authorities (LEAs) were first established under the Education Act, 1902. The LEAs were the counties and county boroughs of the day and they had the power to provide both elementary and higher education. The emphasis, however, was firmly on elementary education, and it was not until the Education Act, 1944, that the distinction between elementary and higher education was abolished and the now familiar categories of primary, secondary and further education were introduced. The 1944 Act has remained the most important development in creating a national system of education and it is still the principal act governing the provision of education in England and Wales. Among other things the Act created the Ministry of Education, with the responsibility for directing national education policy; it made it a duty of every LEA to ensure that sufficient primary and secondary schools are available for its area; it specified the duties of LEAs with regard to the provision of further education and leisure time occupation; it defined the compulsory school age (then any age between 5 and 15 years); and it required LEAs to appoint a chief education officer.

Since 1944 there have been many amendments and modifications to the public sector education service. In 1968, for example, an Education Act provided for polytechnics to be constituted and a further Act in 1968 introduced the establishment of comprehensive schools. The principle of comprehensive education was confirmed under the provisions of the Education Act, 1976, but these were then repealed by the Education Act, 1979, and it is now not compulsory for LEAs to adhere to a system of comprehensive education. The Education Act, 1980, confirmed the principle of parental preference as to choice of schools and created an appeal mechanism for dissatisfied parents. This Act also introduced an assisted places scheme to enable pupils to attend independent schools and made significant changes to the school meals service. These changes were made to bring about major economies in the running of the school meals service and included the removal of the duty to provide milk or a meal to pupils (except for free meals to pupils whose parents are in receipt of supplementary benefit or family income supplement). National nutritional standards were no longer to be set and local authorities could charge what they considered to be appropriate for all meals other than those required to be provided free.

However, at the time of writing it seems clear that the next few years are likely to see the introduction of a variety of measures that will bring about a radical change to the nature and structure of public sector education. Most of the measures seem designed to restrict the powers and duties of LEAs. The government has already introduced city technology colleges outside the control of LEAs, and plans to introduce legislation to remove polytechnics and certain other colleges from LEA control. A consultation document has now been issued outlining proposals for a national curriculum with national attainment tests for children at specified ages. A further consultation document proposes that a simple majority of parents, voting in a secret ballot, could lead to their school opting out of local authority control and being administered as a grant-maintained school with funding provided directly by central government.

However, it is a third consultation paper which contains the proposals with the greatest implications for financial management in the education service. These proposals relate to financial delegation to schools by which the money available for running each school, excluding certain centrally determined items such as debt charges, central administration etc, would be allocated by the LEA to the school in the form of a delegated budget. Subject to certain statutory duties and minimum standards being met, the manager (head-master) and governors of the school would then be able to spend the delegated budget at their discretion. Several LEAs have experimented with such a scheme and the experience of one of these, Cambridgeshire, is examined later in this chapter.

The traditional role of management accounting

In local government there are no legal requirements referring specifically to management accounting but there are requirements concerning financial administration. Thus, for example, section 151 of the Local Government Act, 1972, requires that 'every local authority shall make proper arrangements for the administration of their financial affairs and shall secure that one of their officers has responsibility for the administration of those affairs'. CIPFA (*FIS*, Vol. 9) believes that this confirms the importance of the chief financial officer's contribution to management control, and states that 'the accounting, financial administration and financial control systems of a local authority shall be the specific responsibility of an officer – a chief financial officer – who shall maintain the integrity of the financial administration and control system'. The precise nature of the relation between the chief financial officer's department and other departments is likely to vary from authority to authority and would be very difficult to capture. Even so, the chief financial officers' role as 'guardians of the public purse' does mean that they will almost invariably have a significant role to play in the design and implementation of management control systems. The discussion that follows in this section is based on the results of interviews with both the senior finance department staff and education department staff of several local authorities.

Management accounting and budgeting

One of the principal means of securing sound financial management in local government is through the annual budget process. Most of the authoritative reference works in local government recognize the importance of the budget. For example, Marshall (1974) states that:

> Local government would be unworkable without the annual budget, the centre piece of the financial year. All departments and most officers participate in its making; and most abide by its contents. It is the most pervasive financial activity . . . Legally its purpose is to fix the rate; managerially it is both a decision making and a control document (p. 73).

Management control systems can of course be both formal and informal. While local authorities undoubtedly make use of informal systems, it is the very obvious, highly formalized process based on the annual budget that tends to dominate.

The reliance on the budget for the purpose of management control might, at first glance, seem perfectly reasonable. After all there is much authoritative support for the planning and control purposes of the budget.[3] However, it must also be recognized that the annual budget suffers from major weaknesses as a planning document. A one-year budgetary cycle is generally accepted to be too short a time horizon for effective planning; in addition, annual budgets tend to be incremental in nature and are analysed in a line item format, which reveals the nature of the expenditure (e.g. wages, supplies etc) rather than the purpose of the expenditure (e.g. science education). Several suggestions have been put forward to overcome these weaknesses, ranging from the very radical to those that are more modest and therefore more easily attainable.

The more radical reforms are based on what is often described as a 'rational model' of decision-making, and examples include planning, programming, budgeting systems (PPBS) and zero-base budgeting (ZBB).[4] In the UK, although these approaches have been discussed extensively, very few serious attempts to apply them have ever been made and even in the USA examples of their successful implementation are rare. The causes leading to the widespread failure of PPBS and ZBB have been analysed at length and it is generally agreed that one of the principal reasons is that economically rational models of control are totally inappropriate for activities and services for which political or judgemental control models are required.

One of the more obvious of the modest reforms might be to attempt to overcome the limitations caused by the annual budget's preoccupation with the short term by introducing a longer-term planning perspective. Thus the annual budget would represent the most immediate stage of a continuous process of short-, medium- and long-term planning. A further reform might be to adopt the philosophy of reviewing base budgets from time to time without actually introducing a formal ZBB system. In a recent questionnaire survey of the actual budget preparation practices of local authorities Pendlebury (1985) found that less than 20 percent of the respondents prepared detailed medium-term financial plans on a regular basis and over 60 percent never undertook such an exercise. Thus the annual budget, in spite of its limitations, does tend to dominate forward planning.

The survey by Pendlebury did find evidence of a readiness to review base budgets, with almost 50 percent of the respondents indicating that the base element of the budget was subject to some sort of review. This was supported by the findings from our interviews. Although in no cases had a formal 'decision-package' approach to ZBB been attempted, all the respondents claimed to make some attempt at a priority review of the base budget. For example, the practice of one county council can be described as follows. In previous years, about May or June, the chief officers had been asked for 1 percent, or 2 percent or 3 percent savings to be identified. When this had first been done 4 or 5 years ago, it had proved to be a useful exercise, but more recently chief officers had responded by suggesting the same savings as in the previous year, knowing that they would be politically unacceptable. For the most recent year a small group of officers at assistant chief officer level had been formed into a budget advisory group, and each department had been asked for a 15 percent cut in budget. The choice of 15 percent was quite arbitrary and was based on a general feeling that the statutory requirement to provide minimum levels of service would take about 85 percent of the current budget figure. In addition to identifying savings of 15 percent, each chief officer was then requested to reinstate the savings in priority terms. In other words, the individual items making up the 15 percent were to be ranked. Although these priority rankings were not always accepted by the political leaders of the county council when formulating budget strategy, the exercise was thought to have been extremely useful, because it forced service managers to think carefully about the relative importance of the different activities that made up their service.

The importance of the annual budget lies of course in its central role in financial control. The budget determines how much can be spent by each service, and it is usual for the standing orders of a local authority to include specific rules prohibiting expenditure in excess of the budget. Whereas responsibility for ensuring budgetary compliance usually rests with the spending departments, it is generally accepted that the finance department has a responsibility to supply the basic budgetary control information. The survey by Pendlebury (1985) found that the most widespread method of providing information on actual expenditure to date was from detailed 'hard copy' tabulations issued by finance departments, which formed the basis of the formal budgetary control system. But the survey found that they frequently suffered from obvious defects: they lacked timeliness, the absence of profiling prevented variance analysis, they failed to distinguish between controllable/non-controllable items, and they ignored non-financial output measures.

We might have expected these defects to be a major cause for concern, but discussions with senior finance staff revealed that budgetary control and budgetary compliance were seen to be achieved not so much through the formal budgetary control systems but through informal but frequent contact between finance department staff and spending department staff throughout the budget year. The finance department's role is seen to be of great importance, for the department initiates the annual budget preparation process, lays down the ground rules for preparing budgets, understands the complexities of the grant process, knows the latest position on actual spending against budget, authorises virement, and so on. The position is well summarized by the following observations of a senior finance department official with many years' experience in local government:

What we have may not be very scientific but it works. It works because everybody knows the danger areas in their budgets and these are closely checked by my staff and by the (spending departments') finance officers. If someone really wanted to overspend they could – and it wouldn't be detected until it's too late. But that doesn't happen. Everyone respects the need to keep to budget. I still get 'phone calls asking if its OK to spend on something; sometimes its because they need to vire but often it's in the budget anyway. I suppose we still do expect the overall budget to be underspent, or only slightly overspent.

One reason for the underspending can be seen from an examination of the budgetary-control process for the education department of the same authority. The examination also reveals how the ability to be 'in charge' of the budget strengthens the power and importance of individuals or departments.

In the first place the district education office for each of the four regional divisions of the education department built up the budget request in line with the finance department guidelines. However, for most of the significant items, such as teaching and non-teaching salaries (about 70 percent of the total budget), the calculations were left to the finance department, which also calculated the amounts for heating, ground maintenance, debt charges and central administration costs. The district offices built up the relatively small proportion that was left of the total budget request in terms of November prices, a fairly usual practice in local government, but the finance department then converted these into estimated outturn prices. This meant that the district offices were left with budget figures they did not understand but because they were usually higher than their own calculations were happy to accept. All of this reinforced the importance of the finance department. When allocating the capitation element of budgets to individual schools (i.e. the amount for books, equipment etc, allocated to individual schools on the basis of school population), the district offices tended to keep something back for contingencies. However, the finance officer in the education department had included a global contingency element when allocating the budget between nursery, primary and secondary education etc, and this natural tendency to keep something back to deal with unexpected events tended to lead to underspending in practice. The finance department limited its control of actual spending to the fairly high level of aggregation of 'sub-division of service'. In other words, it was only concerned with the control of the level of expenditure for nursery education, primary education, secondary education and further education, the detailed control of districts and of individual schools being the responsibility of the education department.

The budget document and the philosophy of budget discipline was at the heart of the district offices' control process. The ability to be able to say 'if there is nothing left in the budget you can't spend any more' enabled them to resist requests for spending and at the same time the possibility of being able to 'find something extra from somewhere' gave them increased importance. Cooper (1981) suggests that 'order may be achieved in organisations not so much by formal rules but by an elaborate system of shared meanings: an organisational culture' and goes on to state that 'ritual, magic and myths offer some of the means by which organisational cultures are sustained'. In our example of the education department the budget can be seen to be very much a part of the 'ritual, magic and myths'. The budget is in effect a record of organizational history. For services where outputs are traditionally never subjected to any precise form of measurement the financial inputs included in the budget are the only 'hard' measurements that are available. Changes in the level of inputs are frequently equated with changes in the level of service. The budget provides the common language and framework for obtaining a negotiated agreement on the allocation of financial inputs. Once it becomes accepted, it is important for the maintenance of the organizational culture that the budget is adhered to.

The example described above is typical of a traditional centralized approach to the financial management of the education service. The finance department deals with budget preparation and control. The education department employs a qualified accountant as finance officer, thus tending to reinforce the centralized control, and although much of the detailed work is delegated to district offices, the schools' role is very limited. In many local authorities the control of the capitation element of the budget is delegated to the schools, but in our example even this was a district-office function. This is in very distinct contrast to the totally decentralized system of devolved financial management for schools discussed later in this chapter.

Management accounting and costing

It was pointed out previously that although the bulk of education spending is on the 'soft' services, there are activities whose outputs are more easily measurable and for which routine, mechanistic control models might be appropriate. Examples are ground maintenance, cleaning and school meals. For all of these it would be possible to prepare a budget showing operating costs against expected output, and this would enable targets to be set, with variances from target being investigated and corrective action taken where necessary. In practice ground maintenance and cleaning are rarely controlled in this way and tend to be dealt with as part of the general education budget. It remains to be seen whether current proposals to make competitive tendering compulsory for these activities will cause this to change.

One service that does make some use of costing techniques is that of school meals. Many local authorities have introduced cafeteria-style catering for their secondary and some primary schools and, since the Education Act, 1980, removed many of the requirements and restrictions on the school-meals service, the opportunity to run the service as a profit centre has arisen. As with most local government activities, the costing emphasis is largely ex-post and related to the preparation of unit costs. As a control mechanism, this is of limited use, but it does permit comparisons to be made. One of the local authorities we examined had recently been the subject of a report that drew attention to its higher than average costs of provisions per meal and employee costs per meal, and the reasons for this were being investigated.

If the service is to be run as a profit centre, however, there is need for some measure of rate of return which can also be used as a target. Many authorities do now use this approach. The problem is in choosing the appropriate rate of return. Revenue expressed as a percentage return against full cost might be achieved at the expense of inferior provisions, and the more usual ratio is revenue as a percentage of provision costs. The target has to be set as a matter of policy because of the need to reflect a reasonable balance of financial and nutritional requirements. In one of the authorities we examined the finance department had had to take on the task of preparing the rate of return data. This was done on a termly basis but it was clear that there was much scepticism about the benefits the exercise provided, because there were so many variables that could be offered as an excuse for not achieving the target. In fact scepticism over the relevance of costing is not unusual among local government accountants. One assistant chief financial officer put it this way:

> I've seen many fashions come and go and costing is one of them. There was a time when we costed just about every lamp post. Then we realised that nobody ever looked at most of it so after reorganisation a lot of it got forgotten. Now the fashion seems to be moving towards costing again. We can do it but I'd like to be sure it was going to be used properly.

An obvious problem in the public sector is in providing incentives. Where rewards are tied to performance, there is an incentive to monitor costs and rates of return, and there is a demand for the information to enable this to be done. The local government accounting profession has to convince itself of the benefits of cost-accounting information before it can begin to explain the benefits of such information to others, and encourage its use.

Devolved financial management

The traditional approach to financial management in the education service is for budget preparation and budgetary control to be highly centralized. Several authorities, however, have been experimenting in recent years with a scheme of devolved financial management which gives schools much greater control over their own budgets. Cambridgeshire Education Authority, for example, introduced a pilot scheme in 1981 in which seven volunteer schools (six secondary and one primary) were given a hitherto unprecedented amount of responsibility for budgetary control. The pilot scheme became known as the Local Financial Management (LFM) initiative, and comprised delegating to each school headmaster and body of school governors the responsibility for control of over 75 percent of the budgeted cost of running the school. The budget items that came within the LFM scheme were the following:

1   Staffing (teachers, supply teachers, ancillary staff, caretakers and cleaners).
2   Rent, rates and fuel.
3   Capitation (books, equipment, examination fees, postage, telephones, stationery, furniture).

4 Staff travelling and advertising.
5 Community education.
6 Income.

The school governors and headmaster were given the power to transfer amounts between budget heads, provided that the total budget for the school was not exceeded and overspending and underspending were permitted to be carried forward from one year to the next. Not only does this give greater flexibility in the planning and incurring of expenditure but it also overcomes one of the perennial behavioural problems that affects traditional approaches to budgeting, i.e. the rush to use up the budget before the end of the year so as to avoid losing the current allocation and also to avoid the possibility of the budget being cut in later years. The only items that were controlled centrally by the education/finance department and excluded from the LFM were the following:

1 Transport (home to school), school meals, playing-field maintenance, insurance and debt charges.
2 Costs of education officers, and school inspectors.
3 Reorganization and redundancy costs.
4 Supply cover for long-term absences.

The governing bodies of each of the seven schools in the pilot scheme found it essential to delegate responsibility for LFM to a sub-committee. Although the precise composition of the sub-committees varied from school to school, the membership in all cases consisted of the headmaster plus representatives of both staff and governors.

In 1985 Cambridgeshire County Council took the decision to extend the LFM pilot scheme to all its forty-six secondary schools and to develop a new pilot scheme for eleven primary schools. The extended scheme came into effect on 1 April 1987. Under the original pilot scheme, budget allocations were built up in the traditional way, i.e. the starting point was the historically determined base for each detailed budget line item, which was then adjusted for known and expected changes and price increases to arrive at the revised budget figure. Such an approach clearly offered the potential for arguments about the fairness of a system dependent on past spending patterns, and under the extended LFM scheme a cash-limited total budget allocation is to be made to each school, with responsibility for constructing detailed budget allocations resting with schools. The simplest and most easily understandable system of allocating cash to schools is to use a formula approach based on age-weighted pupil numbers, but this can then be criticized for failing to take account of the special needs and circumstances of individual schools. Cambridgeshire has adopted a formula based on pupil numbers, but other bases for the formula, such as curriculum-led staffing needs, are also being considered.

After several years of experimenting with the scheme Cambridgeshire County Council can point to many benefits, as the following comment from their entry in the CIPFA/Arthur Anderson Financial Management Compendium (CIPFA, 1986) shows:

> The LFM system provides an ideal framework in which local managers, the Heads and Governors of Schools, can set clear objectives for the management of their establishments. The scheme gives considerable freedom to these managers to determine an allocation of resources to secure the best delivery of educational facilities in their school. The system recognises that local managers should have freedom to respond to local circumstances and needs, albeit within the overall policy parameters and in accordance with the broad objectives of the Authority (p. 149).

The LFM scheme clearly offers other advantages as well: freedom from the traditional constraint of end-of-year cut-off and the ability to carry forward underspending and overspending permits planning for longer periods than the traditional annual budget period; it provides the flexibility to respond quickly to local 'crises'; the increased responsibility should lead to improvements in the quality and participation of school governors; and it follows the sound management principle of permitting decisions to be taken by those most affected by them.

A further potential benefit of LFM is its contribution to value for money. There is an obvious incentive to avoid waste and extravagance on items such as heating and lighting if the savings are going to have a direct and identifiable advantage to the school, an often-cited benefit of the Cambridgeshire scheme. The philosophy of achieving better use and control of public resources through devolved management responsibility can be found throughout the public sector. Devolved financial management is the flavour of the month, and under such circumstances it is not surprising to find much attention being given to highlighting its benefits. However, it is not without its costs. In Cambridgeshire many of the pilot-scheme schools found it necessary to employ full or part-time help to handle the extra work load and there was also an increase in central education department costs, owing to the extra monitoring and inspection requirements.

If LFM is to work properly, it also requires regular, accurate and timely budgetary control information to be provided, and this may result in further costs to some local authorities. Cambridgeshire (see CIPFA, 1986) produces monthly reports for each school, giving the following information for each detailed line item expenditure heading:

1 Revised total budgets updated monthly for inflation to date.
2 Expected expenditure or income for the month to date generated from computerized expenditure profiles.
3 Actual expenditure or income to date.
4 Variations between expected and actual.

A monthly printout shows the source document supporting each debit or credit that has been incurred against each line item, and another printout gives details of staff on the payroll.

As part of the government's proposals to introduce devolved financial management for all education authorities, attempts are now being made to produce a financial reporting model for all schools. Adapting existing systems to comply with the new model will add to costs. The government sees a role for the internal audit departments of local authorities in auditing the budgets of individual schools,[5] and there will also be a need to train school headmasters in both financial and general management skills – adding more to the costs of the scheme.

The experience of Cambridgeshire, and others, will undoubtedly be of great value in any extension of decentralized management of schools within state education. Not the least valuable will be the lessons learned in developing the new accounting information systems.

However, it is also important to realize that the principles of management accounting in the public sector have not fundamentally progressed in all this. Financial management may or may not be more efficient or more effective in a decentralized system, but the essential problem of how better to understand the relation between input and output in education is no nearer solution. Partly because of this, we suspect that LEAs will tend to adopt a 'cash limits' system of financial control. An individual school receives a budget from the centre based on a chosen formula, for example, and the headmaster/mistress is told to manage within that cash limit. As has been increasingly pointed out in the context of the central government's cash limits system, this is not so much an attempt by the centre to solve the management problems of government as to avoid them – by passing them lower down the hierarchy. Moreover, the prognosis for better management accounting in local government is not too good. The private sector literature is well versed in the problems of budgeting and control of cost centres. A very broad conclusion might be that the best solution is to avoid having cost centres, by creating as many profit or investment centres as possible!

Perhaps, at bottom, the same thoughts lie behind decentralizing the management of schools: the creation of cost centres is simply a step along the way to an education service where state schools compete with each other and with independent schools, as profit centres. Until that time, however, we assume it is the task of management accountants in the education service, as in much of the rest of local government, to find better ways of providing information for efficient and effective management in the still-public sector.

Notes

1 Hofstede (1981) produces a typology for the management control of not-for-profit activities which shows that when the objectives of the activity are ambiguous and its outputs non-measurable, then the appropriate control model is 'political' control. If the ambiguity can be resolved but outputs remain non-measurable, i.e. acceptable surrogate measures cannot be found, then the appropriate control model is 'judgemental' control.

2 Source, *Local Government Financial Statistics England 1984/85* (1986). London: HMSO, Table 2.

3 See, for example, Schick (1966) and Friedman (1981, p. 99).

4 For a more detailed explanation of the concept and development of PPBS and ZBB see Jones and Pendlebury (1984), Chapters 4 and 5.
5 Pendlebury and Jones (1985) argue, among other things, that the central role of the budget in the financial control of local authorities supports a case for all budgets, not just those of schools, being audited.

References

Anthony, R. N. (1965). *Planning and Control Systems: A Framework for Analysis.* Graduate School of Business, Harvard.

CIPFA. *Financial Information Service*, Volume 9, *Financial Administration.* Multi-volumed, regularly updated manual.

CIPFA/Arthur Anderson & Co. (1986). *Financial Management Compendium 1986.* CIPFA.

Cooper, D. (1981). A Social and Organisational View of Management Accounting. In *Essays in British Accounting Research* (Bromwich, M. and Hopwood, A. G., eds.), pp. 178–205, Pitman.

Friedman, L. (1981). Budgeting. In *Management Policies in Local Government Finance* (Aronson, J. R. and Schwartz, E., eds.). International City Management Association.

Hofstede, G. (1981). Management Control of Public and Not-For-Profit Activities. *Accounting, Organisations and Society*, 6, No. 3, 193–211.

Jones, R. and Pendlebury, M. (1984). *Public Sector Accounting.* Pitman.

Marshall, A. H. (1974). *Financial Management in Local Government.* Allen and Unwin.

Pendlebury, M. (1985). *Management Accounting in Local Government.* ICMA.

Pendlebury, M. and Jones, R. (1985). Governmental Budgeting as Ex Ante Financial Accounting: the UK Case. *Journal of Accounting and Public Policy*, Winter, 301–16.

Schick, A. (1966). The Road to PPB. *Public Administration Review*, 26, No. 4, December, 243–58.

2 Management accounting in the police service

Desmond Farry

Introduction

The steady increase in crime over many years has led successive governments and other agencies to consider and implement various means and measures designed to deter and prevent, detect and punish and rehabilitate criminals. The front-line attack in this war against lawlessness is carried by the police service. The growth in the size and importance of the police service can best be illustrated by examining and comparing manpower and expenditure over the last two decades (Table 2.1).

Table 2.1 *Manpower and expenditure 1965–85[1]*

Year	Police officers	Civilian staff	Expenditure net (£m)	Adjusted to constant price level (1980=100)
1965	64,440	15,466	132	776
1975	84,222	27,107	578	1,156
1985	118,623	43,592	2,734	1,925

Such a major and high-profile service is worthy of closer examination and this chapter looks at the evolvement, organization and structure and the budgetary methods used within it, with particular emphasis on the second largest police force in England – Greater Manchester Police.

A brief background to the police service

The current police systems in England and Wales have developed from a series of compromises between conflicting principles and ideas which recognize that there is a balance to be struck between maintenance of law and order without unnecessary restriction on personal freedoms. Historically, maintenance of the peace was seen as a local duty, with forms of policing prevalent from the Middle Ages. The Industrial Revolution proved existing arrangements inadequate, and between the Gordon Riots in 1780 until the Metropolitan Police Act 1829 no less than seventeen parliamentary committees investigated the problem. The Municipal Corporations Act, 1835, established a form of democratic local government and police forces in chartered boroughs. The County Police Act, 1839, made similar arrangements for the county areas. The control of police forces was a source of controversy, and by 1856 some central government control was achieved by making a grant of 50 percent of the cost of running the forces, subject to a report by HM Inspectors of Constabulary (HMIC) on the efficiency of the forces in question.

Under the Police Act, 1946, all but two of the non-county borough forces were merged with their respective county force. After 135 years of public enquiries and Acts of Parliament the Police Act 1964 settled the present format of police forces, the role and status of police officers, and had the main effect of reducing the number of police forces to forty-six in England and Wales. That number was further reduced to forty-three after the Local Government Act, 1972.

Organization of the police service

Police organization today is a partnership between central and local government. Each of the forty-three separate police forces has its own police authority, but there is a considerable degree of co-ordination, both nationally and regionally, through regional crime and drug squads as well as technical support units. The organization of the police service can be split into the following categories:

(a) Police authorities.
(b) The Home Secretary.
(c) Police advisory staff and investigatory bodies.

Police authorities

There are thirty-one county (including former metropolitan county forces) and ten combined forces, in addition to the Metropolitan and City of London forces, each with a police authority. Membership, of the police authority is made up of two-thirds councillors from the constituent areas and one-third magistrates.

The general functions of police authorities are:

1   To secure the maintenance of an adequate and efficient police force for the area.
2   To appoint, subject to the Home Secretary's approval the chief constable and determine the number of officers in each rank.
3   Subject to the Home Secretary's consent, to provide adequate and sufficient buildings as are required for police purposes.
4   To provide equipment, clothing and vehicles as may be required.
5   A combined police authority may use the services of officers of the constituent authority if this is authorized under the amalgamation scheme.

While a police authority, by its composition, will reflect the viewpoint of, on the one hand, the local political groupings, and, on the other, that of the sentencing authority, its capacity to influence the style of policing locally can be considered to be more persuasive than executive. Thus, though a police authority has a duty to provide and finance an adequate police force for the area, the size of the force is determined by the Home Secretary, and the disposition of it by the chief constable. This three-way split of responsibilities is a difficult situation to cope with, and is frequently a source of conflict between police authorities, chief constables and the Home Office, over the style and manner of policing pursued. This conflict over roles and responsibilities can best be illustrated by the various questions arising from the policing of the NUM dispute in 1984–5.

The Home Secretary

The Home Secretary exercises a central authority in some matters, and has to see that a number of important facilities are provided on a national basis under common police services. The Police Act, 1964, gives the Home Secretary a number of specific powers which he is required to exercise to promote the efficiency of the police. These principally cover the following:

1 *Amalgamations.* He has the power to approve voluntary, or initiate compulsory, schemes for the amalgamation of police authorities.
2 *Appointments.* The approval of the Home Secretary is required for the appointment of chief constables, and deputy and assistant chief constables.
3 *Police regulations.* The Home Secretary has the power to make regulations as to the government, administration and conditions of service of police forces after consultation with the Police Negotiating Board or Police Advisory Board.
4 *Inspectorate.* The chief inspector, the eight inspectors and assistants are responsible to the Home Secretary for reporting on the efficiency of all police forces in England and Wales.
5 *'Directions to chief constables.* The Home Secretary has the power to require a chief constable to submit a report on the policing of his area, to make collaboration agreements with another chief constable, or give him assistance.
6 *Common services.* The main common police services are police colleges and training centres, the forensic science laboratory and research services, and the national computer.
7 *Discipline.* Every chief constable is required to record and cause to be investigated any complaint by a member of the public against a member of his force. Serious complaints are referred to the Police Complaints Authority, set up by the Police and Criminal Evidence Act, 1984.
8 *The Metropolitan Police.* The Home Secretary is the police authority for the Metropolitan Police.

Police Negotiating Board

This is composed of the official side and the staff side. The official side comprises (a) representatives of the Home Secretary and (b) representatives of local authorities who are either current or recent members of the police committee, one-third being magistrates. The staff side represents the Commissioner of Police of the Metropolis, the Association of Chief Police Officers, the Superintendents' Association and the Police Federation. The Police Negotiating Board considers draft regulations on recommendation allowances, hours of duty, leave, pensions, clothing and equipment.

Police Advisory Board

The Edmund Davies Committee of Inquiry on the Police in 1977 made recommendations on police staff associations which said that because of the unique position held by police officers, limitations had to be placed on their freedom of association. This prevents affiliation to the TUC, political and other such organizations which might be prejudicial to the impartiality of the police.

The main police representative organizations are:

(a) *Police Federation.* All members of a police force below the rank of superintendent are automatically members of the Federation.
(b) *Superintendents' Association.* This body represents super-intendents and chief superintendents.
(c) *Association of Chief Police Officers* (ACPO). This body represents officers of substantive rank above chief superintendent.

Police Complaints Authority

The Police Complaints Authority is a group set up to investigate serious complaints against the police. It is independent (no serving or past police officer can be a member), directs enquiries, and records whether it is satisfied with the conduct of the enquiry. It was set up under the Police and Criminal Evidence Act, 1984.

Police finance

Finance for the police service is provided by specific grant, rates and rate-support grant. Of all eligible police expenditure, 51 percent is met by specific grant (one-third City of London). The amount which is not so financed by specific grant counts also as relevant expenditure for rate-support grant purposes, along with other non-police current expenditure by local authorities. Payment of the police grant is conditional upon the Home Secretary being satisfied with the efficiency of the force, which is inspected annually by the Inspectorate Branch of the Home Office. The Home Secretary controls the size of the police establishment, the capital expenditure of the force, and pay and allowances of police officers.

Total income in 1986–7 for the Greater Manchester Police, in percentages, was received from the following sources:

	%
Police grant	46.4
Rates and rate-support grant	45.8
Fees, sales and charges	2.3
Pension contributions	5.5

The sources from which police authorities derive their income from 'fees, sales and charges', include the following:

1 Fees and charges centrally promulgated by the Home Office and ACPO, e.g. firearms' certificates, alien registration, accident reports.
2 Fees and charges determined locally by the police authority, e.g. private special duty (mainly policing of sporting events), police training college fees.
3 Recharges to the Home Office for supply of police officers to staff central service units, e.g. Police Staff College, district police training centres.
4 Sales of used or redundant equipment or unclaimed property.
5 Awards of court costs.

Capital expenditure

Capital allocations are decided by the Home Office on the basis of bids submitted by police authorities. The division of resources between minor works, housing, energy conservation, etc. is decided after consultation with HMIC to determine that these are deployed as effectively as possible. There are three categories of scheme:

(a) Minor works up to £200,000.
(b) Intermediate schemes from £200,000 to £1,000,000.
(c) Large schemes in excess of £1,000,000.

In the case of (a) bids are invited by the Home Office in May of each year for schemes police authorities wish to commence the following financial year. Successful bids are approved in December of that year. For (b) and (c) bids are invited and schemes are provisionally approved, placed on a provisional planning list, and selected for a start date, as determined by financial resources available and priority. The main difference in procedures between intermediate and large schemes is that investment appraisals have to be submitted to the Home Office for the latter but not for the former, though authorities are strongly encouraged to carry out appraisal of the larger intermediate schemes for their own purposes.

Routine management accounting issues

Organization and structure of Greater Manchester Police

The organizational structure of Greater Manchester Police is based on the allocation of various policing responsibilities to six assistant chief constables, who head the following departments:

1 Community Relations/Development and Inspectorate.
2 Personnel and Training.
3 Criminal Investigation.
4 Administration and Technical Services.
5 Uniformed Operations.
6 Discipline and Complaints.

The uniformed operations department is made up of fourteen territorial divisions, and except for the City of Manchester, which is covered by five territorial divisions, the remaining nine divisions are co-terminous with the boundaries of the nine district councils making up the GMP area. Budgets are prepared for departments and territorial divisions over selected headings only:

(a) Supplies and services.
(b) Training.
(c) Crime prevention.
(d) Accident prevention.
(e) Detective allowances and expenses.
(f) Car allowances.

In addition, non-financial budget information is prepared for manpower, overtime, vehicles and mileage.

The Chief Constable, together with the Deputy Chief Constable, directs and controls the force. In addition, there is a 'twinning' arrangement between assistant chief constables, whereby each one keeps close contact with a specific department other than his own, as well as being aware of the broad activities of the other departments. This arrangement ensures a continuity of the corporate management philosophy employed within Greater Manchester Police. The Chief Constable is advised on policy matters by his Policy Review Committee, which comprises the six assistant chief constables under the chairmanship of the Deputy Chief Constable, and he meets his chief officers daily to review force activities over the preceding 24 hours.

The main areas where management accounting practices are used are in:

1 The deployment of staff resources and investigation of current working practices.
2 The preparation of budgets, medium- to long-term plans, and the measurement of performance against the plan.
3 The use of functional budgets.
4 The use of commitment accounting.
5 The use of cost-control and cost-reduction techniques.

In 1976 Greater Manchester Police committed itself to putting more officers back on the beat, and to building and opening more local police stations. These commitments clearly had an impact on the capital and revenue budgets. However, the use of functional budgets and cost centres to collect cost data enabled costs to be ascertained and helped implementation within the timescale required.

A major weakness of the traditional local authority budget is that it follows a subjective structure rather than a functional or objective one, i.e. an analysis over headings for employees, premises, supplies and services, etc. (what we spend the money on) rather than analysis by department, function or activity (what we get for the money). To attempt to remedy the shortcomings apparent in the traditional analysis, the CIPFA recommended layout of accounts identifies six divisions of service, as a minimum, to be used from 1987 onwards. These are as below:

1 Police general.
2 Regional crime squad.
3 Police pensions.
4 Police canteens.
5 Transport and moveable plant.
6 Police training centres.

In addition, GMP has always maintained separate objectives for:

7 Technical support unit.
8 Traffic wardens.
9 Community liaison.

These functional headings have also been broken down into cost centres, to division, location within division, type of activity or operation.

Though the CIPFA revised financial management information layout is an improvement on past practice, it neglects major and growing expenditure areas, such as computer-assisted policing and communications, wrongly classifies items of expenditure (e.g. common police services is a central Home Office apportionment based on establishment *not* an agency or contracted service), and apportions pension costs to the training function (past service costs have nothing whatsoever to do with future training and development needs).

Other obvious defects are:

1 Lack of uniform bases within a uniform costing system.
2 Yearly issue of statistics is too infrequent for planning and control purposes.
3 There is an almost total lack of trend data.
4 Undue importance is placed on averages by HMIC, particularly when these are taken as a performance target. This can result in mediocrity in delivery of the service if one's own unit cost is above the norm and attempts are made to reduce it to the average.

5   Major public order incidents, e.g. the NUM dispute, can have a distorting effect on the figures supplied.

The policy commentary

A policy commentary is prepared by Greater Manchester Police each year, and the budget strategy is based on it. Since the bulk of police expenditure is controlled by the government, it is of necessity the custom that the proposed budget strategy is based on the government's expenditure plans for the police service. The policy commentary reviews what has actually happened in the previous year, and includes costed proposals over the next 4 years. For planning purposes the objectives included have to be both realistic and verifiable, e.g. capital projects need Home Office approval and are only included if this has been granted, or has a reasonable expectation of being granted.

A searching appraisal is necessary to ascertain force strengths and weaknesses in relation to the declared objectives. This serves two main purposes:

(a) It determines the immediate changes in structure and policies necessary to achieve the objectives, e.g. the training, organization structure and building works required for the police and criminal evidence legislation.
(b) It aims to make more effective use of existing resources, e.g. by use of value analysis techniques for civilianization programmes and privatization exercises.

The main areas in which the force strengths/weaknesses are assessed are:

1   The use of financial resources.
2   Functional strengths and weaknesses.
3   Services offered.
4   Human resources and organization.

A typical appraisal takes the following form:

Financial resources

(a) Analysis of operating costs and measures of efficiency.

(b) Inter-force comparisons.

Functional strengths and weaknesses

(a) What is the force's specialized knowledge?
(b) In which activities has it established a position of leadership?
(c) In which areas of activity is it most vulnerable?

Services offered

(a) What contribution is being made by each branch of the force to force objectives?
(b) Is it suitably responsive to meeting force objectives and satisfying public needs?
(c) What resources does it utilize?
(d) What are the trends in recorded crime?
(e) What effect will new legislation have on the force?

Human resources and organization

(a) Do new methods of work, new technologies need to be introduced?
(b) Are training facilities and education requirements satisfactory?
(c) Is the motivation of the force receiving sufficient attention?
(d) Are commanders uncertain as to their role/priorities?
(e) Are there delays in decision-making and breakdowns in communication?
(f) Is there overmanning in some areas and staff shortages in others?
(g) Is there preoccupation with procedures and red tape at the expense of the overall task?

Environment

Since policing is a highly political issue, it is impossible to engage in medium-term planning without considering the external environment. A failure to gather the correct information, assess and interpret it, and make reasonably accurate predictions concerning environmental changes, can result in a police force being left with an inappropriate or ineffective strategy. The environment needs to be scanned and information collected, collated, and analysed to enable forecasts to be made to assist in medium- to long-term planning. This aspect was mentioned as being defective in the District Audit

Services Review of West Midlands Police (District Audit Service, 1985, p. 25):

> There appears to be scope for more systematic gathering of sub-divisional intelligence. One other metropolitan force assigns an officer, initially full time, to build up and maintain a 'profile' of the sub-division. This contains all available information about the area, its social, demographic, housing and employment characteristics, an analysis of its crimes and incidents, and its problems generally. The profile then presents this information in such a way as to be easily understood by all officers in the sub-division. Once it is set up, operational officers in the sub-division can keep it up to date, and add to it if suitable material comes to hand. Once the strategy has been decided upon, it is translated into specific short-term goals for the force, and for divisions, departments within the force, broken down into budgets.

Each year the results achieved are compared against the budget, are reported on in the chief constable's report and the corporate plan is amended accordingly.

Budgetary control in Greater Manchester Police

The police budget is analysed over the divisions of service mentioned earlier. These divisions of service are further broken down into:

(a) Standard group, e.g. employees.
(b) Sub-group, e.g. operational, support, administrative and clerical employees.
(c) Detail head, e.g. salaries.
(d) Sub-detail head, e.g. basic pay, overtime, etc.

It should be emphasized that while the budget is split down to the sub-detail head, and expenditure is classified into cost centres within department or territorial division, divisional budgeting, with definitive needs-based assessment and budget profile, has only been introduced over selected sub-detail heads.

The aim is to achieve full territorial division and departmental budgeting within 3 years. There are many reasons why this has not been done previously, but mainly the following:

1 Inadequate computing arrangements to achieve it.
2 Lack of training in financial management for senior officers, a common problem in police forces.
3 The rigidity of the annual budget and precept-fixing, with its emphasis on financial stewardship rather than financial management.
4 The insurmountable fact that the vast bulk of the budget is tightly controlled by the Home Office.
5 In an incremental budget there is very little review of the base budget.
6 The need for regular examination and review of base costs and the cost/benefits arising has only come about through constraints on income.

At this sub-detail level budgetary control is exercised by fourteen budget-holders with operational responsibility located within the headquarters departments.

Preparation and control of the revenue budget

A budget manual has been prepared and disseminated to all divisions and departments in the force. This shows the following:

1 Objectives of the system.
2 Budgetary procedures.
3 Defined responsibilities and duties.
4 The classification and coding system in use.
5 Specimen forms and reports produced.
6 An explanation of the terms used and examples of how a budget-holder's allocation is built up.

In Greater Manchester Police, in common with other local authority services, the principal budget factor is the level of precept (or rate) to be levied, closely followed by those of authorized expenditure and control. Planning, motivational and communicational aspects assume a lesser importance, and the emphasis is on financial stewardship rather than the behavioural aspects of budgeting. Since the bulk of the budget comprises fixed costs, due to establishments being fixed by the Home Office, it follows that the discretionary element over which budget submissions are mainly concerned is quite small.

Budgets are split into base, growth (committed and un-committed) and inflation elements. Reviews of the base for departmental and divisional manpower elements have been under-taken in part, since examination of the base can release further resources previously tied up in high fixed costs, with a lower level of fixed costs, e.g. for civilianization exercises. Anyone in the force seeking resources puts these requests in writing, with justification for the requests, to his/her senior officer, who collates these into a budget submission for presentation to the relevant budget-holder. The budget-holders' submissions are then put together in a draft revenue budget by the finance branch, and this results in calcu-lations of the Home Office grant and precept required to finance the proposals. Financial modelling techniques are used for assessing the impact of inflation rates, grant levels, etc., and predicting their effect on the plan, and consultation takes place between the finance branch and the budget-holders to attempt to make budget submissions conform to the total arrived at through interpretation of the budget strategy. The position is reported on a regular basis by the financial controller to the Assistant Chief Constable, Administration and Technical Services.

The timetable for this process is based on July to November for a revised budget for the current year, and extends to January (or later) for the following year's budget. As the deadline for submission of a complete budget to the police authority draws near, formal budget meetings take place with all budget-holders under the chairmanship of the deputy chief constable. Any further necessary adjustments are made with reference to the chief constable, should differences remain. It should be emphasized that differences are not submitted to the chief constable for him to resolve disputes, but to decide such matters as the order of priority between what appears to be equally pressing items. Upon approval of the budget by the police authority, budget-holders are advised of their budget allowances and allocate these accordingly.

Though it has been stated earlier that territorial division and departmental budgeting had not yet been fully introduced, there are advantages to the present limited devolution of financial management which will be more apparent when full devolution comes about.

First, decentralized budgeting forces management to anticipate problems and plan corrective action in advance. The entire management team is compelled to coordinate its activities, and a greater understanding between functions is usually forthcoming, resulting in better decisions being taken.

Second, it promotes a feeling of 'cost consciousness' and gives a sense of purpose to the organization. Wholehearted cooperation, enthusiasm and participation are essential on the part of management, and this can be difficult to achieve, particularly if savings generated through 'cost consciousness' are retained by the finance branch, rather than being utilized, whether wholly or in part, for local initiatives. If divisional/departmental commanders are unable to utilize savings in this manner, they can perceive their role as being merely that of an adjunct to the finance branch. A common problem in police forces is to view the use of resources separately from their financial management, so that the cost of resources used in operations is not 'an operational police matter' but is a matter for the finance branch to tussle with.

Budgetary control data is provided on a weekly basis to budget-holders in the following format:

1 Actual to date on an income and payments basis.
2 Budget allowance for the year.
3 The budget profile for the period and year to date.
4 Variances between actuals and profile shown in financial and percentage terms.

Control data is provided on an income and payments basis. A full expenditure basis is not possible as yet, since commitment accounting has only been introduced in Greater Manchester Police for building maintenance and minor works. In this budget area slippages occurred on a regular basis, owing to delays inherent in the application of standing orders and tendering procedures, the nature of the industry itself (highly fragmented and of variable quality), and inclement weather. To alleviate the problems caused by these factors, a commitment accounting system was introduced in 1984, and this has led to budget allowances for the various categories of building maintenance being more fully utilized by reducing under-spendings. At the same time a planned programme of maintenance work was introduced, and this resulted in improvement programmes being less demand-led (by emergencies) and produced savings in other budget areas, e.g. rewiring of police buildings with standardized fittings led to a smaller variety and quality of electrical accessories being stocked by central stores.

Budget profiles, except for basic pay and related items, are modified on a regular basis, by looking at the patterns of expenditure in previous years, and allocating period and cumulative allowances accordingly. Profiles for pay follow a regular pattern, whether weekly or four-weekly, but these can be upset by delayed settlement of pay negotiations, or where an anticipated event has not occurred as planned in the profile.

Non-financial output measures

These apply to some areas of the budget. Police overtime is shared out on a divisional/department basis, and comparisons between allotted hours and hours used are made. The reasons for overtime, which are analysed, might include the following:

(a) Attendance at Court.
(b) Retention on duty
      – charging prisoners/continuing enquiries
      – the cover of beat patrols/additional operational cover.
(c) Extended hours by administrative staff.
(d) Rest-day working to complete urgent enquiries.
(e) Rest-day working to provide cover for beat patrols/additional operational cover.
(f) Football duty
      – inside ground
      – outside ground
      – unspecified.
(g) Special events.
(h) Major incidents.
(i) Routine public-holiday duty.

Mileage is used to exercise control over the use of transport, and in the case of the training school, which has residential accommodation, planned and actual student weeks are monitored. In addition, for the residential accommodation, capacity and usage are monitored on a weekly and cumulative basis.

For telecommunications, management statistics are produced on a 24-hour basis from the 'Touchdown' telephone system. These cover the following:

1 Number of calls received.
2 Number of calls abandoned before answer.
3 Number of calls made.
4 Number of calls answered, waiting 0 to 30 seconds, in bands of 5 seconds.
5 Average time to answer calls.
6 Average duration of a call.

Non-financial output measures, particularly those related to response times, are useful in assessing performance of police as perceived by the public. Response and the type of response can lead to questions about style of policing. For example, in a recent court case in Merseyside it was alleged that the style of policing, i.e. foot patrol, contributed to an undetected robbery, which could have been detected had a response and pursuit by police vehicles been used instead.

Crime statistics and clear-up rates have not been dealt with in this section, since they are considered to be misleading. Crime is recorded in the period in which it is reported. Clear-up rates are made up of crimes detected in the period (which includes crimes recorded in this period or previous periods) and then expressed as a percentage of the recorded crime. Theoretically, this calculation could lead to a clear-up rate in excess of 100 percent!

Revision of budgets

Revision of budgets is undertaken once a year to take the effects of pay and price increases into account, but revisions of parts of the budget are undertaken throughout the financial year. It must be emphasized that these are not revision variances – the budget itself is revised, and the revised budget then becomes the target. Virement is regularly undertaken in GMP, generally when increased efficiency or cost reduction have been identified, or where the effects of legislation, e.g. the Police and Criminal Evidence Act, have been misjudged. Virement was made specific mention of in the district auditor's report in the West Midlands Police, i.e. 'virement between budget heads is not allowed even when it can be shown to be cost effective'.

Cost accounting

The Metropolitan Police distributes a ready reckoner of costs to assist commanders in terms of resource allocation. This covers manpower, transport, mileage allowances, police dogs and horses, and has the stated aims of:

(a) Costing various elements of MP plans, including any new proposals and improvements contained in these plans.
(b) Measuring the extent to which any financial targets or estimates quoted in these plans are achieved.
(c) Making cost comparisons between different approaches to particular problems requiring different mixes of resources.
(d) Costing any other kinds of police activity requiring specified resources.
(e) Providing cost information to consultative committees and more generally to the local public.

Such an approach as this is not yet common among police forces, but there is movement towards it, hastened in recent years by the occurrence of large-scale outbreaks of public disorder or events requiring large-scale policing, such as the NUM dispute.

The lack of standard methods of costing police officers led to acrimony and delay in settlement of accounts for mutual aid between aiding and aided police authorities in the NUM dispute, over whether the amounts to be charged should:

(a) be the fixed cost of employing a police officer (basic pay plus allowances) plus overtime costs, *or*
(b) the additional costs of overtime only (recognizing the fact the fixed cost would be payable in any case).

Though the above is an exception, most mutual aid being small-scale and short-term in nature, this lack of a standard method of costing, in cases such as private special duty (e.g. football duty), leads to wide discrepancies in the hourly rate charged because of the differing treatment of the overtime premium. In the Audit Inspectorate's survey *Civilianisation and Related Matters* it was found that supplements of between 30 percent and 100 percent were added, leading to a difference of 135 percent between the lowest and highest rate per hour charged for an officer of the same rank.

Innovative examples of management accounting

The previous sections of this chapter have been concerned with the routine aspects of management accounting. In this section attention is turned to some of the innovations that have been introduced in recent years as part of the 'value for money' exercise. Value analysis and cost reduction surveys have been undertaken and the following examples have been selected for examination: (a) the investigation of civilianization opportunities, (b) an analysis of fleet management, and (c) energy savings.

Civilianization opportunities

In civilianization investigations the procedure used has been to set up a small project team to make recommendations to the chief constable on posts to be civilianized. The team's task can be summarized as below:

1 *Information stage*. Collection of information regarding non-operational posts occupied by police officers.
2 *Speculative stage*. Consideration of whether the posts are necessary, whether they should be occupied by police officers and what benefit is received from them.
3 *Analytical stage*. Examination internally within the force and externally with other forces on means to restructure posts to permit civilianization.
4 *Planning stage*. Reporting to the chief constable on those posts which can be civilianized, with a suggested implementation programme.
5 *Execution Stage*. Putting the programme into effect, modified as necessary to comply with the objectives of the force.

It is important that this exercise is not seen purely as an attempt to cut costs. The object needs to be viewed in much broader terms as one of achieving the correct relation between cost and performance, eliminating unnecessary functions, while giving satisfaction to the public in delivery of the service, i.e. there are posts, principally in crime and accident prevention, where the esteem factor as perceived by the public of having these performed by police officers outweighs other considerations. This esteem factor is of vital importance to a police force and is often neglected in studies concerned with value for money. For example, a recent study (Department of the Environment, 1986, paragraph 10.) concludes that 'a ratio of 24 civilians to 100 police officers could save £26 million annually'. This takes no account of the pro-active aspects of policing, and is too concerned with savings for savings' sake. The downside of civilianization is that staff turnover in many civilianized posts is considerably higher than in those posts which have been traditionally held by civilians, because a purely cost-savings exercise does not provide a civilian career structure nor job satisfaction. Neither does it particularly aid police morale if prestigious posts are no longer open to serving police officers.

Even the district auditor service has shown lack of consistency over the issue of civilianization. A recent report (Department of the Environment, 1986) identified finance and computer development posts among those offering the greatest potential for further civilianization. However, in a further report (District Audit Service, 1985) surprise is expressed at how little training is given to police officers in 'subjects such as management and management techniques, resource management and financial control, and new technology'. There would seem to be little advantage in training police officers in these skills if these are the areas recommended for civilianization.

Value analysis in fleet management

The number of vehicles in police fleets is fixed by the Home Office, but the composition of fleets and replacement policies are determined locally. The costs of running and maintaining a fleet of vehicles are made up of the following elements:

(a)   Initial purchase price.

(b) Running costs (fuel, oil, tyres).
(c) Maintenance and repair costs (parts and labour).
(d) Standing charges (depreciation, licences, insurance, workshop premises).
(e) Resale value of vehicle on disposal.

The total of these factors will give the lifetime costs of owning and operating the vehicle, yet the initial purchase price, which typically will account for only about 20% of the lifetime cost of ownership, will assume the major significance, or indeed be, the sole criterion in the purchasing decision (Andrews, 1983).

Subject to other constraints, a police force's objective should be to minimize the total life-cycle costs resulting from the ownership of vehicles during their economic lives, which may be shorter than their operational lives. The aim has to be the minimization of future expenditure arising from the acquisition, use and replacement of vehicles. To achieve this, the following is necessary:

(a) To specify correctly the technical and functional attributes at the acquisition stage.
(b) After acquisition the appropriate level of servicing and care during the life of the vehicle needs to be determined.
(c) Use of the fleet efficiently.
(d) Determining the optimum replacement period.

The life-cycle costing system developed needs to generate relevant financial information relating to these activities. In specifying the technical and functional attributes of a vehicle, the force must also identify the life-cycle costs of alternatives, of the same nominal capacity and type but built to different standards. The use of terotechnological appraisal procedures in this evaluation should expose the short-sightedness of a 'lowest tender price' attitude (Sizer, 1976).

In the Greater Manchester Police the management information system developed to cater for this type of evaluation comprises:

1 'Timeplan' fuel-monitoring system.
2 Vehicle availability system.
3 SAVE fleet-management system.

Fuel monitoring

Each vehicle has a unique coded key to operate computerized fuel pumps. This key identifies the vehicle, its mileage, amount of fuel issued, time and date, and this information is passed on to the vehicle record held on the SAVE fleet management system. Secondly, since the system also records bulk fuel receipts and capacity availability in storage tanks, it enables orders to be placed for the optimal amount of fuel, to take advantage of volume discounts as well as giving early warning of tank leakage, or recalibration of pumps. This does away with the uncertainty of 'dipstick' methods.

Vehicle availability system

This gives information on the availability of vehicle types in divisions and identifies surplus or deficient resources by area or time period.

SAVE fleet management system

This gives the following information:

1 Full life history of individual vehicles.
2 Full maintenance and repair costs.
3 Running costs by vehicle, by type, by manufacturer, by year.
4 Standing costs.
5 Exceptions to user-defined parameters.
6 Reports by time period and year-to-date.
7 Workshop stores control.
8 Hired vehicle control facilities.
9 Scheduling of maintenance for workshop loading.
10 User-defined reports.

The use of such a system fulfils the requirements of terotechnological appraisal procedures. Cave (1986) suggests that the benefits of terotechnological appraisal are that it:

(a) Enables purchase decisions to be made on whole life history backed by the facts relating to past performance, costs and comparisons with other vehicles in the fleet.
(b) Produces better maintenance information, with consequent

reduction in the number of breakdowns, and an early indication of problem area and rogue vehicles.

(c) Improves purchase decisions and reduces downtime, so that greater utilization of vehicles will be achieved.

(d) Gives facilities to analyse the performance of individual components and make comparisons between different manufacturers' components on similar vehicles in the fleet. This results in efficient purchasing decisions.

(e) Compares the performance of common components (filters, tyres, etc.), resulting in greater use of more effective and reliable parts.

(f) Makes use of history files, which makes it easier to predict failure times on individual components; this facilitates the replacement of relevant parts before actual failure (just-in-time replacement).

(g) Permits better management of existing resources in accurate scheduling of workloads. By implementing a parts stock control system, a more economical value of stock is held.

Cost reduction through energy saving

A fuel conservation policy was implemented in the Greater Manchester Police in 1984 by the purchase of an automated energy management system, to cover six selected large police complexes. This crash programme recognized that energy expenditure follows a pareto distribution (20 percent of the buildings account for 80 percent of energy expenditure) and, aiming for a 15 percent reduction in total energy use at these premises, would produce savings of £50,000 pa. Savings of this magnitude would mean payback of the original investment of £84,000 in under 2 years.

The equipment was installed in March 1984, and a progress report was presented to the Police Committee in June 1985.[2] In the six complexes heating needs were satisfied by gas and oil (four by gas, two by oil). A comparison of consumption between 1984–5 and the base year 1982–3 showed, first, a reduction in consumption of 26 percent in gas-heated buildings, producing financial savings of £44,000; and, second, a reduction in consumption of 22 percent in one oil-heated complex, producing financial savings of £9,000. No reduction was achieved in the other complex, owing to contractual delays in boiler replacement, and difficulties caused by asbestos removal work.

The performance targets for consumption reductions and financial savings had therefore been surpassed. A crash programme of this nature does not, however, constitute an energy policy, though it does demonstrate two elements essential to a cost reduction exercise: the setting of predetermined performance targets, and the measurement of progress against the targets, to demonstrate that they have been achieved.

An energy policy statement has therefore been formulated for the efficient management of energy consumption throughout the force which encompasses the following:

Definition of objectives

To reduce energy consumption by 20 percent by 1988, from a baseline established in 1983.

Establishment of responsibility centres

Each police station to be given an annual budget, based on an average of its consumption over the previous 3 years. This figure would be adjusted to take into account the following factors:

(a) The weather (measuring the annual mean temperature).
(b) The size and hours of use of the building.
(c) The efficiency of the building fabric.
(d) The site's exposure to the weather.

The active participation and cooperation of staff are essential to a cost reduction scheme. Management has to accept that effective management and cost savings are so closely related that they cannot be separated. By using the force newspaper *Brief*, together with regular bulletins and seminars, staff will be informed of any proposals or measures taken and subsequently encouraged to cooperate in achieving agreed objectives.

Obtaining clear understanding of cost structure

What costs are incurred, why they are incurred, and how they behave, are fundamental to effective cost control and cost reduction, so the annual energy consumption and target consumptions will be established for all buildings.

Selection of factors of control

Cost reduction demands the selection of a number of factors, and determines the priority of projects with the following in mind:

(a) Projects with a 4-year payback or less to be generally developed in order of priority.
(b) Implementation of technical improvements and adaptations to plant and buildings.
(c) All new buildings or refurbishment works to incorporate energy-conservation measures.

Measuring effectiveness of cost-reduction programme

The previous statements stress the need for a continuous programme. The force surveyor will be responsible for recording data, monitoring consumption, technical improvements to buildings, equipment services and publicity. An annual report will be submitted to the police authority detailing savings, good housekeeping measures, work completed and proposals for new investment.

The second phase of extending the energy management system to a further twenty-one police buildings, was completed in 1985–6, at a cost of £133,000 and target savings of £33,000 pa. In the part year after installation savings of £13,000 were achieved.

Since a cost-reduction programme requires teamwork to succeed, other departments apart from the suveyor's branch are participating in:

1 Identification of areas where 'zoning' can take place and allow heating to be carried out separately in these areas.
2 Individual light switching, rather than banking.
3 Identification of activities carried out on a 24-hour basis which can be grouped together to allow 'zoning' to take place.
4 Reviewing catering facilities, e.g. use of foil containers rather than tins and traditional ovens.
5 Energy pinching from areas containing heat-producing plant (computers) to boost temperatures elsewhere.

Conclusion

It is recognized that effectiveness measurement in the public sector is fraught with difficulty. There is often undue importance placed on the measurement of inputs rather than outputs achieved. The use of management accounting methods can help, and some routine as well as innovative aspects of management accounting that are used and adapted in the police service have been described and documented. It is certain that this usage will extend further into the police service, and it is hoped that this chapter will stimulate further action in this area.

Notes

1 The information on manpower and expenditure 1965–1985 has been taken from CIPFA – Statistical Information Service. However, because of incomplete data for 1985 the CIPFA estimates have been adjusted by the author.
2 Much of the information in this section has been taken from a series of reports submitted to the Greater Manchester Council, Police Financial Control Sub-committee, during the period 24 February 1984 to 27 September 1985.

References

Andrews, D. (1983). Value Assurance – Detailed Attention to the Needs of the Customer. *Management Accounting*, December, 32–3.
Cave, B. (1986). Getting value for Money from Fleet Management. *Municipal Journal*, July, 1188.
Department of the Environment (1986). *Civilianisation and Related Matters*. Report of the Audit Inspectorate, Police Service.
District Audit Service (1985). *Review of the Management of West Midlands Police*, October.
Sizer, J. (1976). Life Cycle Costing. *Management Accounting*, July, 13.

3 Management accounting in direct labour organizations

Tony Hope and Linda Kirkham

Introduction

This chapter will look at the specific requirements placed on direct labour organizations (DLOs) by the Local Government Planning and Land Act, 1980 (henceforward 'the Act'), and will discuss how they are currently being met. As the 1980 Act requires DLOs to earn a positive return on capital employed, it seems sensible to devote most of the paper to a discussion of the major management accounting issues this exercise will raise.

The chapter is in five sections. We begin by giving a general background to the Act and explaining some of the organizational changes it produced. The following section discusses general issues relating to the calculation of the return on capital employed. We then look at the impact of different organizational structures on the types of management accounting systems used by particular DLOs, and follow this with a discussion of some accounting issues attendant on the tendering procedures used by DLOs. A brief concluding section then highlights some common problems arising from the analysis, and makes some tentative predictions as to future issues to be faced by DLOs.

A word of explanation is necessary at the outset. The chapter will argue that, given the very diverse natures and organizational structures of DLOs, it would be a fruitless exercise to attempt to describe or prescribe universally appropriate management accounting systems. Rather it is necessary to appreciate the different objectives and environments of DLOs and thus to understand management issues within such a framework. Our emphasis throughout the chapter is on tendering procedures and accounting systems which we have observed in the small and diverse sample of DLOs we have studied, and our descriptions of the more extreme management accounting systems we have encountered are intended to convey a flavour of the sorts of problem facing DLOs which have different organizational relationships to their local authorities. For example, some DLOs operate as virtually autonomous organizations, whereas others are under the close supervision and control of a parent department, e.g. housing or technical services. All DLOs have, nevertheless, direct responsibility for some aspects of their work. The responsibility for, and control of, the DLO rests with a specific committee. In a recent study (El-Deen *et al.*, 1985), 89 percent of DLOs surveyed had undergone some reorganization as a result of the Act, and many had created new committees and sub-committees. However, whatever internal arrangements exist, the changed profit-oriented emphasis of the DLO requires it to be regarded as a contractor in its relation with other local authority departments.

The 1980 Act and its effects

Direct labour organizations exist within local authorities to undertake construction and maintenance work. The first DLO was established in 1892, partly as a response to the housing crisis then pertaining but also as a result of the corruption associated with contracts undertaken by private sector companies for public sector agencies (Langford, 1982). Their initial role was not limited simply to the provision of building and maintenance services and the prevention of exploitation of the public purse, but was perceived also to encompass wider socio-political objectives, e.g. the maintenance of decasualized employment, and the improvement of conditions of service and site welfare.

Since their inception in the 1980s the role and nature of DLOs have undergone a number of changes. Until 1980 the development of DLOs did not have a clear statutory base but came from a combination of political and administrative events both at a local and a national level. While their precise role has never been defined in any one authoritative statement, those commentators who have offered one have recognized the elements of service and effectiveness as central to understanding the role of DLOs. Thus for example: 'DLOs exist to provide specific services to the authority and the community they represent, and the production of proper "value for money".' (Minister of Housing and Construction, 22 August, 1978).

From the mid-1970s a stream of reports on the management of, and the accounting by, construction and maintenance DLOs have argued that they could be more efficiently managed and that they should be operated on a trading basis (CIPFA, 1975; CIPFA, 1978; Department of the Environment, 1978). Before 1980 a number of authorities already operated their DLO as a trading department (e.g. Wandsworth Borough Council), whereby the DLO acted as a contractor in competition for council contracts. It was argued that, since DLOs enjoyed a 'special status', defined by the amenability of their operations to commercial comparison and competition, this should be reflected in their accounting systems and requirements; furthermore, the change in the accounting requirements and procedures of DLOs to the production of trading accounts was seen as an important factor in the system of management control and performance measurement (CIPFA, 1975).

Part III of the Local Government Planning and Land Act, 1980, claimed to put these principles into practice. The Act has five main features:

1 A requirement to keep separate accounts for different categories of work – namely that relating to highways and sewers, major new construction and routine building maintenance.
2 A requirement to earn a 'real' rate of return on capital employed (currently 5 percent) within each category.
3 A requirement to compete for certain work and to provide a prior written estimate for all work. Basically this entails tendering for all jobs over £50,000, and for up to 60 percent of construction jobs under £50,000 and maintenance jobs under £10,000.
4 A requirement to produce a balance sheet, a revenue account and a statement of rate of return for each description of work.
5 A power is given to the Secretary of State to close down a DLO if it fails to make the required rate of return, or for any other reason.

Before the act was passed, the main function of DLO management was to provide a service within a given budget. Maintenance and construction work was carried out for client departments and recharged at actual cost. Financial controls sought to ensure that the DLO's budget was not overspent. The Act changes those functions. There has been a shift in emphasis away from the control of inputs to stay within the budget, and towards the production of the output necessary to attain the rate of return. This in turn has necessitated a change in management style and, in many DLOs, a change in organization and control. Management is now faced with the conflicting and qualitatively different objectives of, firstly, providing a service to the community and, secondly, and more importantly, of producing a 5 percent real rate of return on capital employed.

Any money allocated by the authority to building or maintenance work is no longer guaranteed to finance the DLO's operations – instead the DLO must compete openly for most contracts as if it were a private sector firm. Any surplus generated by the DLO may be allocated in accordance with the policy of the individual local authority and in keeping with the spirit of the CIPFA Code of Practice, 1981, which recommends that any surplus should be used firstly to repay any deficits previously charged to the rate fund or general fund and any remaining amounts may be transferred to either central reserves or a special DLO reserve, bearing in mind the capital requirements of the DLO.

The increased emphasis on financial targets and control has resulted in increased prominence for accountants and accounting within DLOs. There is now a greater role for accountants as part of the management team. Some of the more traditional management functions previously fulfilled by individuals who had 'worked themselves up from the bottom' within the organization have been replaced or usurped by the conventional role of accountants within contracting organizations – roles relating to planning, financial control and other operational procedures. Apart from a shift in emphasis within the management function, the provisions in the Act have resulted in the employment by some authorities of additional non-productive staff to produce estimates and monitor and control costs. The requirements to monitor individual jobs and to maintain four separate accounts have, on the one hand, decentralized more control to individual depots, whereas key controls have been centralized, e.g. the monitoring of key statistics on work output, preparation of tenders and negotiations with client departments.

Capital employed by DLOs and achievement of rates of return

Before examining specific accounting issues, such as those relating to tendering and cost control, we must address ourselves to a significant issue arising from the profit test imposed by the Act on DLOs, and which thus defines the context within which DLO management must make decisions. Ultimately the survival of a DLO rests on its ability to pass the 5 percent profit test. In order to measure the rate of return for each category of work, it is necessary to assign operating assets to each category and, further, to value such assets at their current equivalents. From our interviews we have identified a number of recurrent problems in defining the parameters of the rate of return – parameters which go directly to the heart of the issue of *defining* the DLO as a separate entity within the local authority. In other words, to compute the DLOs' rate of return it is necessary to define its assets and its operations, and to define its assets and operations is tantamount to defining the DLO as an entity. These problems stem directly from the provisions of the Act and the burden of their resolution lies heavily on the management accountant. Although the CIPFA guidelines provide information on how assets and operations might be classified, the diversity of structure and organization among DLOs makes such general prescriptions difficult to operationalize. For example, how are DLOs to deal with assets drawn upon by different departments in the local authority? How should assets used by different categories of DLO work be allocated? Are the extra costs incurred in effecting such allocations justified by better management information? Should allocation be on the basis of past or estimated future asset use?

The nature of the issue can be illuminated by some examples. Thus our research encountered organizations which experienced difficulties in determining who, within the local authority, actually owned the capital assets. The distinction between the role of contractor (DLO) and that of client (LA department) is often artificial, and thus the ownership of assets can reflect the same artificiality. Other organizations used 'creative decision-making and accounting' to minimize the asset base and thus to aid the achievement of the rate of return. This entailed extensive use of internal and external leasing arrangements, for which the economic justification was unclear. These issues influence most management decisions within DLOs and, as our interviews revealed, may help to decide how cost control and tendering problems are resolved.

The problems faced by DLOs' management are not confined to technical issues such as measurement and allocation, but are compounded by the sceptical attitude of some local authorities towards the underlying philosophies of the rate of return. Our survey suggests that this scepticism is concerned with the following issues:

1 The rate of return is only one method of measuring performance, and the achievement of such a return is not in itself a measure of efficiency, e.g. the rate of net profit to turnover may be a more appropriate figure in certain cases. Indeed, in attempting to achieve a rate of return, it may be found that efficiency and service are sacrificed in meeting this arbitrary target. This can be illustrated by the conflict between the need for the DLO to hold sufficient stock to carry out emergency and other repairs efficiently and the necessity to minimize stock for rate of return purposes.

2 The requirement to earn a rate of return on a current-cost basis is inconsistent with the requirements of private industry. In addition, the principles of current-cost accounting have not been accepted by the accountancy profession.

3 Cross-subsidization between different categories of work is commonly carried out in the private sector, whereas the DLO has to make a rate of return in each category. This puts the DLO at a disadvantage in competing for work in the market place.

4 In considering the financial performance of a DLO, it should be borne in mind that the underlying objective is to undertake the maximum amount of work at minimum cost. This is in direct contrast to a private organization, where the attainment of a substantial operating surplus would generally be considered to be one of the principal aims.

Success in achieving rates of return has been mixed. The data

Table 3.1 *Direct labour organizations – comparison of rates of return on capital employed*

	1984–5 Birmingham	1983–4 Birmingham	1983–4 Leeds	1983–4 Manchester	1983–4 Sheffield	1983–4 Average all metropolitan districts
	%	%	%	%	%	%
Maintenance work	38	55	26	12	88	39
New construction						
– jobs individually valued at less than £50,000	(623)	25	16	19	39	50
– jobs individually valued at over £50,000	(461)	17	13	9	–	17
General highways	19	26	7	9	28	32
Rate of return	28	49	25	11	74	36

The rate of return on capital employed is shown for each type of work and is calculated on a current-cost accounting basis in accordance with DLO regulations. Current cost takes inflation into account.

provided in Table 3.1, which has been taken from Birmingham City Council's annual report for 1984–5, compares the rates of return achieved by large metropolitan districts.

Since the 1980 Act was passed, one DLO, Haringey, has been closed down for failure to meet the rate of return requirements. Extreme cases also abound. For example, in 1982–3 the Edinburgh DLO made a loss of 41 percent, while the Walsall DLO achieved a profit of 1006 percent.

To achieve its targets, the DLO must have an up-to-date, comprehensive and relevant management accounting system. As no recompense is offered by client departments if DLO costs exceed estimates, DLOs must ensure both the accuracy and competitiveness of their estimates and the control of their costs. It is to the context in which these issues arise that we now turn.

Organizational structures and management accounting

Few management accounting issues relating to DLOs can be properly understood until the relationship of the DLO to the local authority is clarified. The effects of this relationship determine in large measure the quality and appropriateness of the accounting information used by DLOs. This information is used for a variety of purposes – determining costs for tendering (an issue to which we will return for detailed discussion in the following section), providing information for the control of costs, and determining profit figures for profit-sharing bonus systems, for example. Our sample of DLOs revealed a spectrum of relationships, varying from relatively strong dependence on information provided by the local authority's central finance function, to relative autonomy in the provision of information. All our organizations stressed that the accounting function within the DLO, where such existed, was considerably under-resourced, and that this led to major problems.

Yet it was anticipated that, as a result of the Act, there would be an '. . . increased cost-effectiveness which authorities should achieve when their DLOs are operating under the strict management accounting system which the legislation prescribes . . .' (Department of Environment Circular, 10 January 1981, paragraph 29). A survey undertaken by UMIST (El-Deen et al., 1985) revealed that, while most authorities already operated computerized systems, many authorities made extensive changes to their systems as a result of the 1980 legislation.

Some problems are, however, common to DLOs whatever accounting autonomy they possess. To be successful they must be able to provide services on a competitive basis. To provide competitive services they must be charged for central local authority services at a competitive and equitable cost. This is a thorny issue, raising as it does issues of overhead allocation, make or buy and transfer pricing – classic problems of private sector organization structure.

As Flynn and Walsh (1982) have suggested, it is imperative to be clear as to what is and what is not DLO work, i.e. it is necessary to separate the client and agent aspects of work. Thus, for example, a DLO worker doing pre-inspection work is performing such work on behalf of the client (e.g. the Housing Department) and not for the DLO, and thus the cost should not be charged to the DLO. In principle, the argument is that, as far as possible, the DLO should be organized as a separate entity within the authority, or, at least, there should be a clearly identifiable point of separate responsibility for the DLO – preferably near the top of the organizational structure.

A correct split of functions between the DLO and other departments within the authority is clearly a major issue in defining the DLO's responsibility for costs and profits. Thus, for example, DLOs must, as far as they can, exercise control over such activities as the purchase and use of material and the use of transport in order to avoid potential clashes of interest with other departments. In particular, DLOs should bear only those costs of carrying services which would be born by private contractors in normal circumstances. But how should these costs be evaluated? How should one deal with the problems of spreading overheads among fewer local-authority departments if DLOs are permitted to use external facilities?

That these are problems for DLOs are evident from our discussions. Specifically, our research suggests the following as being some major areas of difficulty:

1 The evaluation of technical and in-house consultancy, often at no extra charge, to other authority departments.

2   The evaluation of the contribution made by DLOs via their reputation as stable employers providing superannuation and holiday payments, to remove the 'casual' form of employment traditionally offered in the building industry. This is a theme to which we will return throughout the paper.

3   The lack of flexibility available to DLOs to shop around for cheaper and more appropriate services (e.g. computing services, legal advice, and external transport facilities).

4   The problems attendant on an understanding of the nature of, and the allocation basis used to charge, central overheads.

These problems are more or less important as a result of the organizational structure in which they reside. The following subsections detail three short case studies of particular DLOs in relation to these and other issues. We look first at some management accounting problems encountered by a large DLO which operates via a number of different depots having profit targets; we then examine some of the problems encountered by a medium-sized DLO which is totally dependent on its local authority for the provision of accounting information; and lastly we look at how a largely autonomous DLO, which grants a high priority to 'social' objectives, designs its management accounting systems.

Case Study 1 – the divisionalized DLO

This large DLO carries out the physical execution of works for building repair, maintenance and refurbishment for the local authority's housing department. Head office is responsible for obtaining work by tender or quotation, for producing the required rate of return, and for the overall direction and control of five areas or depots. The individual areas are responsible for the quality and completion of work on time at tender or quotation figures, for control of labour, transport and plant, and for the execution of work safely, as set out by legislation.

To help tendering and control, a computerized management information system, developed specifically for the local authority, is employed. The system consolidates the many sources of information on, for example, repairs. There may be as many as five requests for the same repair – a problem magnified by the sheer volume of repairs during the year. The system, which has been in force since 1982, is based on a schedule of rates approach, and produces a series of reports for the five individual areas relating *inter alia* to the value of work, planned and actual, physical and financial, and authorized and received; profitable and unprofitable jobs and cost centres; work-in-progress; and completed job reports covering all contracts, reports on overdue jobs, etc. The nature of the system is intended to reflect the DLO's status as a quasi-commercial organization.

Broadly speaking, the system acts as a method of area assessment. Area managers should receive monthly statements (though presently these are subject to up to 3-months delay) with budget and actual figures, showing contracts analysed by type of work, e.g. planned maintenance. The aim is to inculcate, via the use of area profit and loss accounts, an ethos of competition between depots – for example, in terms of void contracts, supervision levels and cost minimization. Much depends on the depot manager's understanding of the determinants of his 'bottom-line' profit figure. The manager is responsible for his prime costs – labour, bonus, transport and materials – and is charged a proportion of housing-department and central DLO overheads.

The nature and method of calculating these overheads threw up major problems of understanding. There is little input from any of the depots in the budgeting procedures, and there is no 'bargaining' in the amount of overheads to be borne by depots. Thus the manager of one of the larger depots dealing with 400 completed jobs per week, who was initially wary of the new performance measures, enthused about the bottom-line targets and their motivational effects, but confessed to doubts as to the exact determination of his proportion of allocated overheads. He believed that overheads were allocated to the five depots on a simple percentage basis, (i.e. 20 percent each, irrespective of the depot's size or identifiable costs. Subsequent explanations given to us by the central accountant revealed the situation to be otherwise. Overhead allocations are expressed as recovery rates on the depots' prime costs. If the prime costs of department x are twice those of department y, the former department will pick up twice as much administrative overhead. Thus there is a great incentive for depots to minimize their prime costs. The accountant added that many hours had been spent explaining the nature of the depots' profitability structure to the individual managers, and was most surprised that their perceptions should be at variance with his own.

The accountant suggested the most important report produced by the system to be the monthly monitoring report, which summarizes the results of each depot. This report goes to all DLO officials, both from central office and from depots, and evokes a variety of responses from divisional heads. The younger, more profit-oriented, depot managers raise critical questions on the determinants of their performance – the older managers are more concerned with the quality of service provided by their depots and argue that the management accounting system should produce indices which better measure the quality of service. Thus, for example, it was argued that a system which distinguished between depots which performed their jobs in strict chronological order and those which completed the 'easy' and more financially rewarding jobs first should be encouraged to operate.

Case Study 2 – an example of organizational dependence

For this DLO the accounting function and information require-ments were provided directly by the central authority. DLO management considered that the central finance department had been slow to respond to the new commercial environment faced by the DLO, because of an apparent lack of concern about the DLO's management-accounting needs. This lack of concern was attri-butable to a variety of factors, among which were the following: the extreme political pressures placed upon local government finance; the relatively low priority given to the development of appropriate DLO systems, owing to the dominance of the informational requirements of the education department, i.e. the DLO was seen as a peripheral activity; and the physical distance between the DLO and the central finance function.

The dependence of the DLO on central finance gave rise to a number of problems, many of which are common to DLOs that share a close relationship with central finance. While many of these problems are at the operational level, e.g. control over purchasing and stock levels, our research has indicated that there are a number of organizational problems which may act as a powerful hindrance to such a DLO in trying to monitor and control costs. Thus the aforementioned DLO failed to make its required rate of return in 1985–6 and yet its failure to do so was not obvious throughout the accounting year. Information relating to actual costs incurred during the first month of the year was not received until the fourth month, by which time, it was argued, it was too late to rectify the problem. Nor did the DLO feel that sufficient training had been provided by the local authority in the new requirements of the Act.

Furthermore, the resources required for the DLO to cope with the booking of thousands of small jobs (180,000 in 1985–6) were not made available, owing to lack of foresight concerning the technical supervisory requirements of so many jobs. The DLO must not just recover its costs on particular jobs, it must also claim its income. The claiming of income on 180,000 jobs, 30 percent of which were subject to variation orders, is a major task. Instances cited suggested that by the time the client department was ready to pay the DLO, the computer system was no longer in a position to process the information quickly. There was, in other words, no mechanism within the central accounting system which allowed quick income recovery by the DLO.

Thus a lack of understanding within the central authority resulted in inadequate information systems and consequent lack of control over DLO costs. Managers were seen to be resentful of the additional amount of paperwork, which was unaccompanied by a commensurate understanding of the purpose of such an exercise. Though some new lower-level accounting personnel had been appointed to work within the DLO, most of the older DLO hands were not capable of initiatives which might alter the degree of DLO dependence on central finance for its day-to-day operations. What was needed, argued the DLO manager, was an innovative management accountant who could persuade central finance to move more of the work in-house. The logical implication of this argument, it was suggested, was for large, more autonomous DLOs that could provide their own resources from the surpluses they generated. This was seen to be the only way of breaking out of a complicated local authority structure which emphasized centralized decision-making and centralized control.

Case Study 3 – organizational autonomy and social objectives

Our final DLO was almost wholly independent from its parent authority, both in management decision-taking and in physical location. Its major problems, concerning accounting systems and cost control, stemmed from the conflict between its operation as an independent contractor and its formal links with the local authority. The authority had anticipated that more effective control would stem from the DLO's independence from central accounting and management systems. It had recruited and re-allocated staff at all levels, e.g. estimators, personnel, accountants, to ensure a self-contained organization, housed in a single location to provide fast, accurate and relevant information flows.

The DLO considered itself to be 'the council's own builder' and, consequently, not to be governed excessively by the profit motive in the same way as private contractors. It thought its primary role to be the provision of a service to tenants and the community. There was a general recognition among those interviewed (accountants, management, trade unions) that the organization should strive to improve its efficiency and effectiveness, which was interpreted as a need to improve the quality of service by 'responding more efficiently to repair requests and by developing a preventative maintenance programme'. While this interpretation subsumes cost-effectiveness and value for money, the emphasis is on qualitative output rather than financial achievement.

The DLO's major problems related to the maintenance side of its operations (as distinct from capital works section). They were seen to result from a number of factors.

Firstly, there had been problems in controlling labour productivity costs, owing to a perceived lack of consultation and co-ordination with the client housing department. This in turn resulted in sub-optimal planning of workloads. Controlling labour costs in an organization constrained by 'no redundancy' agreements requires an ability to plan work to ensure labour costs are not incurred when there is no compensatory income source. It was argued that a decentralization programme undertaken by the client's housing department had resulted in the creation of area and district boundaries which did not mesh with those of the DLO, resulting in wasteful and complicated job planning and control. The unproductive elements of labour costs, such as travel and wet and waiting time, were also adversely affected by uncoordinated planning. Thus, while decentralization of control to depots might overcome some problems, it is only an effective solution if the DLO maintains and promotes its links with client departments to ensure the avoidance of dysfunctional decisions taken independently by the two departments.

Secondly, problems were caused by the authority's hasty response to the legislation in terms of organization and control. While separation had led to improved communication between management, estimators, operatives, etc. on a verbal level, the accounting reporting system was slow to respond. The following quote from the management accountant of the DLO conveys the nature of the problems:

. . . So in local authority accounting, you have two different areas of accounting. You've got what we call the general overheads which only come in at the year end and about which we argue a lot. So that's a bit of an unknown. They're things that you have to estimate, the salaries, the costs of the buildings, loan charges, depot charges. You just have to attempt to budget for these. But during the year we produce management information from my section which has a two-fold purpose. Firstly, it attempts to satisfy our profit-share bonus system, by two-monthly reconciliations of income and expenditure, which is a goal that we will attempt to achieve once we're properly resourced. But we've had a shot at it over the last couple of years. We've done it for all areas periodically, but not every two months. In some areas it's just once a year. You provide that sort of profitability information to satisfy the bonus agreement for the management and the Union side. Then secondly, you provide other management information that attempts to tell them how their capital scheme or how their maintenance organisation or how their service trades are going on during the year; whether it looks like at the end of the year they're going to make a profit or a loss, which takes all other aspects into consideration, including general overheads. But because we are considerably under-resourced – it is to a great extent crisis management in the accounting section. We respond to immediate crises so there isn't any planning and there isn't any back-up service. In fact we'd like to take the initiative and say to managers 'Look here, if we were only to look at that area, there could be a considerable saving there'. Or, 'If we were only to take this approach, or tender for this work, or not tender for this work'. There isn't that initiative in my section because of a lack of resources. So we produce printouts, hand-written reports or whatever to the best of our ability, given our resources. I suppose a lot of the quality of that information hangs on the computer systems that we use to draw our accounting information together. Our authority is part of a consortium of x Local Authorities. What happened was that in the

1960s those x Authorities joined together as a consortium and thought they'd get in at the beginning of the computerisation of accounting in the public sector. They set up this quango, bought massive IBM mainframe equipment and we get our accounting information basically from that mainframe. But over the years it's proved to be a disaster. It was a large error to make that decision because with a consortium of Authorities all you get in all decisions is the lowest common denominator – what's the least unacceptable to anyone in the end. So there just isn't the flexibility in that computer system. So what we're doing is bolting onto that – or even going totally independent – our own computer systems as well.'

Thirdly, and perhaps most importantly, there was the issue of meeting social policies outside the power of the DLO. The local authority in question had a very positive attitude towards employment and working practices. The accountability of the DLO was seen to be directed towards the community and the tenants it served. Both the local authority and the DLO had a strong commitment towards training, which was evidenced in policies of high apprentice–operative ratios. These ratios included a number of female trainees, reflecting the equal-opportunities policy of the authority. While these conditions were not resisted by the DLO (in fact they were welcomed), no account is taken of these additional costs in terms of measuring performance for statutory purposes. Indeed these problems were envisaged by the working party on DLOs which noted 'We recommend that extra costs arising from decisions taken on social grounds, e.g. employment of extra trainees as a contribution to the employment of school-leavers, should be identified and charged not to DLO but to the appropriate authority vote' (Department of the Environment, 1978, para. 11.4). While a number of 'creative accounting' measures had been undertaken to offset the detrimental financial impact, e.g. by the use of MSC schemes which 'fall outside' the DLO accounts, there was, nevertheless, the feeling among management and operatives that the DLO could not compete fairly unless either contractors met their obligations as employers (i.e. training, security of employment, safety standards, etc.) or performance measures incorporated their 'social' achievements.

It is instructive to note that, although panic response had resulted in a number of problems, this DLO did perceive that change had been necessary and that a number of positive developments had resulted.

Tendering

Tenders win or lose work. Winning work provides continued employment and minimizes 'dead time', i.e. expenditure incurred with no compensating income. Successful tendering is thus an important first step in the achievement of the DLO's rate of return. Nor can DLO management afford to drop its standards – the quality of tendering for every contract for which the DLO bids is critical. DLOs are expected to be competitive on all contracts, for they simply do not have the portfolio of opportunities to be as selective in their tendering as the private sector. They cannot afford to accept, for whatever reason, 'loss-leader' contracts, nor can they, by statute, tender for new building work outside their own area. Furthermore, unlike private contractors, they cannot cross-subsidize operations, even in the short term.

The amount of work for which DLOs must tender has increased sharply since the introduction of the 1980 Act, and thus the quality of professional management and expertise demanded by the new requirements has necessitated a fundamental change of thinking on the part of many DLOs. This change has resulted in the employment of more professional surveyors, accountants, estimators, and systems analysts than previously – often by 'poaching' such expertise from the private sector. Education and training, which had formerly been given a low priority by DLOs, is now seen to be an integral factor in future success.

As might be expected, these professional changes have been greeted with mixed emotions by many DLO staff used to a more paternalistic mode of management. Staff see a change from a system of supervision by building tradesmen who have been brought up through the DLO system – and for whom the quality of service was, and is, the overriding objective of the organizations – to one of more structured, formal planning by 'new' professionals – for whom achievement of profit targets is more important than the provision of service. In one large metropolitan authority we noted a marked dichotomy in philosophy, and in practice, between younger managers seeking the achievement of formal profit targets, and more experienced managers seeking to maintain close relations with tenants and a more painstaking approach to the provision of service. The requirements of competitive tendering are thus imposing different, profit-oriented private sector values and methods on DLOs, and in many cases strengthening managerial (and not least accounting) power vis-à-vis labour, which views the more rational and strategic methods of decision-making with some scepticism and distrust.

We shall here confine ourselves to just three of the many issues raised by the tendering system – the nature of the tendering system, some possible tendering methods, and, finally, a brief look at the effect of competitive tendering on planning with DLOs.

The nature of the tendering system

Since October 1983 DLOs have been required to tender for most local authority construction and maintenance work. Specifically, they must tender for all new construction jobs and general highways work over £50,000 and all maintenance jobs over £10,000. In addition, 60 percent of non-exempted jobs (jobs other than those classified as emergency, gritting and snow clearance of highways, and certain extension jobs) under new construction and mainten-ance work and 30 percent of non-exempted jobs under general highways work must be put out to tender.

For *all* work that falls outside the tendering requirements the legislation requires the DLO to provide written statements of the estimated cost of each job, or the method by which that cost will be calculated, before the work is undertaken. It is on the basis of these estimates and tender quotations that charges are made to client, e.g. housing, departments.

It can readily be seen from the above requirements how vital is the role of the estimating department in ensuring the DLO's continued existence. Indeed in many cases local authorities require their DLOs to tender for more than the law demands. Thus one large North West council in 1985–6 demanded tendering for 80 percent of work below the compulsory threshold, and has an objective (approved by its DLO manager) of 100 percent tendering. It is, however, not always incumbent on the local authority to accept the lowest tender received – for example, local authorities might argue, and indeed have argued with some vehemence (witness the 1986 furore surrounding

Burnley's acceptance of its DLO's tender for a major contract) that acceptance of the DLO tender gives work to employees who would otherwise be idle, and in the final resort avoids the payment of redundancy monies. However, details of the reasons for non-acceptance of the lowest tender must be published in the DLO's annual report, and the local authority must, if necessary, justify its position to the auditor (who will not be pacified in perpetuity that the costs of redundancy or of surplus buildings justify the acceptance of internal tenders which are not the lowest received). In *extremis* the secretary of state can order the DLO to change its position.

But how efficient is the tendering system in practice? A typical situation is that prevailing in a major local authority in the North West. Here the DLO is invited, along with four major local contractors, to tender in one amount for the major £3.5m contract for the following year's council house repairs and maintenance. The tender is 'secret' – the sealed bids are opened and the winner is announced. In the case under discussion the DLO won the bid – considering that the contract represented 75 percent of the DLO's total income, any other outcome would have been catastrophic for the DLO. The idea is that the DLO is competing with the 'efficiency' of a selected number of private contractors. But as *Management Today* argued in 1983, tendering systems are fraught with inconsistencies. Discussing tenders in the private sector it stated that:

> The safeguards provided in theory by the secret tender system became an exercise in futility. The fact that major housing projects were sure to be subject to architectural changes, errors, additions and delays meant that the tender price was often an irrelevance. A nominal million pound contract might produce double, treble or quadruple that total as a result of claims for additional or disrupted work. For this reason, it was usually more important to secure the contract at any price than to ensure that the bids tendered were economically sound.

The evidence from our own research suggests strongly that private contractors have greater freedom to vary from their original tender offer, and, further, that in many cases repair work resulting from poor standards employed by private contractors has had to be completed by DLOs.

In tendering for this work the DLO is required to compete with at least *three* outside contractors. The choice of competing private contractors, and the compliance with contractual terms, are integral to the whole process and success of competitive tendering. DLOs have, since the 1980 Act, often observed that they are at a competitive disadvantage because of their very organizational nature, and have argued that they are more closely supervised than private contractors. Thus, for example, DLO tenders must accommodate public sector working practices on health and safety requirements, training of apprentices, and trade-union rights – in fact, all the requirements imposed by local authority standing orders – but many of these requirements may not be as extensively followed in the private sector.

Here is an obvious role for managers wishing to avoid the simplistic 'cheapest is best' philosophy and wishing to ensure that private contractors are placed on an equal footing with DLOs in competitive tendering. Many local authorities have set up contract vetting and contract compliance units in order to impose the same standards on private contractors before they are allowed on to the select tendering list and after they have started the contract. Three examples will illustrate the type of vetting constraints imposed by local authority management.

1   In Islington the council requires contractors who wish to be placed on the tendering list for repair and maintenance work to show that they can provide a 24-hour call-out service, and also demonstrate that foremen are in constant contact with depots – a necessity if there is to be an effective response to emergency-repair requirements.

2   In Manchester the council requires contractors to belong to the NFBTE and recognize the standards of the industry. It also provides that companies found to have breached the Working Rule Agreement for the Building Industry can suffer the penalty of being removed from the tendering list for up to 3 years.

3   In Sheffield the council asks contractors to maintain the minimum pay and conditions requirements of the Fair Wages Resolution – though the resolution itself has been abolished – and also to show that they comply with a minimum ratio of one apprentice to ten craftsmen (the standard ratio in local authorities being one to five).

The scope for management to ensure its broader objectives are met when private contractors are successful in tenders has not gone unnoticed by the government. A recent government green paper 'Competition in the provision of local authority services' (1985) states the government's intention to take action against the imposition of contract conditions not directly concerned with the ability to do the work. It is already illegal for authorities to require trade-union membership. Nevertheless, many of the contract compliance units that have been set up have emphasized legal requirements such as equal opportunities and health and safety policy (Walsh, 1985). To ensure private contractors do not break the law can hardly be construed as conferring an unfair advantage on DLOs.

The importance of managerial competence in dealing with competitive tendering is well illustrated by the following quote from a leading official of a DLO:

> . . . we appointed a new supremo from the private sector. He bought in a research team consisting of architects and surveyors to sort out the corporate problems . . . I think we are surviving, and if you look at the accounting restrictions in the 1980 Act, our antidote has been contracts compliance as a measure of dealing with these. That's what's kept the DLO afloat and kept us in work, over the past 2 years certainly. That's why we've got a fuller order book now. We were able to get around the accounting restrictions of competitive tendering by operating a very strict selective list and by inserting fair competition clauses which evened up the balance in terms of the starting point. We start from x amount of overheads and the private sector starts down there. We're bringing them up to a closer level . . .

But organizational, and thus accounting, differences between DLOs and the private sector still rankle. Our interviews with DLO managers reveal strongly that they believe DLOs still suffer relative to private sector contractors by, for example, having to bear in the tender price the additional costs of training a higher ratio of apprentices. Managers argue that these costs should be financed from outside the DLO accounts, since they are often imposed upon the DLO by the authority and are not controllable by DLO management.

The choice of work to be undertaken by DLOs is a matter of

policy, often determined at higher levels within the local authority. For example, many DLOs have a policy of not quoting for work other than from their local authority clients. Others, on the grounds of their riskiness, do not tender for new construction projects, arguing that the private sector is better able to absorb the risk. But innovative and imaginative managements are weighting the diversification benefits more heavily than before. Thus we have encountered examples of DLOs diversifying into work for the Boy Scout movement, housing associations, other local authorities in direct competition with other DLOs (one North West DLO currently performs up to one-third of its work outside its authority, primarily because its investment in a specialized UPVC window plant requires a broad area of possible work to recoup the attendant overheads), universities, the armed services and the police. DLOs often benefit from mutual reciprocity: we have found instances under which painting contracts have been lost to the private sector by one DLO, but idle time and possible redundancies have been saved by employment of the same painters by an adjacent local authority which had a shortage in the particular area. All these initiatives lessen the likelihood that failure to win a major tender will result in the demise of the DLO, with the attendant redundancy costs and personal heartaches.

Tendering methods

Evidence gathered since the 1980 Act came into force shows DLOs to be using a variety of tendering methods, though the stated intention of the Act was to persuade local authorities to implement a standard schedule of rates (SOR) approach, primarily on the grounds of comparability and ease of monitoring subsequent operations. These rates are based on statistically determined median costs for a range of typical jobs, and are widely used by private sector companies in budgeting and controlling their operations. The data provided in Figure 3.1, which has been extracted from Birmingham's 1985 report, shows the variety of different methods used by certain metropolitan districts in estimating tendering charges.

Although the SOR approach is the most widely used – particularly by Birmingham itself, which agrees the rates with the DLO and two leading building employers' organizations, and revises them every two years – it is far from being the only one used. Its lack of

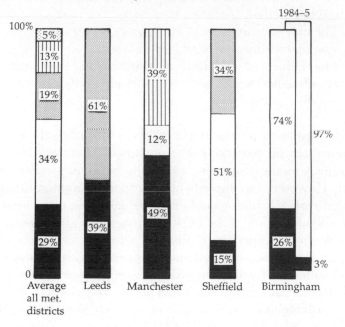

Comparison of extent to which different charging
methods make up total DLO income 1983–4

DLOs are required to keep to their original quotation or tender for work
carried out. There are several ways of estimating the charges:

Schedule contracts: charging is on the basis of a schedule of rates.
Each operation or job has a unit rate, e.g. re-run putty – £x per metre.

Lump-sum contracts: the most comprehensive charging methods
whereby the operations and quantities involved in the specific
work are detailed and a price built up.

Target hours: measured times are set for the jobs and the charge is
based on these target hours. Bonus schemes are used as incentives
to complete the work within the target time.

Day-work contract: this is simply a charge based on the number of
hours spent on the job.

Other

Figure 3.1 *Use of different charging methods*

widespread acceptance may be attributable to certain factors,
enumerated by the Association of Metropolitan Authorities in its
1983 survey. Among these are:

1   The excessive cost of preparing *standard* SORs, both for local authorities who have their own SORs, and for those who do not use the method.
2   The excessive number of SORs in existence.
3   The unwieldiness of SORs for daily use.
4   The failure of standard descriptions to cover all types of maintenance work, and the different needs of local authority building stock.

One argument against the blanket use of SORs is their difficulty of application in particular circumstances. For regular, planned, routine work they constitute an invaluable management accounting tool. However, for unpredictable and thus unquantifiable emergency work, e.g. finding and mending gas leaks, their use is limited.

Implementation of the SOR approach has also proved difficult. One authority experienced difficulty when the change in legislation required an increase from 30 percent to 60 percent in the amount of work subject to tender. The authority recognized its need to develop a detailed SOR quickly, but it had neither the technical expertise nor the available time to do so. The result, according to the DLO chief executive, was disastrous. The DLO submitted its bid on the SOR basis for the major repairs and maintenance tender put out by the local authority, and in fact won the contract – at a price which was £1.4m and 23 percent lower than the nearest competitor. The result of winning the bid led, according to the manager, to a lack of motivation by DLO operatives, because the tender price caused a large loss to the DLO. The operatives realized that the loss was outside their control. Paradoxically, of course, the client's housing revenue account benefited by having the work performed at such a competitive price.

It is unlikely that the client would have known about the DLO's situation. At council level DLO accounts are discussed in sub-committees and most of the discussion is held in camera. Much of the information is confidential and thus the DLO may not tell the client anything it believes the client should not otherwise know. Thus the DLO may argue that, because of the nature of the arm's length transaction between client and contractor, the client may have no right to know what it costs the DLO to perform a contract; the only information provided is that relating to the cost of the job, a situation analogous to that between private contractor and customer. In fact our experience is that many DLO managers see it as their duty to hide such information from their client, irrespective of the percentage amount of total DLO work done for the client. This approach is consistent with the spirit of the 1980 legislation and separates DLO management from the rest of the local authority, with potential dysfunctional decision-making for the authority as a whole.

The costs of implementing more sophisticated tendering methods should not be underestimated. The following extract from the 1985 Annual Report of the City of Aberdeen's Department of Building and Works expressed the point well:

One of the aims of the legislation is to impose competition for construction and maintenance work undertaken by a local authority. However, the very requirements of the legislation, not least in the accounting provisions and extensive administrative procedures, have caused DLOs and other Departments of Local Authorities to incur considerably increased costs which, in themselves, undermine the efficiency of DLOs.

In addition, the legislation makes no allowance for the administrative costs that are borne by local authorities when using private contractors as compared with their DLOs. A detailed investigation undertaken by the Association of Metropolitan Authorities reveals that increased costs of the order of 7% results to local authorities in the tendering, supervision, certification and extra administration necessitated by the legislation. Whilst the Council is making every effort to minimise these costs, the legislation will result in local authorities either reducing much needed maintenance budgets or having to increase costs at a time when they are being told to economise.

Planning issues

Competitive tendering has changed the rules of the game beyond recognition for DLO management. If, as we have seen, DLOs are unsuccessful in winning important contracts, the long-run effects are bleak indeed. Short-term planning overrides any systematic attempt to plan in detail for the future. DLOs are thus caught in a dilemma. The 1980 Act positively encourages and indeed even requires DLO management to act as would a short-term profit-oriented private contractor, while, on the other hand, local authority policies, objectives and statutory restrictions constrain the options available to the DLO to a mere subset of those available to private contractors. For example, DLOs cannot easily adjust their management structure, because of trade-union agreements, they find it difficult to react to changing workloads and speedily recruit extra staff needed for new contracts, and they are unable to divert and adapt capital resources without seeking time-consuming political and financial approval.

Conclusion

It has not been the purpose of this chapter to discuss the many issues and problems faced by DLOs as a result of the 1980 Act, or to prescribe standard solutions. Indeed, as we have suggested elsewhere in the paper, we believe such an approach to be impracticable because of the extreme diversity of DLO organizations and operations. Instead we have focused on a number of issues which emerged from our detailed interviews with individual DLOs.

It soon became apparent that the operational problems of DLOs are merely symptoms of the greater problems of organizational structure and conflicting objectives. It has been suggested here and elsewhere (e.g. Walsh, 1985) that many of the problems relate to providing management information for trading purposes. These could be overcome, at least in part, by the separation of the DLO from both central finance and client department constraints. Autonomous decision-making by DLOs in itself raises a number of different problems, which are, to a large degree, similar to those experienced by the private sector.

For example, the imposition of a profit target on four different parts of the organization has exposed DLOs to management accounting issues relating to the measurement of divisional performance. Furthermore, if the DLO is viewed as a division of a local-authority unit, there may be conflicts between the objective function of the latter and the objective function of the secretary of state.

In particular, the internal management accounting function has now become subservient to the external reporting function. This has resulted in an overemphasis on achieving current profit targets.

Kaplan (1984) has observed that when profit targets become hard to achieve because output is not increasing as fast as expected, or variable and operating costs are rising faster than expected, managers may try to minimize the adverse impact on short-term earnings by reducing other expenditures, e.g. quality improvement, human resources, customer relations and other such intangibles. The immediate impact of such expenditure reductions is to improve the reported profitability of the division by risking the long-term effectiveness of the organization. This problem may be insurmountable for marginal DLOs, since their long-term future is limited by legislation to just 3 years. A DLO which tries to improve its long-term effectiveness and as a consequence suffers reduced reported earnings in the short term may not survive long enough to reap the benefits, since the secretary of state may use his power of closure.

The conflict between short-term pressures and long-term planning is accentuated by the use of a single financial measure (return on capital) to both evaluate and motivate managers. Even within the private sector it has been suggested that multiple performance measures, comprising both financial and non-financial targets, are crucial to the success of an organization. Indeed Peters and Waterman (1982) suggest from their study of American companies:

> We find among the excellent companies a few common attributes that unify them despite their very different values. First, these values are almost always stated in qualitative, rather than quantitative terms . . . Furthermore, financial and strategic objectives are never stated alone. They are always discussed in the context of other things the company expects to do well. The idea that profit is a natural product of doing something well, not an end in itself, is also almost universal.

Thus, if the role of a DLO is, as the government has suggested, to act 'as if' it were a private contractor, then the imposition of rigid profit targets may not necessarily be the way to achieve success, either financial or otherwise. Other measures, perhaps relating to productivity, employee skills and morale, and customer satisfaction, may be much better indicators of effectiveness, and even of future profitability, than annual profits. These multiple performance measures are even more important when it is recognized that DLOs are not surrogates for private sector companies; they were conceived out of social and political needs, and these roles are still of paramount importance. To treat DLOs as wholly separate organizations has given rise to dysfunctional decision-making and the elevation of departmental and professional interests over broader authority-wide interests represented by the community in general and tenants in particular.

Furthermore, the heterogeneous nature of DLOs raises the question of the validity of a unitary set of accounting rules or a standard system of management information as measures or controls either among or within DLOs. Management accounting cannot exist as a separate discipline by employing one set of accounting and measurement procedures. It must have regard to the underlying values, goals and strategies of particular DLOs. DLOs should be exposed to multiple performance measures which encompass both the financial and non-financial objectives placed upon them by their dual masters, the parent authority and the secretary of state. These are difficult but not insurmountable tasks. The private sector is already beginning to examine and react to these related issues. The government has signalled its intention to extend the principles of the 1980 Act to other local authority departments. If it is successful, these accounting problems will no longer be confined to DLOs.

References

Chartered Institute of Public Finance and Accountancy (1975). *Direct Works Undertakings Accounting*. CIPFA.

Chartered Institute of Public Finance and Accountancy (1978). *Direct Works Undertakings (Maintenance) – A Discussion Document*. CIPFA.

Chartered Institute of Public Finance and Accountancy (1981). *Direct Labour Organisation, Code of Practice*. CIPFA.

Department of the Environment (1978). *Working Party on Direct Labour Organisations – Final Report*. DOE.

El-Deen, M. B., El-Kady, B. and Johnson, D. K. (1985). *A Comparative Study of the Accounting Systems of Direct Labour Organisations and Their Implementation – a survey study report*. Department of Management Sciences, UMIST.

Flynn, N. and Walsh, K. (1984). *Managing Direct Labour Organisations*. Institute of Local Government Studies, University of Birmingham.

Kaplan, R. S. (1982). The Evolution of Management Accounting. *The Accounting Review*, July.

Langford, D. A. (1982). *Direct Labour Organisations in the Construction Industry.* Gower.

Peters, T. J. and Waterman, R. H. (1982). *In Search of Excellence; Lessons from America's Best-Run Companies.* Harper & Row.

Walsh, K. (1985). *Contracting Local Services. A consideration of the impact of Competition in the provision of local authority services.* Institute of Local Government Studies, University of Birmingham, August.

4 Management accounting developments in British Rail

David Allen

Introduction

British Rail essentially comprises five business sectors, three of which are passenger businesses presently supported by government and local authorities, and the others a freight business and a parcels business. Taking each in turn, their main spheres of operations are as follows.

Passenger: InterCity

Fast, high quality services largely based on London and its links with major population centres. Services operate over four radial routes from London as follows:

1 The East Coast main line via York to Edinburgh.
2 The West Coast main line via Birmingham and Manchester to Glasgow.
3 The Midland main line to Nottingham and Sheffield.
4 The Western Region main lines via Bristol to South Wales and the West Country.

InterCity also operates a cross-country service from the North East to the South West.

Passenger: Network SouthEast

Commuting services, roughly within a radius of 60 miles of London.

Passenger: provincial

All other passenger services, including cross-country routes and commuting services into all major conurbations except London. In particular this will include the British Rail services sponsored and paid for by local authorities through seven passenger transport executives: Strathclyde, Tyne & Wear, Merseyside, Greater Manchester, West Yorkshire, South Yorkshire and the West Midlands.

Freight

Mainly based on trainload business in bulk commodities, such as coal, iron and steel, oil, aggregates, etc. However, it also operates a network of dedicated wagonload services from major centres under the brand name 'Speedlink'.

Parcels

This business is based on speedy delivery of small packages, newspapers, letter mails, etc., partly through the operation of specific parcels trains and partly trading on the spare capacity of passenger trains.

Having briefly introduced the railway's businesses, the focus of this chapter, for completeness it is important to note that British Railways Board has two important subsidiary businesses:

1 Freightliners Ltd, a rail-based container business with a turnover of £105m.
2 British Rail Property Board, which is concerned with the management and development of the Board's property interests. Its annual letting income is £75m.

In total British Rail moves 660 million passengers per annum, and 140 million tonnes of freight, and has a total income of some £2,300m from Railways Operations. It drew support of £714 million from government and £73 million from local authorities in 1986–7.

Organization

Until 1982 the railways' management had been based upon

traditional lines, with a chief executive sitting on the board controlling the business through five geographically based general managers (the regions). Regions in turn exercised control through functional departments covering:

(a) Operations.
(b) Civil engineering.
(c) Signal and telecommunications engineering.
(d) Mechanical and electrical engineering.
(e) Finance.
(f) Personnel.

In essence BR was a production-led organization, though there was a business presence within the regional structure represented by freight, passenger and parcels marketing management.

While this structure was well understood and effective in cost-control terms, through some 4,000 cost centres, it was not perceived to be right for managing the trade-offs between costs and income in an increasingly competitive environment, responding effectively to customers' needs, achieving clear accountability for net results at all levels, and shaping business requirements in a number of different markets.

The change which followed, referred to internally as 'sector management', saw the creation of five sector directors, and was designed to produce a cultural switch from the largely production-led organization to one which is business-led. This has been achieved by disaggregating 'bottom-line' responsibility, thus focussing attention, as far as possible, on the profit/loss performance rather than receipts and costs in isolation, as in the past.

The top structure which has been produced as part of this change is as shown in Figure 4.1. The vice-chairman exercises control through two joint managing directors, and all three are main board members.

Reporting to the sector directors there are some thirty sub-sector managers, located in the regions. The number of sub-sectors and their nature are related to the business characteristics (markets) of the individual sectors. Sub-sector managers have bottom-line responsibility for the contributions earned by groups of profit centres (services, of which there are roundly 700).

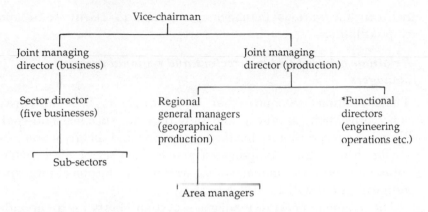

* Excluding those who are corporate in nature,
  e.g. finance and personnel, which respond
  direct to the board

Figure 4.1 *Top structure of railways' business*

The management team shown at Figure 4.1, plus the finance and personnel directors, meets as a group each 4 weeks to ensure effective coordination within the matrix. Chaired by the vice-chairman, this is known as the Railway Executive, the key forum for communicating the board's policies, ratifying the work of a number of specific sub-committees and agreeing action required. On several occasions over the year this meeting turns itself into a planning conference and devotes itself to progressing and updating the 'Rail Plan', thus giving direction to sector directors, regional general managers and functional directors. A standard item on the 4-weekly agenda is financial performance, which means that this executive grouping is constantly concerned with control from inception (the Plan) to delivery (budget and outturn).

In financial control terms the most significant sub-committee is the Business Review Group. Chaired by the joint managing director (businesses) and attended by joint managing director (production), the 5 Sector Directors and Director of Finance and Planning, its major role is to settle control budgets for each of the businesses and monitor performance against them each 4 weeks. It is the springboard for most of the control action generated during the year.

Before moving forward it is essential to outline the relations between the various management groups to clarify roles and responsibilities.

Relations between sector directors and regional general managers

These relations recognize that sector directors have authority concerning their 'products' and how they are specified and sold. They have responsibility for the bottom line and quality standards set for their sectors. As indicated above, each sector director has sub-sector business managers to whom this responsibility and authority is delegated.

The regional general manager's accountability is to provide services at a cost and quality agreed between the sector and the region. Apart from the above accountabilities to sector directors, regional general managers are also accountable for the management and coordination of their regions, for maintaining quality and improving productivity, and for representing and safeguarding the interests and reputation of BR within their regions.

Relations between functional directors, regions and sectors

In order to ensure that regional general managers have complete authority over resources in meeting their accountabilities to sector directors, areas of overlapping responsibilities with headquarters functional directors have been identified and eliminated. Functional directors are responsible and accountable for identifying, developing and monitoring, implementation of the technical policies and corresponding action plans for improvement in medium- and long-term cost trends, and for standards and technical safety in support of sector policies and objectives. Generally they have no direct responsibility or accountability for functional budgets other than for their own headquarters staff and services. Consequently, responsibility for shorter-term actions and day-to-day management lies, for the most part, with regional general managers and their regional functional chief officers. However, the functional directors still retain responsibility for a number of limited activities which require day-to-day coordination on a national basis, e.g. coordination of the shopping programme for the servicing of locomotives, etc., and management of the national telecommunications network.

Relations between area managers, regional general managers and sectors

In the early stages of sector management the pivotal relationship, below HQ, was between the sub-sector managers and regional functional managers. As the management style has evolved, the emphasis has shifted to one where the main 'contractual deals' are struck between the sub-sectors and area managers. The areas' relationships are therefore:

1 Direct responsibility to regional functional managers for current performance and professional standards.
2 Settlements of a performance 'contract' with the appropriate sub-sector business manager for expenditure targets against agreed specification.

Figure 4.2 summarizes the key features set out above, emphasizing the nature of the various contractual relations between the sector director with bottom-line responsibility and the region as the production department.

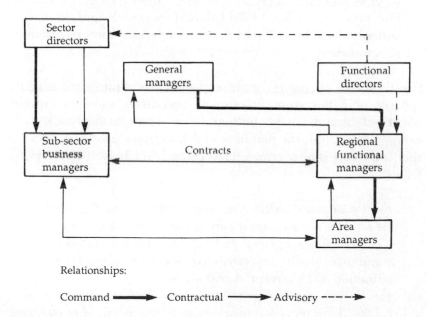

Figure 4.2 *Organizational relations*

It is this fundamental change and the attendant complex relations which represented the challenge for the management information and control systems. It is vital as a backdrop for understanding the developments which have taken place.

Objectives and the budgeting process

The British Railways Board currently operates within a financial framework set by Government in the form of:

1   A predetermined limit on external financing which covers all external funds required by the board for its operations whether in the form of grants or borrowing.
2   A predetermined cash limit on the amount of grant which government is prepared to pay for the services it requires the board to operate as part of the Public Service Obligation (PSO). The obligation currently requires the board to operate a network of passenger services broadly in line with that which existed in 1975. As such, the board receives support for its passenger services whether InterCity, Network SouthEast or Provincial. However, from 1 April 1988 InterCity was no longer eligible for support. Freight and parcels do not receive any grants from government.

Clearly these cash limits condition the policies of the board in all its railway activities from investment and asset sales to current operations and business bottom lines. Their achievement is a primary input into the planning and budgetary processes. Within this framework the government has recently set 3-year objectives, as follows:

(a) *For the supported sectors (Network SouthEast and Provincial, post-1.4.88)*. To reduce support from the 1986–7 level of £736m to £555m (at 1986–7 prices) by 1989–90 while maintaining quality standards (quality objectives are separately agreed). This is a reduction of 25 percent in real terms.
(b) *For the non-supported sectors (freight, parcels and InterCity, post-1.4.88)*. To achieve a return on assets employed, after charging depreciation at current cost, of at least 2.7 percent by 1989–90.

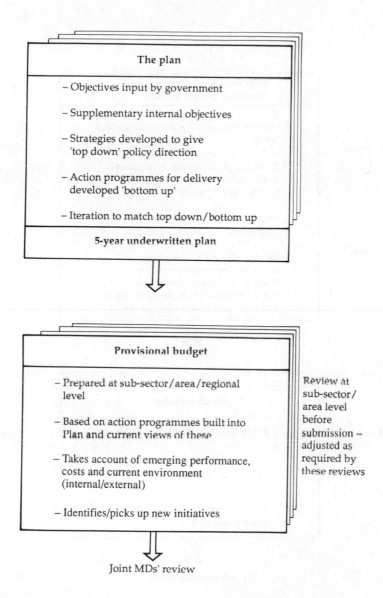

The plan

– Objectives input by government

– Supplementary internal objectives

– Strategies developed to give
  'top down' policy direction

– Action programmes for delivery
  developed 'bottom up'

– Iteration to match top down/bottom up

5-year underwritten plan

Provisional budget

– Prepared at sub-sector/area/regional
  level

– Based on action programmes built into
  Plan and current views of these

– Takes account of emerging performance,
  costs and current environment
  (internal/external)

– Identifies/picks up new initiatives

Review at
sub-sector/
area level
before
submission –
adjusted as
required by
these reviews

Joint MDs' review

Figure 4.3   *Business budget and monitoring cycle*

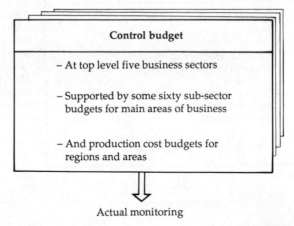

Joint managing directors' review (Business Review Group)

– Reviews the aggregated sector budgets in the context of objectives and the Plan for the year

– Identifies policy and tactical change to get back on course/exploit new trends and initiatives

– Ensures all changes are fed down and underwritten at level of delivery

– Finally, after further meetings as necessary, determines the Control Budget. This fixes delivery for net business result (sector/sub-sector) and production costs (regions/area)

Control budget

– At top level five business sectors

– Supported by some sixty sub-sector budgets for main areas of business

– And production cost budgets for regions and areas

Actual monitoring

Figure 4.3   *continued*

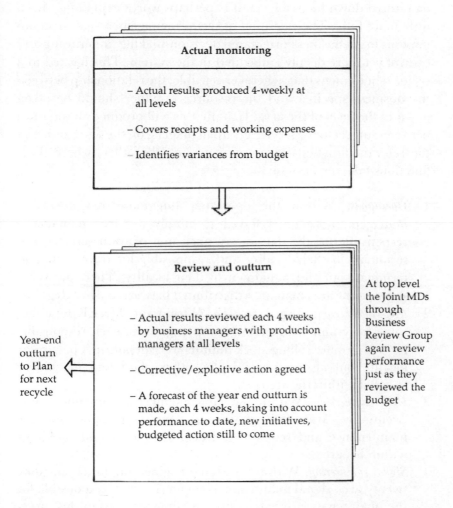

Figure 4.3 *continued*

These then are the starting points for the development of internally generated sector targets, and strategies for their achievement.

The business budget and monitoring cycle are best described in diagrammatic form, as shown at Figure 4.3. It starts with the Plan, through which government objectives are translated into board policy and performance goals, and concludes with the year end outturn being fed back to the next plan rolled forward.

While Figure 4.3 indicates that budgets are compiled and monitored down to area level, it is perhaps worth explaining this a little more fully. The evolution of sector management has given an impetus to get business-orientated decision-making, monitoring and control yet more deeply embedded in the system. This has led to a sector requirement that, wherever sensible, the relationship between the business specifier and the resource provider should be taken down to the level of the area. Usually this will produce an interface between sub-sector or service group managers, on the one hand, and the relevant functional area manager, on the other, where these functions take the form of:

1   *Operations*. Within the operating function, area operating managers (normally referred to simply as 'area managers') responsible for the day-to-day operation of train services and terminals in their locality and responsible for train crew and terminal staff and signalmen in their locality. There are some seventy-one area managers distributed between the five Regions.

2   *Mechanical engineering (M&EE)*. Within the M&EE function, some forty-nine area maintenance engineers, each responsible for one or more rolling stock maintenance depots in a particular ˙ locality but also responsible for other plant and machinery situated within the area.

3   *Civil engineering*. Within the civil engineering function, some twenty-five area civil engineers, each responsible for the maintenance and renewal of track, structures and buildings within his area.

4   *Signal engineering*. Within the signal engineering function, some twenty area signal maintenance engineers, each responsible for the maintenance of signalling equipment within his area, together with a slightly smaller number of works engineers,

responsible for signalling renewals, and telecommunications engineers, responsible for telecommunications.

In order to take the business dimension down to the level of the area in whatever function, and in order to provide the appropriate degree of debate, creative tension and agreement as to what level of resources of what quality is to be provided to the businesses, it is necessary that two basic conditions are met. These are:

(a) That the individual sectors' requirements for resources (whether train crew, terminal staff, rolling stock or infra-structure facilities) can be identified at area level.
(b) That the spending functions can allocate money sufficiently precisely to the relevant local disaggregations of staff/assets.

In respect of budget compilation and review, all budgets now start with the planning process. Sector plans/strategies produce sub-sector goals and these provide the targets which must be met. Thus a sub-sector manager in determining and agreeing his specification, and its cost consequences, with the relevant area functional managers (engineering or operating) will be aware of his target bottom line. The specification provided by the sub-sector managers and the undertaking given to deliver at an agreed cost by the relevant area production managers will form a 'contract', its basic expression being sub-sector budgets, on the one hand, and area production volume and cost budgets, on the other. Sub-sector/profit centre managers, in addition to setting a specification, will review and agree area budgets. In turn, sub-sector budgets will be reviewed/agreed by sector directors. All necessary budgets will be recycled to the appropriate level to secure a control budget which meets the sector's objective.

In respect of monitoring, the same process will be followed, in that sector directors monitor in total and review sub-sector performance. Action will be called for as necessary by the subsector/profit centre managers. Sub-sectors will seek action for change by reference back to those responsible for production – area production managers. The role of the general manager is in the nature of a coordinator of all production units (areas) within his region. Key responsibilities therefore are professional/technical guidance, and management audit/quality of performance.

The whole thrust of this approach, in whatever function, is to more closely relate what the functions provide with what the business managers require and can afford. In addition, it will give the sectors (at local but more particularly at regional and national level) comparative indicators of performance, which, when treated with care to isolate particular local circumstances, will provide further leverage in terms of bringing performance up to that of best practice.

Development of cost identification

In setting our hand to the development of information systems, it was of paramount importance that they reflected the organizational arrangements outlined above. To this end a matrix of information has been created whereby the functional nature of production and engineering endeavour located in geographic regions is now inter-faced with the five sectors. This can be seen in Figure 4.4.

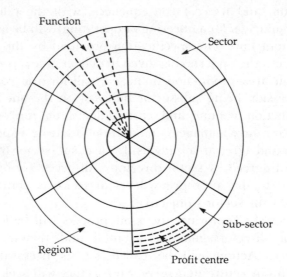

Figure 4.4 *Geographic/functional management information/business sector management information*

Sector influence over costs thus touches all regions, all functions within regions and every area within them both. To achieve this, it was necessary to develop a completely new computing package to replace former manual systems for business information. Production budgets were already largely computerized. Computerization made it possible to produce actual results to a comparable depth of analysis which had hitherto only been attempted in an annual exercise. Simultaneous renewal of expenditure-accounting computer and clerical systems enabled this to be enhanced to four-weekly actual and budget reporting. This transformed the nature of the product from a tool of strategic direction to an instrument of financial control.

The primary objective of the new systems has been to create five separate financial entities as far as possible within the limitations of joint and shared resources. In doing so, it was important to encompass the following requirements if sector control was to have meaning:

1   Managerial responsibility for all costs and receipts to reside with sectors.
2   A direct link between physical assets and financial consequences to be established.
3   The capacity to trace back to source.
4   The facility for business managers to talk to resource managers in the same financial language.
5   Information to be provided at intervals appropriate for management to react to evolving circumstances.

The three planks of the development process were:

(a)   To construct a financial language common to both business and production management.
(b)   To build on the cost-centre structure which had already proved robust in cost control.
(c)   To produce a series of conventions which identified production costs with businesses in a manner that clarified business responsibility and management signals.

Cost centres and classification of costs

The basic building block adopted for the control system is the cost

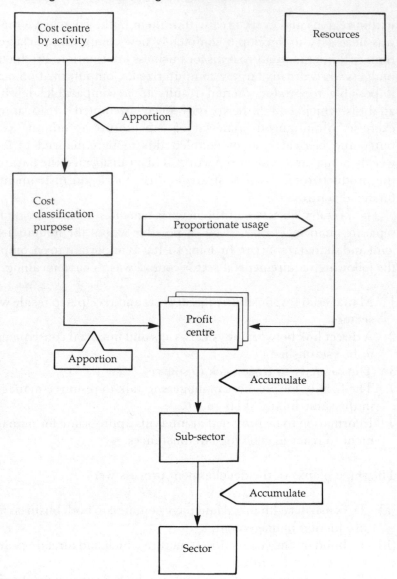

Figure 4.5 *Former analysis by sector*

centre. However, in order to make business control more effective and to meet the requirement for tracing costs back to source, several key enhancements have been introduced.

The entire classification of expenditure was recast in 1983 and cost centres re-established so that the first stage of complexity in the former analysis was eliminated. This allowed for the establishment of a common financial language between sectors and line managers, which had not been possible under previous conditions, where dual systems of purpose and activity classifications had run in parallel.

The redefinition of cost centres presented the opportunity to maximize the identification of staff resources with sectors, where this was managerially sensible for day-to-day control purposes. A significant degree of sector specificity was achieved by this means, and minor changes have continued to be made in this area to that end.

Some of the sophistications and economic niceties in the identification of costs and resources to sectors have been replaced by more robust and accessible conventions designed to forge a more direct link between physical assets and the financial consequences of their management. It can be seen from Figure 4.5 that the former system required extensive allocation from cost-centre appropriations to a large number of small profit-centre traffic flows. The allocations to each of the many hundreds of profit centres had then to be accumulated in order to achieve a sector perspective.

It has been possible to reverse the sequence so that identification with sector is sought first, often now without resort to any allocation at all, and only after that to sub-sector, by way of new conventions. As can be seen in Figure 4.6, the analysis to individual profit centres is relegated to a secondary analysis, which is conducted at a lower frequency than that for sector and sub-sector. In this way the capability to assess economic performance at a low level has been retained, but the main thrust of the financial control mechanism is aligned with sectors and business managers of the sub-sectors.

Under the new regime the easier and more meaningful task of identification of whole blocks of resources with a small number of large business units – the sectors – is done first. Allocation and apportionment are only resorted to at a late stage in finer breakdowns within the sector – particularly the breakdown to profit centre. The new regime therefore minimizes the extent and consequences of arbitrary allocation, whereas the old regime, starting from the lowest levels, tended to accentuate it.

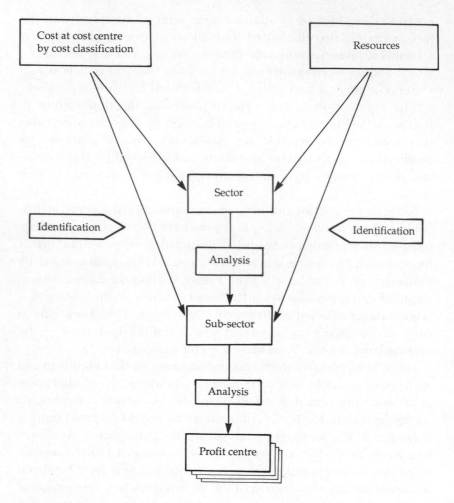

Figure 4.6 *Current build-up by sector*

Cost conventions

Since any analysis of costs by business will require the adoption of cost conventions, where resources cannot be uniquely identified (through cost centres, etc.), it is worth looking more closely at this issue. The range of possible approaches is constrained only by the power of the imagination and, in some cases, of the computer itself. However, in the context of a budgetary control regime it is important to remember what is the prime purpose, i.e. to secure control by identifying accountability.

Given this as a starting point a number of important guidelines for the development of conventions emerge:

1   They should be managerially clear. The main aim of the system should be to focus managerial attention and accountability, rather than pursue economic truths. It is important to note that these guidelines are related to conventions' development in the context of budgetary control. They would not apply to financial modelling, where the basic objective is different. As far as possible, rail business models rightly do attempt to pursue economic truths.

2   Conventions should be defensible and developed on a rational basis. They should treat the businesses even-handedly, as to do otherwise would inevitably distort the allocation of resources (physical and financial) and fundamentally undermine the principle of accountability upon which business management is based.

3   They should be developed within the bounds of accounting propriety.

4   They should provide stability in the relations between the businesses, so that changes thrown up by the system have meaning, i.e. that they are not just the results of the convention in operation.

5   Once agreed by the businesses and production, they should only change through joint agreement.

Specificity

The driving force behind the review of attribution conventions was always the search for greater specificity. It is possible to construct an approximate sliding scale of specificity across the major cost headings and to show against each the predominant costing philosophy which applies. No diagram at this level of generalization can be comprehensive, and there are significant elements of absolute specificity in both general expenses and infrastructure. Nevertheless, Figure 4.7 does provide a flavour of the cost characteristics and the general approach adopted in each case. Later sections look in a little more detail at each major cost heading.

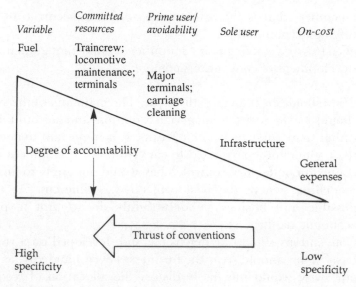

Figure 4.7 *The spectrum of specificity*

Thus, wherever possible, costs which can be identified directly or specifically with a sector/sub-sector are handled in this way. Where this is not possible, the remaining conventions of underwriting committed resources, prime user and sole user are applied to clarify accountability.

Underwritten and committed resources

Resource management is a key feature of sector management. This has been enhanced by the introduction of the principle of underwriting, whereby a given quantum of assets or jobs are agreed in advance through the budget mechanism. The agreements cover a wide range, from staff numbers at terminals, through permanent way relaying jobs, to the investment programme. In practice this has worked very well, but is conditional upon the common unit of measurement being simple and well understood, which was one of the major factors behind the need to review methodology at the time of computerization. Complementary to the principle of underwriting is the committed resource rule, whereby a sector which has undertaken to make use of a given number of resources, say locomotives, will be held to that commitment even if in practice demand does not materialize to enable full use to be made of them.

Only by removing the assets from the system, or by mutual agreement to transfer to another sector, can a sector improve its position. This rule holds good over time, so discussions of budget or plan can concentrate upon change and not repeat debates about the base.

Prime user/avoidability

In order to ensure that the dialogue between business managers and functional line managers is conducted efficiently, it is essential that there is no doubt as to who is responsible for what. Prime user is the means by which responsibility is determined for, *inter alia*, carriage cleaning, depots and terminals. While it is not so difficult to identify specifically the sector which sponsors a particular train service, it is a much more difficult task for a large passenger station.

It was possible to identify prime usership from the experience gained in measuring comparative usage under earlier business analysis, but this only provided the first step. The true test was to decide which sector basically determined the character of the route or terminal in question, and on this basis to assign notional ownership to sectors.

This is not to imply that sponsors (prime users) should be charged the full cost of all that they sponsor, but it does mean that the matrix for decision-making is very straightforward and robust. The subordinate subset of rules for allocating costs between prime users and other interested sectors is governed by the convention of avoidability. The avoidability test is applied at each cost centre in response to the question: 'If this Sector ceased to exist, all others continuing, what facilities and costs would be avoided?' In this way it has been possible to assess an appropriate charge for secondary or tertiary users. In turn avoidability is applied within sectors to their constituent sub-sectors.

Sole user

The sole-user convention essentially builds on prime user and is the basis of the current methodology for analysing infrastructure costs by sector. Of all the cost headings, this was without doubt the most difficult to handle in a managerially coherent way. It is perhaps worth tracing the earlier approaches which ultimately led us to settle on the sole-user approach.

Before the present regime was adopted, there had been four different approaches to infrastructure – the cost of providing and maintaining bridges, tunnels, earthworks, track and signalling. Each was a logical development of what went before and a direct response to managerial pressure for knowledge about the business. All have been concerned with attribution of infrastructure to individual parts of the business. The development of new theories did not necessarily devalue earlier work nor indeed mean its abandonment. For instance, contribution accounting is still relevant and applied for profit centres of the business, avoidable theory forms an essential part of the prime user approach and sole user builds on the central assumptions of prime user.

Approaches to infrastructure

Total cost allocation. This approach, widely used by railways throughout the world, sidesteps the basic problem of relating costs with actual performance of an operation. In essence a share of the joint indirect cost of track and signalling is allocated to traffics on the basis of a measure of their physical use of the facility, e.g. gross tonne miles for track and train miles for signalling. The insidious danger of such full cost allocation, on the basis of arithmetic, appears to make it possible to determine the total cost of any traffic movement within the network, however small, and confers a spurious numerate precision on such estimates.

There is little doubt that over the years the qualifications attached to cost estimates, warning that a true total cost could not be produced, came to be viewed merely as a form of technical purism. This resulted in an authority which would not have been claimed by analysts producing the information being attached to it by the layman.

What made it worse was that this system was adopted 'lock, stock and barrel' for the calculation of grant aid for unremunerative passenger services under the terms of the 1968 Act. (From that time it became known as the Cooper Brothers formula, after the consultants then employed to pass judgement on costing methods.) It was at this time that it became clear that the system was giving false impressions of the potential for cost saving on withdrawal or reduction in the level of service. The system was not primarily designed to provide for Business Management being neither related to cost behaviour nor attempting to identify responsibility.

Contribution accounting. Although grants continued to be paid on the Cooper Brothers' formula through to 1974, contribution accounting was used internally from 1970. This deeply conservative retreat from full allocation made no attribution of infrastructure costs at all, save those that could incontrovertibly be specifically identified without allocation. The pretence that there was any direct relation between volume changes and expenditure levels was ended abruptly.

Admirable though the theoretical method was, in stating that infrastructure would be funded from the corporate excess of income over direct expenses, there were problems. It was not always clear what appropriate level of contribution each service was expected to make. As a means of business control it did not even begin to address the issue of responsibility for infrastructure. There was also a suspicion that, combined with market pricing, there was a risk of under-achievement and extending short-run activities into a longer period. However, the major theoretical justification for its retention was the supposed invariability of infrastructure costs to changes in volume. This was put to the test in the avoidability studies.

Avoidable costs. The thrust of the analysis here is directed towards answering the question: 'If this sector ceased to exist, with all others continuing, what facilities and costs would be avoided?' The first test of this approach was for grant purposes under PSO conditions from 1975. The task was to identify the infrastructure charge avoidable to freight and parcels, as the PSO convention was that the railway was primarily a passenger network. As parcels generates a minuscule incremental requirement over the network, we have effectively provided a sector infrastructure facility since 1975 to freight. The sector recognized that it had clear responsibility and by persistent management pressure successfully reduced its infrastructure charge. The right environment for action had been created. This provided the encouragement to develop the application of avoidability to the passenger businesses as well.

When the preparatory work had been completed, it became clear that by expanding the analysis out to five sectors, the basic facility cost, which was left not avoidable to any, amounted to over 50 per cent of all infrastructure. This did not meet the basic requirement of managerial responsibility for all costs. In order to break out from a grant mechanism to an instrument of management control, the vital link to provide total responsibility had to be added. This is what prime user and sole user add to the basic tenet of avoidability.

Prime user and avoidability. Prime user attacks the problem of responsibility for infrastructure head on. All routes are assigned to one sector or another. Freight and parcels had already been identified, InterCity took the principal radial routes out of London and the NE/SW corridor, Network South East took the Southern Region and the Liverpool Street division and a few other branches on the Midland and Eastern, leaving Provincial the balance. In this way all expenditure had a business sponsor.

The principle of avoidability was invoked so that the prime-user sectors did not have to shoulder the full cost of their routes if others made significant demands upon them. So an individual sector was charged for the full cost of its routes, less the avoidable costs of secondary users, plus any avoidable costs where it was a secondary user of another sector's routes.

In practice the clarity of responsibility worked very well, and the sense of corporate interest was strong enough to hold back the temptation to disown routes in almost all cases. Although the mechanism of avoidability is rigidly hierarchical, and great care was taken to ensure that judgements were those of operators or engineers with sectors, not accountants, there was a natural bias against the sector in the primacy.

Included in the charge borne by the prime user was often an undisclosed element of surplus. Managerially it was correct that one sponsor was given responsibility, which created the environment for change and promoted pressure for cost reduction.

Robust though prime user is, it is at the point of taking action that its major weakness becomes apparent. A system geared to today's railway, replete with hidden surpluses, is no guide to business decisions for the future. The sole-user convention, which was approved in August 1984, was introduced to address this issue.

The present regime. This is illustrated diagrammatically in Figure 4.8, which sets the prime-user approach alongside sole user and contrasts the two.

The first distinction is that it is 'bottom up' rather than 'top down'. Prime user worked by hypothetically removing first the tertiary and then the secondary sector, leaving the sector in the primacy to take the rump. Sole user does exactly the same thing but

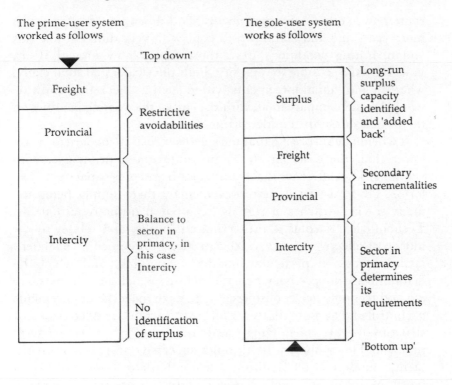

Figure 4.8 *Prime user and sole user*

in reverse order, introducing first the sector in the primacy, then the secondary and finally the tertiary sector. The next and fundamental distinction is that sole user, working 'bottom up', starts with a 'blank sheet of paper' – essentially a zero-based budgeting approach. It then hypothetically introduces the physical requirements of each sector in turn and incrementally in modern form. In other words, it lays down the railway infrastructure appropriate to today's conditions and in the most fitting modern technical form and does not work within the infrastructure which is actually out there on the route now – often dated technically, laid down 20, 30, 40 or even more years ago and laid down to cope with very different markets and operating conditions from those which now prevail. It is, however, still possible to quantify, both physically and financially, what the individual increments within such a 'theoretical railway' would be and compare them with the cost of the existing facilities on the route as described under prime-user costing.

It will not be surprising that the sole-user costs in modern form are lower than the costs for the same route under prime-user conventions. The difference is accounted for by surplus capacity, in two forms. Physical surplus is represented by there simply being too many tracks, switches or signals for modern traffic requirements. Technological surplus is rather more complex and relates to the more cost-effective layouts which can often be obtained with modern facilities and, in particular, modern signalling, and which by definition are not present where the facilities which actually exist are old and technologically obsolescent. So as to meet the requirements of control and accountability for all costs, surplus is added back in a structured way, identifying responsibility for its longer-term removal. This will often be through successive tranches of investment to modernize the facilities. Sole user has already proved to be a powerful means of analysis for investment projects, where all infrastructure schemes are now required to be assessed on this basis. This means they are subjected to the rigours of business specification and scrutiny at an early stage of appraisal.

Cost Treatment for major cost heads

While the conventions are considered philosophically above, it is perhaps worth looking briefly at their application over some major cost headings.

Fuel and power

This can to all intents and purposes be charged directly to sectors. Consumption rates for the various types of rolling stock can be established and held as constants with the system. Monitoring actual mileage run by sub-sector, while relating this to consumption rates, allows fuel to be operated as a variable cost.

Traincrews

The costs incurred at each traincrew depot are attributed to sub-sectors and sectors in proportion to the number of productive shifts worked for that sector, weighted for the cost characteristics of the shift in question (bonus payment, etc.). Manning levels at depots are derived from the planned workload, which in turn is a response to the timetable (service) specification demanded by sectors. Train-crew costing has been strengthened in two crucial ways. Firstly, the local costs of employing staff are now reflected in the costs attributed to the sub-sectors using that depot, so that there is a direct link between the area cost centre and sub-sector. This has enabled local business managers to underwrite the workload of particular depots and negotiate change commensurate with current experience and market demand. Secondly, the committed resource rule, whereby sectors are charged on the basis of planned workload and not day-to-day variations, applies. This is a safeguard to ensure that poor utilization of resources or disputes are contained at source and innocent sectors are not adversely affected by the performance of others. We are developing further refinements in the treatment of unproductive work and depot overheads in order to strengthen the sub-sector to area dialogue about the level of resources and their associated costs.

Rolling-stock provision and maintenance

The cost of maintaining each sub-class of rolling stock (circa 200 different types) is attributed to sector and sub-sector in relation to the resource commitment demanded by each sector. In many instances the identification of a particular type of stock with a sector or sub-sector is direct. But for the common-user assets, such as main-line diesel locomotives, a means of sharing the cost of provision between users has had to be provided.

The traditional approach of measuring the performance of rolling stock under the dual criteria of time and mileage has been withdrawn. Instead a pseudo prime-user regime has been intro-duced: now a sector is allocated the full cost of each diagram its stock is planned to work, less the proportion of the total time in the diagram spent on productive work for other sectors. Although this might appear to represent a harsh burden on the predominant user, because he has to pay for all unproductive time, it does provide an unambiguous identification of which sector is in the lead with regard to the drive for improvements in productivity. Strong sector identification with specific rolling-stock fleets has been aided by investment where sectors have sought greater specialization, such that many types of stock are now virtually sector-specific. Dedication of the fleet by sector and sub-sector is the ideal in control terms.

The modernization of expenditure-accounting systems, completed in 1985, provided the opportunity to record actual expenditure on rolling-stock depot maintenance in unit sub-type detail and interface with the new business reporting systems. Although the 1986–7 budget was prepared for each unit sub-type by every region, it was only in the 1987–8 budget that this was done for each depot. This has meant that the direct link between cost centre (regional maintenance depot) and sub-sector, through depot level attribution, was realized in the 1987–8 budget.

Yet more progress towards dedication of the fleet was possible as a result of the revised trading arrangements with BREL for the heavier repair and modification of stock. Now it operates as a contractor to the rail businesses, and invoices for work by type of work, which has provided an opportunity to charge rail sectors on the basis of ownerships of individual vehicles. In the minority of cases where stock is not already operationally dedicated, an allocation, which was sensible in terms of the long-term future of individual classes, was used. This experiment, known as allocation by painted number (the unique reference number for locos, etc.) proved a success and will be validated into a permanent commitment this year so as to form a solid basis upon which to found all budgets, including regional depots, for the following year. We plan to supplement the managerial robustness of fleet dedication with a controlled inter-sector charging mechanism, to encourage the use of resources in marginal time, thus maximizing the corporate benefit of stock with a common-user capability.

The consolidation of this, the framework for rolling-stock accounting, will take place concurrently with fundamental re-organization of the engineering function itself. That will be placed on a business footing at headquarters, with direct access to strengthened area teams on the ground.

Terminals

The prime-user methodology is used for terminals, carriage cleaning, and shunting and marshalling. In each case the major item of expenditure is staff costs, which are organized in cost centres. Prime ownership was derived from past experience of administering systems based on comparative usage. For many terminals no other means of attribution has been required, but where it has, an avoidability calculation has been invoked. At some terminals there is more than one secondary user, so fixed hierarchies have been established to determine the sequence of the avoidability test. For sectors, the order is InterCity first, followed by Network SouthEast, then Provincial with freight and parcels last. Within sectors, hierarchies have been established for the sub-sectors. Prime user has been the mechanism which has enabled sectors to take a leading role in the determination of appropriate staffing levels, investment decisions and the broadening of trading opportunities at 'their' terminals.

General expenses

As with any organization, BR has had to wrestle with the problems of overheads and how to inject effective business control in a difficult area. Although it has been possible to monitor the budget each 4 weeks against actual spending, it has remained a difficult area for sectors to deal with. The basic problem has been the absence of a tangible product in an extremely varied collection of costs. Recent attention has been focused upon this problem, and a programme of initiatives has been agreed with sectors to address these issues.

The main thrust of the attack on general expenses is to identify layers of expenditure with the sectors as specifically as possible, thus reducing their size to the real core overhead. The process by which this is being achieved is to move through a progression of methodologies or relationships as follows:

1 *Dispersal of central provisions.* The first step is to strip out the large provisions for items such as pricing, retirement benefits and uniform clothing, and recognize them as true costs of manpower. In this way the size of headquarters general expenses is greatly diminished and sectors are charged the full costs of manpower, through the activities on which the staff are engaged.

2 *Change of responsibility*. Where a department or function performs a task exclusively for a sector, it may be more appropriate for that sector to take direct responsibility for it. There may be other instances where the activities are seen to constitute such a fundamental part of the sector team effort that it would be more effective to manage them as a cohesive whole from within the sector. This route home is by organizational change, for which sectors must determine the scope and timing.

3 *Sector sponsorship*. Where a department cannot be wholly or substantially identified with a particular sector, but where its work, or individual elements of its work (projects), can be sponsored by sectors, this should be developed. Sectors have already developed a working relation with the research department, whereby the majority of research projects are sponsored and the charge to each sector reflects its sponsorship. The departments remain autonomous under this option, but their workload is directly controlled by sectors. The departments suitable for this type of relation usually service more than one sector. Coordinated action is therefore required of sectors to set up these new relations.

4 *Zero-based budgeting*. Having in this way identified the core general expenses, we have advocated a zero-based budgeting approach. This will apply to those departments falling outside the scope of organizational change or sector sponsorship. What is required is that sectors spell out their joint requirements for each department. These are then debated and recycled until an acceptable level of workload and resource requirement is determined. This technique is being introduced on a trial basis in the first instance.

The above changes are being implemented, but will not come to fruition overnight, as the delineation of true requirements is a lengthy and iterative process. Nevertheless, an agreed direction of change has been determined and a positive start made.

Income

The main purpose of this chapter is to explore BR experience in the treatment of costs, following the move to a business-led style of management. This is not because income is considered less important, merely that it is more easily handled than costs, and indeed the first generation of systems in the late 1960s had already tackled many of the problems. It is easier because the nature of the business and the source documents themselves (e.g. invoices for freight and parcels, and tickets for passenger journeys) identify as a minimum the first basic split between the businesses and in most cases (through commodity, or journey) more refined sector and sub-sector analyses. That is not to say that there are no problems with income nor indeed further developments taking place. Passenger income in particular is a sensitive area and sectors are anxious to ensure that what is generated by their energy finds its way into their bottom lines.

Thus for completeness it is worth noting that income for all sectors is identified by sector, sub-sector and, where appropriate, for freight-and-passenger, by main flows of business (profit centres). As indicated the major problems in securing this arise on the passenger side where the customer does have choice in the journeys made. A ticket, once sold, can be used for travel by any train during the period of validity between the two points specified on it. In a number of cases the passenger has a choice of alternative routes and services. There are five possible situations:

(a) The journey is entirely on one service, with no alternative available (this accounts for the vast majority of journeys).
(b) The passenger will not change trains en route, but has a choice of service direct to his destination.
(c) The passenger will change trains en route, but has no choice of service on any section of the journey.
(d) The passenger will change trains en route, and has a choice of service on one or more sections of the journey.
(e) The passenger has a choice of route, and within that choice any one of the previous four alternatives may apply.

In a business-led environment the analysis of earnings to services is clearly fundamental to the production of information for management. Perhaps the most important element therefore is the careful definition of the service entities by sector. While they should be small enough for local-management focus, they should be large enough to measure up to the requirements of market and cost integrity. It is on this basis that the lowest level of reporting, the profit centre, has been defined. Profit centres are unique to a sector and within it to a sub-sector. The thrust of the system is therefore to identify tickets/journeys with a profit centre or profit centres, and in turn with a sector. For the vast majority of journeys, see (a) above, the income can be directly attributed to the profit centre and sector concerned.

Where the passenger may exercise choice, see conditions (b)–(e) above, journey flows are allocated first to routes (e.g. a journey to Scotland may be via the West Coast Main Line or the East Coast Main Line), then within the routes to change points (depending upon the ultimate destination) and finally within change points to service. This allocation is based upon a mathematical modelling technique which determines likely customer preference and journey patterns, based upon a number of parameters:

1   The timetable and services on offer between relevant points.
2   Restrictions on choice implicit within the ticket type. For example, day returns are invalid on certain peak trains.
3   The journey duration of alternative services.
4   Interchange penalties where travellers are likely to elect for through services.

Each 4 weeks income statements for each profit centre are produced for sub-sector and sector management, giving an analysis by full fares, reduced fares and seasons. Passenger journeys and passenger miles, together with the average fare paid per journey and per mile, are also shown. Marketing information by product, e.g. discounted fares, Capital Cards, first-class travel, etc., is also provided from the same source data.

The corporate dimension

Sector management on British Rail is at best 5 years old, but more realistically we have less than 3 years' experience, allowing time for the organization to settle down. It was introduced as an evolutionary process (and continues to develop), not as a revolution sweeping away overnight 150 years of history. In financial information terms the systems have been functional since the 1985–6 budget year, and their programmed enhancement is still being pursued. In setting our hand to the construction of budgetary-control systems around five separate business entities, where there is significant sharing of resources, we inevitably created corporate tensions and the possibility of dysfunctional behaviour. At the outset we made a conscious decision to emphasize 'control' and the need for managerial clarity, even where this may offend conventional wisdom on joint costs. In that endeavour there is ample evidence that the approaches adopted have generated management signals and a business focus which has prompted questions in a manner and in areas not previously tackled. Nevertheless, it is still possible that one sector could propose action which, through the conventions adopted, would improve its own net performance while being detrimental in corporate terms.

Similarly, it is possible for a sector to pursue cost reductions by seeking transfers of cost from its own responsibility to that of another sector, though there are safeguards to cope with such an event:

(a) The sector structure itself, where each sector is acutely aware of its own costs and income and is unlikely to yield ground lightly.

(b) The fact that a number of elements within the organization 'wear corporate hats' (not least the board and its finance department), which brings an objective view to proposals for action.

(c) The disciplines inherent within the systems demand cross-sectoral agreement to change over an underwritten base.

(d) The conventions have been established within a 'frozen frame', which requires board approval for their change.

(e) All major proposals for investment or disinvestment are subjected to sound appraisal.

The methodology and conventions were developed with management, and their enhancement has been increasingly promoted and led by management. While this does not imply unquestioning belief, it does mean that they are regarded as defensible, robust and workable, and for the most part more reasonable and less capricious than traditional allocative techniques built upon arithmetic relations.

If they are capable of giving misleading signals in perhaps one out of every ten questions which they raise, this is better than a situation where the questions are never raised.

5   Colliery accountability in the British Coal Corporation

Philip Andrew and David Otley

Introduction

General background

The British Coal Corporation (BCC) was created in March 1987 as the new organizational form for what was previously the National Coal Board (NCB). The National Coal Board took over responsibility for the mining of coal in Great Britain on 11 January 1947. At that time coal production was running at a level of about 200m tons a year, and provided some 91 percent of total primary inland energy consumption. This production required the services of over 700,000 men and took place at over 1,000 separate collieries. The 10 years following nationalization were characterized by a strong demand for coal. Production rose to a peak of 224m tons in 1954 and, even then, some coal had to be imported.

In 1957 the demand for coal began to fall, mainly due to the availability of cheap oil, which was also often more convenient to use; and by 1977 deep-mined output had stabilized at around 110m tons a year, produced by about 240 collieries and 240,000 men. Coal then accounted for only about 37 percent of the country's energy consumption, having been overtaken by oil (41 percent) and also affected by the availability of natural gas (18 percent).

These trends have continued into the 1980s. Despite the oil crises of the 1970s, the demand for coal has continued to fall, and in 1986 deep-mined output amounted to just 88m tons, produced from 110 collieries, with the employment of 125,000 men. As mining is an extractive industry, much of the best and easiest coal was worked long ago, and costs of production tend constantly to rise unless these can be offset by improved technical methods.

The objectives set for the NCB in the Coal Industry National-ization Act, 1946, required the NCB to operate in such a way as to break even (after paying interest on its debt capital) 'on an average of good and bad years'. This has proved increasingly difficult to achieve and, although an operating profit (before interest) has generally been made, the 1970s saw a pattern of substantial losses and increasing government grants. Such grants were originally limited to cover items such as social costs, increased pensions for mineworkers and specific operating grants, but since 1980 have included a grant to cover the operating deficit. The BCC's financial objective for each year is now set in terms of an external financing limit and a maximum level of deficit grant.

Current industry objectives

The basic objective of British Coal has now been set in terms of earning a satisfactory return on its net assets and, with government support, achieving financial soundness. It has therefore planned to break even in the year 1988–9, after payment of interest charges and the accrual of grants to meet social costs. Thereafter it seeks to generate an increasing surplus on its revenue account and to move increasingly towards becoming self-financing.

It has therefore decided to concentrate on low-cost production and on those sales which will maximize profit on a continuing basis in competition with other fuels. It has also to plan to achieve an adequate return on new capital investment in accordance with the principles set out in the White Paper 'The Nationalized Industries' (Cmnd 7131). In order to achieve these objectives it is anticipated that it will be necessary to reduce the operating costs (per unit of production) of its mining activities by 20 percent (in real terms) over the period 1985–6 to 1989–90.

Organization and accountability

British Coal is organized along functional lines, with coal production being separated from marketing up to headquarters level. The marketing department is organized on a regional basis, although currently some 77 percent of coal produced is supplied to the electricity generating boards. The remainder is sold for general industrial use (8 percent), coke ovens (4 percent), and for commercial and domestic heating (8 percent).

The production department is organized into coal-producing Areas, together with an Opencast Division. Each of the deep-mining Areas contains around 15 collieries, often situated in fairly close proximity to each other, e.g. in Yorkshire, the East Midlands and South Wales, although sometimes more widely separated, e.g. in the North-West and Scotland. The present Area structure is the result of a series of amalgamations over the years as the industry has contracted, and represents the outcome of a continuing effort to maintain an efficient management structure. A typical colliery now employs in excess of 1,000 men, produces about 800,000 tonnes of coal and has a turnover of around £32m a year.

This chapter is solely concerned with the accountability and control arrangements needed in the running of a single Area, and focuses primarily on the management accounting information used by Area staff in managing colliery activities. The Area is headed by

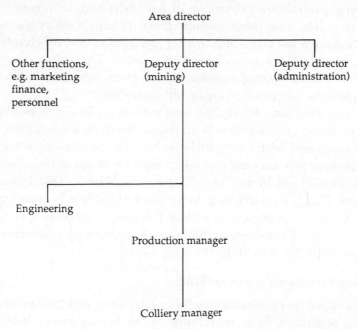

Figure 5.1 *Organization of a typical coal-producing area*

an Area director, and a simplified structure is shown in Figure 5.1. The main line of command consists of a deputy director (mining), responsible for all aspects of coal production and engineering services, with several production managers, each in charge of up to five collieries, reporting to him. Although Figure 5.1 shows an Area marketing function, this is responsible primarily for the logistics of coal distribution and quality control, as the actual selling of coal is handled on a regional basis.

Accountability between Area and collieries is maintained in formal terms by a battery of statistics, which include a comprehensive budgetary-control system, together with a considerable number of other operational and technical data. Less formally, production managers visit collieries frequently and are in daily contact by telephone. It should be noted that coal-producing Areas do not prepare balance sheets, and that their profit and loss accounts are primarily operating statements but do include an allocation of interest charges. Regular accountability meetings are held, including a quarterly meeting at which the Area director holds each colliery manager individually to account.

Accounting for colliery activities

Fixing colliery objectives

It is of note that the industry objectives are set in financial terms rather than in production, employment or social terms. The industry objective is set not only in terms of operating profit but also requires that interest charges be covered, the Corporation essentially being financed by government loans. The bottom-line objective figure is thus akin to a residual income calculation. Rather than allocating interest charges as if they were an overhead cost, the prime management accounting document for a colliery (the F23 profit and loss account) calculates a capital charge as a percentage (currently 12 percent) of the colliery's written-down capital value. The industry's outstanding loans amounted to £4,000m, as at March 1987, and represented over 95 percent of the historical written-down value (WDV) of its assets. The current objective for the industry as a whole, and hence on balance for each area and colliery, is to make sufficient operating profit to give a 12 percent return on the WDV of its assets.

The major customers for coal are the electricity generating authorities – the CEGB and its Scottish equivalents. Within broad parameters, power stations are able to burn most types of coal. However, in addition there are specialist coals and markets: anthracite and free burning large coals for the domestic market, coking coals for steel-making, manufactured domestic fuels, and specially sized coals of particular inherent qualities for the medium and smaller boilers used in industry, schools and hospitals. Anthracite cannot be produced in sufficient quantities in the UK, requiring imports to be made. Similarly, the British Steel Corporation imports the high quality, low sulphur fuels which cannot be produced economically in the UK. For the other markets there is sufficient interchangeability in coal qualities for the scientific constraints to be less important than the price charged. The accepted measure of coal value is its cost measured in pounds sterling per gigajoule, i.e. money for heat content.

For coal to maintain its current market share of 103m tonnes per year (87mt deep-mined, 13mt opencast, 3mt licensed), it requires to be sold at a price not exceeding about £1.50 per gigajoule. If it were to be priced at above this level, then many consumers would find it cheaper to import, limited only by port facility constraints. Pricing much below this level would not substantially increase market share in the short term, since the customer can only consume to the limit of his plant capacity. However, the prospect of coal being available for significant periods at a price below £1.50 per gigajoule would no doubt lead to consumers converting to coal-fired plant. The setting of objectives by HQ to Areas is therefore based almost entirely on the potential cost of production.

Investment decisions

Mining is an extractive industry working in a (geologically) uncertain environment. The same colliery operating in the same way will quite normally have fluctuations in output of 15 percent from one year to another. To some extent these fluctuations can be reduced by designing spare capacity into the coal-production system, but this can only be achieved by investing more capital resources. The skills of the management accountant are needed to help achieve the planning balance between having sufficient spare capacity and wasting capital resources.

The classic investment baseline is to do nothing. In coalmining, however, this does not maintain the *status quo*. Clearly the most attractive coal reserves will have been worked first and future reserves are deeper, thinner or further away from the shaft. Generally the decline in productivity, if no additional investment is made, will occur at a rate of about 3 percent pa. The main production unit, the coal face, has a life of between 3 months and several years, with an average life of 18 months. Since each replacement face has to be accessed by driving roadways and then equipped with coal-getting machinery, the medium-term planning process is heavily concerned with investment options of a mining and technical engineering nature. Longer-term planning will include consideration of investment in new mines, the deepening of shafts to access lower seams or the driving of longer roadways into new reserves of coal. A final option to be considered for a colliery is closure. This has to be considered if it does not appear to be possible to produce coal at under £1.50 per gigajoule after depreciation and capital interest charges. To plan to operate above this cost level is to plan to lose money, and such losses cannot be allowed to persist indefinitely.

Review of the colliery plans in terms of the major resources of men, machinery and money will suggest various options, each having different levels of production and different marginal costs of production. As in normal investment appraisal, the sensitivity of the options to the construction period, capital cost, and likely outcomes need to be recognized. Aggregation of the various colliery plans produces a potential profile for a coal-producing Area as a whole. This profile will indicate possible production levels and costs relating to the various investment options. At this stage a preferred Area plan will be selected, with each colliery having its own optimal plan.

The business plan

Each year, as part of the Five Year Business Planning cycle, there is a formal meeting between Areas and Headquarters. From an HQ point of view, there are limitations on the amount of capital available and there is a need to balance short-term efficiency schemes with the development of adequate production capacity to meet the needs of the twenty-first century. Investment strategy cannot therefore simply comprise a list of projects in the order of a financial measure, be it IRR, payback period or the marginal cost of incremental capacity. For any project to succeed, there is a need for detailed planning and a full assessment of alternatives. Resources are required: management accountants, project planners, project managers, specialist contractors, etc. Too much demand on any resource is likely to reduce its cost efficiency.

Reaching agreement

The result of the meeting between the HQ team and the Area team will be that specific large schemes (over £1m each) are sanctioned and that an investment level is set for the Area. The Area team, which always includes a management accountant, now formulates detailed plans and proposals for each colliery. The process is not one of evaluating detailed production plans, but rather devising broad strategies for the colliery and testing them for practicality. The objective is again to produce plans which will yield a profit after interest charges, given the current market price. Major constraints on colliery output are its shaft capacity and its coal-preparation capacity, since to increase either calls for heavy investment. Underground, the main constraints are coal clearance and bunker-age capacity.

Since about 50 percent of colliery operating costs are related to manpower, productivity is the most important factor in determining cost levels. The wages payment system (Labour Costs Statistics Payroll) is operated by finance staff at collieries. Its inherent costing structure is determined by the management accountant, giving him a unique insight into the utilization and cost efficiency of labour. Detailed comparisons are made between collieries, and the determination of realistic efficiency levels is possible. Production and required productivity levels can therefore be formulated on a realistic basis.

For medium-term planning (2- to 5-year planning horizon), there is considerable input from mining and technical engineers. New technology in the form of more efficient and productive machines permits the design of larger production units with increased productivity. To achieve changes in the mine plans requires development roadways to block out the new production units. Since each of the new units will have a higher rate of production than before, the coal-clearance system needs to have greater capacity and the materials supply system will be required to operate more efficiently. The role of the management accountant is to evaluate these plans in conjunction with the mine planner and line management. The process is inevitably iterative, since many plans will not be feasible, owing to resource constraints.

Colliery planning decisions

Physical planning

Once the broad strategy has been determined for a colliery, it is possible to make more detailed decisions. The 'shape' of the colliery, in terms of number of production units and development locations, has been decided. The colliery planner now needs to draw up a physical layout which will support this 'shape', consistent with the constraints that impinge upon the unit. These are principally the location of geological faults, the need to protect important surface features from subsidence damage, and the requirement to extract as large a proportion of the coal reserves as is economically worthwhile. Design engineers will then consider machine availability, given that most machines have an effective life of 8 years or so, and that maximum utilization for the whole of that period is essential. The total cost of the machinery on a coal face (the production unit) is typically around £5m, making the design of each coal face comparable to designing a small factory.

Detailed coal-face design includes matching equipment from many different manufacturers, and is a specialist function outside the remit of the management accountant. The major components of machinery on a coal face will need to be installed and salvaged at least five times in their life. While being salvaged from the face, repaired and maintained (either underground or in British Coal workshops), and installed on a new face, the equipment is not producing coal. In practice the average asset utilization for face machinery is only just over 50 percent, indicating the importance of managing the salvage, repair and installation process as efficiently as normal production management.

Before the installation of equipment on a coal face, it is necessary to drive access roadways to the area of coal to be mined. From the main roads that already exist, roadways to be used solely for a new production unit can cost up to £3m, if the unit is to be won by the retreat mining method, and take 12 months to construct. Blocking out the coal reserves for retreat mining improves the knowledge of the geology of the coal seam but requires investment in the year before coal, and hence income, is produced. Thus the adoption of retreat mining techniques requires investment, but not of a type normally classified as 'capital investment' in the financial accounts.

Over longer periods of time the coal workings move away from the shafts and the roadways deteriorate under the enormous pressures of the overlying rocks. However, the standard shift length stays constant at 435 minutes, and given average travelling time from the pit bottom to the production unit of 60 minutes each way, the time available for work is usually only 315 minutes per shift. Clearly, greater speed of travelling over more direct routes can give considerable benefit by increasing the length of time over which the prime production machines can be operated. Again, the decision when to drive a more direct roadway or to introduce faster manriding trains must always be considered.

Coal won has to be transported to the bottom of the shafts to be wound up in skips each of perhaps 9 tonnes capacity. Here the speed at which the coal moves underground is not important, the limitation being the capacity of the system of conveyor and bunkers. Bunkers are used to smooth out peaks in coal flows, to ensure even loading of conveyor belts and a constant and continuous flow of coal to the pit bottom, and to allow coal winding in the shaft to be virtually continuous. To assist in the process of design, computer simulation is used, but again this is an area for the specialist, and the role of the management accountant is one of supporting rather than leading.

Manpower planning

As mentioned previously, the payroll system is fully computerized. In addition to details of time worked, the computer system holds in its master file information on the grade, experience, age, etc. of each man. When aggregated, these details produce manpower profiles, which can be used to match available skills to forward plans. This may result in plans for training or retraining, or sometimes for the preparation of a manpower wastage programme. Since all investment is geared to cost reduction and higher productivity, manpower levels are crucial. Typically, the smaller improvement schemes will lead to productivity improvements of around 2 percent pa, compared to a normal deterioration of 3 percent pa. Larger schemes to expand output might require recruitment, or significant schemes to improve efficiency might require redundancy, which can be effected by transfer to other collieries or by voluntary methods.

Inevitably, even a full examination of all alternatives can still result in a position where it is not possible to produce a plan to make the colliery profitable. If no more investment and development work is undertaken, then the total manpower resource can be used on coal production, with no resources being devoted to future development. This will frequently result in the colliery showing a short-term profit, but is a result of actions that inevitably lead to the planned closure.

Overhead costs

While much of the above discussion has concentrated on the major decision areas in colliery planning, administrative overhead costs are also important. Control of overheads needs to be strong in order to minimize the burden placed on the producing units. In 1967 the number of Areas in the NCB was halved to nineteen in a major reorganization. By March 1987 this number had been reduced to eight by a series of mergers and amalgamations. While each Area now produces more coal than before, its resources in terms of manpower and number of collieries is somewhat less, since the number of collieries has been reduced from 438 to 110 over the same period. The role of the management accountant in analysing overhead cost, both by activity and by the functional manager concerned, leads to a greater understanding of the build-up of overhead costs, and such understanding is a prerequisite to effective control.

The budget process

Once the strategic decisions on the design of the colliery have been made, much detailed work is necessary to produce the budget base against which actual performance can subsequently be measured and evaluated. The basic production plan is termed the 'action programme'. This sets out, in bar chart form, the pattern of producing faces, roadway developments, salvage and installation activities which are required to implement the selected plan. Due account is taken of planned holidays, and the production levels and manpower resources used are aggregated by accounting periods. The graphic format is primarily helpful in visually demonstrating the balance between production and development activity, and since it also schedules linked resources, gives an indication of where critical paths might arise.

In particular, the attendance pattern of the workforce varies during the weekly cycle, with absence perhaps being only 5 percent on a Wednesday morning but rising to 30 percent on a Friday night. This variability means that all activities will not be able to work on all three shifts of each weekday. Colliery management determines the priorities of work but, by analysing historical trends, the management accountant is able to advise on the likely percentage performance of each activity. In addition, for mining engineering reasons, the output level declines during the last days before a holiday and builds up again afterwards in the first few days after resumption of work.

Even after all these factors are taken into account, it is still necessary to 'relax' the expected output levels from those planned to give a central estimate of the most likely outcome. The reasons for this are manifold, but the effect is predictable from the historic trends at each colliery. Similarly, it is also necessary to relax the sum of colliery outputs to arrive at a central forecast of Area output. This latter process arises since, despite the fact that 50 percent of collieries will produce more than budgeted and 50 percent less, the amounts by which the budgets are exceeded are considerably less than the typical shortfalls. This effect will occur in any production process where the plan is to produce at a level approaching plant capacity. Levels of relaxation generally amount to around 15 percent at colliery level and a further 9 percent at Area level.

As has been implied, the action programme (production plan) forms the basis for the phased budget. Much detailed work is done on manpower attendance patterns. Forecasts are made of absence due to individual rest days as well as sickness patterns, estimates of number of shifts deployed to capital works have to be made, and finally an overtime budget is required. This latter item can amount to as much as 15 percent of the final wage bill. Detailed computer programs have been devised to assist in the budgeting of wages expenditure. Since employee costs approach 50 percent of total costs, the need for detailed budgeting to allow in-depth analysis of actual results is self-evident.

While the analysis of wages expenditure is mainly carried out by the management accountant, his role is that of a team member for other budgeting decisions and objectives. For example, the engineer will table work needed if the colliery is to remain in sound mechanical order. The need for each significant item is discussed by the unit engineer, his colliery manager, the Area chief engineer and the management accountant. The team decision, when reached, is based on the likely production costs and likely colliery life, as well as the more obvious engineering needs. Perhaps surprisingly, this process is not normally acrimonious. The engineer is quite able to classify repair work into essential, economic or desirable categories. The colliery manager is concerned with managing his unit as a business, the engineer is well trained in commercial practice and the Area chief engineer is able to maintain the balance of standards between collieries. The role of the management accountant is to analyse relevant information and to join in the debate. The management accountant's job is always much easier when he provides well laid out, easily comprehensible data and has taken the trouble to educate the technical specialist in the financial needs of the industry. His job is to offer guidance on what can be afforded and to 'set the tone'.

As the budgeting process nears completion, it is essential to maintain the monitoring to see if the financial objectives are being attained. This is done for each colliery, together with an Area aggregation, using simple spreadsheet packages on desktop personal computers. The final budgeting process is done in much more detail on a mainframe computer. While this process is essential to form the base against which actual results are measured, since it is time-consuming it is only carried out after the full debate has been concluded. The debate is a participative process, carried out by a team of area and colliery personnel. Inevitably it is necessary for senior line management to impose its decisions on key issues. Strong views having been expressed, the budget is always jointly agreed and accepted.

Accountability

During the year the performance of the colliery, and by implication its management, is closely monitored. Formal accountability takes place monthly with production managers and quarterly with the Area director. This process of formal accountability, while taken extremely seriously, is generally accepted as a mechanism having the primary purpose of improving the performance of the industry. Since accountability is a function of line management, the role of the management accountant is confined to preparing the extensive briefing material used as a basis for discussion.

This briefing material, which forms the background whereby the colliery manager is held accountable, and in turn holds his subordinates accountable, determines the budget detail. Once generated via its own computer system, the budget is linked into the main accounting system.

The Integrated Accounting System

The Integrated Accounting System is the core computer system used in managing the corporation's financial affairs. The coding structure for each transaction consists of eight fields and covers sixteen digits. In addition to the sixteen-digit code and its associated sterling amount, the accounting period of the transaction and the transaction type are logged. The transaction type is used to distinguish between budgets and actuals. The accounting system is integrated in that not only does it produce all the management accounting information but it also forms the books of account and hence is used as the basis for all financial accounting records and returns. Not only does the Integrated Accounting system log financial transactions but it also records key statistical information. Primarily these are disposals, stocks (and hence saleable output), manpower levels and manshifts worked. Other more detailed information is logged in separate computer systems, such as the Face Data Bank and the Drivage Data Bank. Computer systems such as these are regularly accessed by the management accountant to extract data to calculate financial indices. Indeed, at colliery level, the bulk of input to computer systems is carried out by the colliery costing staff.

The major underlying principle on which the corporation's computer systems are based is that once a transaction is logged, it is automatically linked, normally on a weekly cycle, into the main Integrated Accounting System. For example, the industry solid fuel system (ISFS) has as its prime function the recording of sales and the generation of invoices. Each weigh ticket is input to the computer and provides the basic information necessary to calculate sales. In addition stock levels are input, which themselves match to stock master files to evaluate the net stock valuation. An interesting feature of coalmining is that it is not possible to precisely measure the weight of coal produced at its point of production. The definition of saleable output (or production level) is disposals plus closing stocks less opening stocks. Clearly this places great demands on the stocktaking procedures, and whenever possible coal is weighed both when it is stocked and lifted. The responsibility for correct measurement and evaluation of stocks is a joint function of the marketing and accounting departments.

The personnel systems are the integrated staff records (ISR) system and the labour, costs, statistics and payroll (LCSP) system. This latter system not only records time worked to be evaluated against grade rates, but also calculates the various allowances to be paid as well as making the bonus payment calculations, although these matters are far too complex to explain in a chapter of this nature. However, the payments for all time worked are costed both by location within the colliery and type of work. This permits costing analyses of the usual standard nature and also allows checks to be carried out on the grade of worker carrying out each type of work, as it is clearly inefficient to use highly trained labour on less skilled work.

All material requisitioned or issued is logged by the materials computer system. Each issue is coded by the location of the proposed usage and also by the requisitioning officer. This permits detailed costing by location and also facilitates the accountability process for each spending officer. The sophistication lies within the stores system itself. Each issue is recorded and aggregated by colliery on a weekly basis. This permits accurate usage information and also makes possible the automatic generation of order suggestions. The timing and quantity of each suggestion is determined by stockholding levels, rate of demand and economic order quantity.

While there are many smaller computer systems, each of which links into the main Integrated Accounting System, the final major system is the fixed assets/project ledger computer system. This system follows the classic model of recording the date and value of every capital purchase and keeping a record of its last known location. The depreciation schedule is automatically generated according to the type of asset, subject to the potential constraint of the remaining life of the colliery where it is installed. The project ledger system collects together the engineers' estimates of progress each month and matches these against invoices received into the supplies accounting system. Additionally, internal recharges of labour or plant hire are automatically collected by weekly computer links. On project completion the asset is consolidated and transferred into the project ledger.

All these linked systems are the gathering grounds for the management accountant, although many systems will produce their own reports. For example, the Integrated Accounting System produces a diversity of reports, including the monthly colliery profit and loss account (the F23). The advantage of having totally linked and balanced computer systems is that the management accountant can select detailed information from any system, knowing that in aggregate it will tally with the profit and loss account and the formal books of account. The mainstream systems will produce all the standard documents, covering comparison with budget on a period and cumulative basis and trends of costs levels in both the current and previous years. However, there is a need to monitor actual results against shorter-term objectives and also to carry out *ad hoc* investigations.

An example of the former is when a colliery encounters geological difficulties, and it may need to deploy additional overtime shifts. A short-term higher standard can be used, often to some extent 'paid for' by lower overtime allowances at other collieries in the same group. Again the principle is working together to overcome difficulties while staying within financial limits. Routine monitoring of financial and statistical indices might reveal abnormalities. In these instances special monitoring reports will be produced until the problem is solved or better understood.

Performance evaluation

Much of the foregoing has indicated the means by which performance statistics are derived. However, in evaluating performance several techniques are used, including:

(a) Comparison with budget.
(b) Looking at the trend.
(c) Comparison with other collieries.
(d) Conventional financial indices.

The *comparison with budget* is well understood, and as a technique depends critically on the quality of the budgeting process. *Looking at the trend* is useful in that it indicates whether improvements are being achieved and also quantifies them. The standard measure used in the coal industry is percentage improvement over previous years on a cumulative basis. *Comparison with other collieries* is particularly helpful for studying the effects of detailed measures, as it can help to pinpoint where improvements can be made. While there is competition between collieries, the sharing of experience with other collieries helps to increase understanding and improve performance. *Conventional financial indices* are increasingly used to indicate the relative performance of the colliery viewed as a business activity.

The first three of the above four techniques use industry indices. The basic unit of production is the tonne, with the heat quantity being the gigajoule. Cost and income levels are measured in pounds per gigajoule, as this facilitates comparison between collieries satisfying different quality markets. Equally the income and hence desirability of each market sector is measured in pounds per gigajoule. However, the measure of labour productivity is tonnes per manshift, and the measure of production unit is tonnes per day, associated with the shift index of machine shifts per day.

In the more specialist sectors other measures are used: energy usage, for example, is monitored by comparing gigajoules consumed with gigajoules produced. However, as the industry faces up to its target of producing a profit after interest charges, the more conventional financial indices are being increasingly used; operating profit as a percentage of assets employed, absolute profit level, and the percentage of capital expenditure which is self-funded, are perhaps the most obvious examples.

Analysis, evaluation and critique

The role of British Coal

British Coal occupies a unique position within the national economy. Although it is a nationalized industry with its own financial objectives and responsibilities, its major customers are also state-owned corporations. Despite the fact that most coal mined in Britain is used for electricity generation, and the fact that most electricity is still produced in coal-fired power stations, the two enterprises are treated as being formally independent of each other.

The major issue raised by this symbiotic relation concerns the price at which coal is sold by British Coal to the CEGB and its Scottish equivalents. From the perspective of the UK taxpayer this is an internal transfer price, but the commercial realism of the figure used is crucial, since the accounting information produced by the two industries is used to make judgements about their efficiency, and as a basis for major decision-making. Attention must therefore be focused on the nature of the contract between British Coal and the CEGB.

There are two main aspects to these arrangements, which have been the subject of intensive debate over the past few years. First, there is the basis on which the price itself is to be set. Second, there is the period to which the price should refer. On the issue of the price itself the CEGB has argued that the world market price for coal should be the benchmark from which discussion should begin. However, the world market for coal is quite small relative to world consumption, and the internationally traded price can fluctuate markedly on a short-term basis. In addition, Britain does not currently possess the port facilities necessary for the importation of coal on a large scale, so the use of imported coal as a major source of supply is not a realistic alternative in the short to medium term.

On the second issue, British Coal has argued that, as it must invest substantial amounts of capital on a long-term basis in order to supply the needs of the CEGB, contracts should also be written on a long-term basis. It would be unfair for the coal industry to be penalized for investing in coal production, only to see the CEGB take short-term decisions to move away from using domestically produced coal.

However, at present the issue is only partially resolved. British Coal is required by the 1946 Act to ensure that it is capable of producing sufficient coal for the country's needs, and thus continues to develop coal supplies potentially required for the next century. But the supply arrangements it has with the CEGB are for much shorter periods, at most 5 years. Under the current 'Joint Understanding' different tranches of coal are supplied at different prices; a basic tranche is supplied at a relatively high price, but additional demand is met at a series of successively lower prices, ultimately reflecting the CEGB's ability to import marginal amounts of either coal or oil at lower world-traded prices.

The current (1986) 'Joint Understanding' provides for British Coal to continue to supply a quantity of coal equivalent to 95 percent of the CEGB's requirements, but that the proportion supplied at lower price levels will be progressively increased. Thus the key features of the agreement are:

(a) Firm commitments for 2 years and statements of intent for a further 3 years whereby British Coal will supply a minimum of 72mt in 1986–7 and 70mt per year thereafter.

(b) The total tonnage supplied is divided into three tranches.
    First tranche: this coal, which is supplied at the highest prices, was progressively reduced from its previous level of 65mt to 50mt in 1986–7, and will be reduced to 40 mt by the fifth year of the understanding.
    Second tranche: this coal is supplied at an intermediate price, reflecting the savings that the CEGB could obtain from burning oil or imported coal at inland power stations. The size of this tranche will increase from 10mt to 18mt per year, as the size of the first tranche decreases.
    Third tranche: ultimately 12mt per annum will be supplied at a price which competes with imports available to coastal power stations.

(c) Further coal is available to meet short-term fluctuations in demand at the same price as the third tranche.

This agreement thus reflects commercial realities by recognizing the opportunities for short-term gains by the CEGB, and the importance to the two industries of continuity and security of coal supply, while at the same time allowing adjustments to be made to meet longer-term conditions.

It is thus apparent that, from the taxpayers' point of view, the total proceeds figure credited to the accounts of British Coal is not a short-term free market price obtained at arm's length. Although these revenue figures are used in national, Area and colliery accounts to produce profit and loss statements, such statements are used with a great deal of care in both decision-making and accountability processes. The remainder of this section will focus on colliery accountability.

The nature of coalmining as a business

Coalmining is an unusual business as its production units are not situated in purpose-designed factories but follow seams of coal of varying thickness and subject to a variety of geological disturbance. Although the aim of the mining engineer is to establish coal faces that can be operated as smoothly as possible, production is inevitably subject to considerable variation, owing to unexpected geological conditions and to the failure of machinery that is operating in a harsh and demanding environment.

The output of a colliery operating the same machinery in apparently the same conditions may vary by as much as 30 percent from year to year, owing to the mining conditions actually encountered. Further, it is precisely the conditions which cause output to fall that demand increased effort to overcome. So it is likely that total production costs will rise at exactly the time that output falls. The evaluation of the performance of a colliery cannot thus be based on short-term accounting results, but requires the exercise of judgement based on the experience gained over a considerable period of time.

A coalmining Area is primarily a production unit. Sales to the electricity industry are handled nationally, and sales to most other customers are handled by the marketing department, which is organized on the basis of sales regions distinct from the coal-producing Areas. Although the various types and grades of coal have list prices, individual customers negotiate discounts of varying amounts for their supplies. These individual discounts are a matter of commercial secrecy, and they are not applied directly to the accounts of the particular colliery which happens to mine the coal. The decision about which colliery should supply which customer is not under the control of local management. A colliery is not credited with the income from its own sales but with the national average net income from all sales of coal of equivalent quality, i.e. rebates are pooled nationally and each colliery is allocatd a *pro rata* share. Thus the revenue attributable to a specific colliery is calculated by multiplying the colliery's saleable output by the appropriate list price of each grade of coal produced, and then deducting a percentage to cover the average level of discount allowed to all customers.

Both the Area and the colliery are therefore primarily production units rather than independent businesses supplying their own individual customers. Nevertheless, they are treated as profit centres, even investment centres, for the purposes of accountability and control. The advantages of such an approach are evident, in that the results as well as the costs of the mining activity at each colliery can be expressed in money terms, and a profit and loss account produced. It also provides an accounting base from which to value the output of a mine, so enabling comparisons to be made between collieries and decisions to be made about the investment of additional capital. However, it needs constantly to be borne in mind that the revenue side of these accounts is subject to a great deal of allocation, in addition to the more traditional cost allocations.

Although, in mining terms, collieries are largely independent of one another, they are highly interdependent in economic terms. As production units they are also managed as a set of interdependent activities, rather than being allowed to act independently. Thus, one of the roles of the deputy director (mining) and his staff is to coordinate the mining activities of all the collieries in his Area in order to balance the production capability of the Area as a whole. The relative proportion of effort that a particular colliery puts into current production as against development work designed to allow future production is subject to central direction.

The economics of coal production is such that, once a colliery is in operation, it is most economic to operate it at its designed capacity. Fluctuations in demand are therefore dealt with by stocking in the short term, by colliery redesign in the medium term, and by the establishment of new collieries or colliery closure in the long term. Coupled with the fact that mining is an extractive industry, the economics of the business ensure that there must be constant reappraisal of the amount, type and cost of the productive capacity that is to be made available.

Coalmining in the UK is therefore a unique business. It operates, to an extent, as a monopoly supplier to a single monopsonist buyer, although both operate in the wider energy market, with competition from other sources of energy. There is central direction and control of both production and marketing to ensure coordination of supply and demand across the country. Being an extractive industry, it has constantly to replace and renew its production capacity both within individual collieries and by opening and closing whole collieries. For these reasons it is inappropriate to consider the accountability arrangements for individual collieries in isolation. Yet a colliery is a substantial business activity in its own right, with an investment value of, say, £35m generating a turnover of £32m a year. Despite the reservations made above, it is treated as an investment centre, having its own profit and loss accounts, and control is exercised over its activities by the normal financial and managerial techniques.

Accountability procedures

The responsibility of a colliery manager is primarily to implement agreed production plans and policies, and to produce an agreed amount of coal safely and efficiently. However, within these broad constraints, he is very much 'master of his own ship' and has onerous legal responsibilities for the proper operation of his colliery according to procedures defined by statute. In addition, as far as the colliery workforce is concerned, the manager is the embodiment of the employer, and held responsible for nearly all aspects of their employment activities. Thus the colliery forms a natural focal point for accountability and control, and the manager is held accountable for the way in which it is operated.

The central plank of the accountability arrangements is the colliery action programme (or production plan). This sets out the major activities that are to be undertaken in physical terms for a period of 2 years ahead. It is reviewed every 3 months and revised, if necessary, every 6 months. The colliery budget is based on the action programme, and is expressed primarily in financial terms, with the inclusion of one or two physical measures, such as output, number of men and metres of development drivage. The budget serves two major functions. Firstly, it indicates the extent to which the colliery is expected to help meet the financial objectives of the industry. Secondly, it permits alternatives to be evaluated when conditions require the original operating plan to be amended. Thus, a colliery manager is reminded of the financial consequences of the various operating decisions he takes on a day-to-day basis.

Accountability takes place on a variety of timescales. There is daily reporting of actual output produced, although these figures are only approximate (as the output is not weighed at this stage) and require considerable judgement on the part of colliery managers. However, such information is necessary to help coordinate the flow of coal to customers. There is a weekly review of development work, to help ensure that new productive capacity will be available when it is required, and also an informal weekly review of the major cost and proceed headings in the budget. This serves an attention-directing function and may stimulate an enquiry into the activities of a particular colliery. However, these daily and weekly reviews are essentially concerned with production and are conducted by the deputy director (mining) and his production managers. The production managers themselves are in daily contact with each colliery for which they are responsible, and will visit each at least once a week.

Formal accountability operates on a longer timescale. The major formal meeting takes place quarterly, supplemented by monthly meetings. At the quarterly accountability meeting the colliery manager, supported by two or three of his management team and his production manager, meets the Area director and the heads of the major functional departments. There is a standard formal agenda, supported by an accountability brief, i.e. a comprehensive set of actual results compared with budget, together with a variety of supporting information. However, it is very much up to the Area director how such a meeting is conducted and the items on which attention will be focused.

It might be argued that such meetings can only be a formality. They take place some 5 or 6 weeks after a quarter has ended and thus concern events which may have taken place up to 5 months previously. Nevertheless, the knowledge that performance will be reviewed in a comprehensive manner can act as a powerful motivator to a manager when he is taking day-to-day decisions. But the main function of the accountability process is not so much judgemental as problem-oriented. The meeting can be used as a means of modifying and restating objectives, and also to provide colliery managers with a formal means of ensuring that their views are transmitted to the Area director personally. Thus the meeting considers three quarters: the one formally being reviewed; the current quarter, to see how effective corrective action is proving to be; and the next quarter, to see if the plans need to be reviewed or modified.

The operation of these accountability arrangements, and the style of management used by an Area director, are quite critical to the effective operation of the Area. Too great an emphasis on evaluation rather than problem-solving, or too much stress on meeting the budget regardless of other consequences, can lead to harmful side-effects. Running a colliery calls for the maintenance of a delicate balance between short-term productive efficiency and longer-term development work. Thus a manager who feels under pressure to meet his budget may well take actions that are not in the longer-term interests of his colliery. This is especially so because of the uncertainties inherent in coal-mining, which make it difficult to distinguish between inefficient operation and the effect of unforeseen circumstances. The methods used to handle such uncertainties in the budgeting process are therefore of some importance, and may have a wider applicability outside the mining industry. They are discussed in the following section.

Dealing with uncertainty

The major uncertainty in coalmining concerns the amount of output that will be obtained from operating a coal face, of a given design, over a particular period. The mining engineer will produce a coal-face design that has a certain output potential, but this potential will rarely be achieved, owing to various possible mishaps. These can be categorized into a number of different types. Firstly, there are machine breakdowns on the face itself, which are, given experience of using the machinery concerned, fairly predictable. Typically these cause stoppages of short duration, although they may occur randomly. Secondly, there are geological conditions that can occur unexpectedly, as when a face runs into an unknown fault. These are generally more disruptive of output over a longer period, and may even cause the premature closure of a face. To some extent such problems can be minimized by the choice of mining methods to be used, such as retreat mining. Thirdly, there are problems un-connected with the specific face, such as breakdowns in the coal transport system or shaft. Here production may have to be curtailed because of problems elsewhere in the mine. Finally, there are interruptions to production caused by industrial-relations problems. These may be specific to a particular coal face, or to a given colliery, or of an Area-wide or national nature. Each type of uncertainty will cause disruptions to production of differing magnitudes and will occur with different frequencies.

These are coped with in three different ways. Firstly, the design potential of a face is adjusted to take account of normal operating delays and known geological disturbances. This gives a standard of production, given the absence of major breakdowns, but requires a great deal of judgement and experience to estimate correctly. Secondly, the total output of a colliery is adjusted downwards from the sum of the expected face outputs by a factor known as the 'colliery relaxation'. This relaxation factor, which is different from colliery to colliery, represents an attempt to cater for colliery-specific uncertainties. Its size will depend upon geological conditions, mining methods, the industrial-relations climate, and a general 'feel' for the colliery. Again, this is a matter of judgement, mainly on the part of the deputy director (mining). Such colliery relaxations may amount to anything up to 20 percent of colliery output. Finally, the aggregate of colliery output budgets is again relaxed by an Area relaxation percentage, to take account of uncertainties that could occur at any colliery in the Area, but which are infrequent enough to make it inappropriate to include them in colliery budgets. However, over some fifteen to twenty collieries the unexpected becomes somewhat more predictable, and a figure of between 8.5 percent and 10 percent is generally used.

Setting relaxation figures requires considerable mining judgment, and is more a matter for senior production managers than for the management accountant. However, the result of the relaxation process is of vital importance, in that it forms the basis on which the budget is constructed.

The intention of the relaxation procedures is for every colliery's output budget to stand an equal chance of achievement. Although this requires mining judgement, it is nevertheless an ideal that can be aimed for, while recognizing that the budgeted output is an expected value, and is subject to different uncertainties at different collieries. For example, a colliery operating the retreat mining system and having a stable industrial-relations climate can have its results predicted with more certainty than another colliery operating advancing faces in poor geological conditions and subject to industrial action. The Area relaxation factor is intended to allow for items not specific to a single colliery.

Unfortunately the system does not always operate in such an ideal manner. Because the worth of collieries tends to be assessed, in part, by reference to their budgeted results, the Area relaxation must be split between collieries for this purpose. In the absence of more detailed information, the tendency is for HQ staff to reduce excess output *pro rata* from each colliery, i.e. if the Area relaxation is 10 percent, then 10 percent of output is removed from each colliery's forecast output. This procedure would have the effect of under-stating the performance of collieries subject only to small variability, and overstating the likely performance of high-risk collieries. This is the opposite result to that desired by most production managers, who spend much of their time attempting to design out variability.

The upshot is that there is a tendency for bias to creep into the colliery budget estimates, with the results of low-risk collieries being somewhat overstated (before Area relaxation) in comparison with high-risk collieries. Thus the budget for a low-risk colliery tends to represent a somewhat optimistic expectation, while that for a high-risk colliery is pessimistic. This produces an unfortunate bias in the budget figures, but can only be avoided by a greater degree of information about output variability being available to HQ staff.

This exposes a fundamental weakness in standard budgetary procedures, namely that they are not designed to cope with significant degrees of expected variability. A budget is a single point estimate of anticipated results. In an uncertain situation what is required is a more detailed, probabilistic forecast which in-corporates information about both expected values and variability. The relaxation procedure used by British Coal can be seen as a means of trying to cope with this issue at the Area level, where it works reasonably effectively. However, it does not seem possible to transmit such rich information upwards to Headquarters; the result is a distortion of the colliery budgets. As uncertainty is such a widespread feature of organizational life, it seems rather surprising that better formal methods of dealing with it in budgetary control systems have not yet been developed in the literature.

It can be seen that British Coal's accountability procedures have to cope with two fundamental issues which are perhaps more important in mining than in other industries. Firstly, there is an important day-to-day balance to be maintained between activities which maximize current production and those which prepare the ground for future production. Because much mining activity takes place in locations which are difficult to visit frequently, and in conditions that vary markedly from place to place and from time to time, this is more difficult to monitor than in the more usual factory situation. Secondly, the inherent variability in mining activities has to be taken into account in constructing estimates of output. Because only some of this uncertainty is localized, there have to be procedures whereby estimates are adjusted at different levels of aggregation.

The preceding sections have described some of the procedures by which these issues are coped with. They are by no means ideal solutions, but represent a serious attempt to cope in practice with the problems that arise in specific circumstances. It may well be that they can be adapted by organizations facing similar problems.

Examples of specific practices

This section contains two specific examples which illustrate the adaptability of the accounting system in coping with both long-term changes in mining technology and short-term demands for particular information. Although neither example is particularly unusual, together they indicate the advantages which can be gained from having a flexible data collection and coding system from which accounting reports can be generated.

Adaption to changes in mining technology

Mining methods are subject to continual evolution, as techniques are tried and adapted to new circumstances. However, the introduction of new methods can change the proportion of costs that are incurred under the main cost headings, requiring new standards for the exercise of control. Here one such change in mining technology is described and its effect on the accounting control system traced.

Pump-packing

As a coal face advances with the removal of coal from the seam, access must be maintained by driving roadways at each end of the face. However, the extraction of the coal creates enormous pressures in the rock strata, which usually manifest themselves in considerable roadway distortion some distance behind the face line. A consequence of this is that roadways driven at a height of 4 metres can be reduced in size to 2 metres or less. In order to maintain access for men, materials and ventilation, it is necessary to maintain, repair and enlarge the roadway continually.

Traditional methods of mining use packs, built either from timber or from stone extracted from the roadway rippings, on the void side of each roadway to support the roof where the coal has been extracted. In addition, considerable work is necessary in back-ripping, or enlarging the roadway, as the pressure of the ground above tends to close it. Both these activities are labour-intensive and represent a considerable cost.

A recent development has been the introduction of 'pump-packing'. Instead of building packs, cement-type materials are pumped into a heavy-duty polythene casing to produce a concrete column between the floor and the roof. In fact two different materials and water are used. Once mixed, they set solid within a few hours. This produces a continuous concrete wall along the void side of the roadway, which is highly effective in providing strata support and in reducing the need for back-ripping. It has proved possible to use this technology in many locations, but it cannot be used universally and, in particular, is not used in retreat mining.

From an accounting point of view, the technique is expensive, costing around £1 per tonne of coal extracted, although it could be cost-effective because of savings in subsequent maintenance work. In addition, the cost is incurred mainly in terms of materials, whereas the savings are made in terms of reduced labour requirements over a period of time. This caused no problems at the experimental stage when the materials costing system routinely identified the costs, and allowed cost-benefit analyses to be carried out.

Once the technology was proven and its cost advantages identified, it was introduced on a wider scale. However, if the costs-recording system had been left unaltered, significant distortions would have been introduced into inter-colliery comparisons. Different collieries would have different numbers of faces utilizing the new system, and the standards for material and labour usage would have been inappropriate. A fifth category of cost was therefore introduced into the routine cost reporting system. Costs which had originally been categorized into roadway advance related, face advance related, project related and other, could now also be coded as pump-packing related. In addition, to allow proper comparison with budget, both the budget modelling system and the trend-reporting system were modified to incorporate standards for the new system.

These changes were important because the basic unit for perform-ance comparison is the colliery. Unless activities within collieries are properly modelled, crude comparisons between them are inappro-priate. In this case comparison of roadway drivage costs between collieries having different proportions of coal faces using the pump-packing technology would not be sensible. However, once the costs are correctly coded, and standards for each technology established, useful information can be gained from such a comparison.

The introduction of new technology, although beneficial, can be expensive and increase expenditure under some cost headings despite showing benefits under other headings, possibly at different times. The flexible costing systems of the British Coal Corporation were able to adapt easily to the new technology, both at its experimental stage in developing cost/benefit analyses, and when it was routinely adopted by producing more meaningful comparative statistics and cost analyses.

Ad hoc reports

Although the timely production of routine control information is the core of a well run accounting department, perhaps the crucial test of a management-accounting system is its ability to produce relevant information in response to *ad hoc* enquiries. To produce information which is actually relevant requires both a good understanding of the production processes and the more obvious analytical management accounting skills. In addition, because within such a large and complex organization as British Coal production and accounting data are spread around different computer systems, the management accountant also needs considerable skill in interrogating those systems to extract the necessary information. In order to ease this process of interrogation, some standard approaches have been developed.

In the South Yorkshire Area of British Coal the main routine accounting reports are produced on a regular basis from mainstream systems running on large IBM-type mainframe computers. The basic principle of the interrogation system is that information from the mainframe systems is downloaded on to a smaller local computer (a Wang Model VS100) before it is processed further. This allows the user to construct and manipulate his own database without any risk of corrupting the mainstream accounting databases.

Once a user knows where the basic data is stored, a standard FILELIST package is used to interrogate the mainframe database and extract the records required. However, this output is not printed directly, but spooled into the local Wang computer, where it can be operated on by the data-management package. The main advantage of this process is that the Wang data-management package is relatively 'user-friendly', allowing information to be extracted from files and then processed in various ways by users having very limited programming skills.

The level of computer knowledge required is perhaps best indicated by the fact that the Area runs a standard 3-day training programme in the use of the utilities available on the Wang computer. This is sufficient to enable cost clerks to carry out the analyses described above, and to bring information initially stored on different mainframe systems on to one document for scrutiny by management. While the quality of report presentation produced by the utilities leaves something to be desired, the necessary information can be produced quickly and accurately. Usually reports generated in this way will be required for only the short period of time while the problem that required them is resolved, as the following example illustrates.

Recently the routine cost-monitoring system showed an unexpected rise in the number of operating manshifts worked per employee. The main factors which affect operating manshifts were known to be overtime, whereby a man may work an extra shift on occasion; the pattern of holidays taken in a particular period; sickness; absence for training purposes; and deployment of men to capital rather than operating work. Because the budgets had been prepared in the necessary detail, it was a straightforward matter to establish budget variances under each cost heading on a weekly basis. However, to understand the causes of the variances required further analysis.

Further information was therefore extracted, to be analysed in conjunction with the operating manshifts worked. Information on overtime working, holiday patterns, voluntary redundancy losses (a major influence on the sickness pattern), and capital roadway drivages (the main consumer of capital rather than operating shifts) was extracted and analysed on a weekly basis. This led to two main contributory factors being identified. First, a changing pattern of capital working emerged, such that a reduced demand for roadway drivage had released men for operating activities. Second, the times at which holidays were being taken was also affecting manpower availability. Once the factors causing the change were understood, the new patterns were incorporated into the budget model and colliery managers were able to plan their programmes of work more realistically. The new weekly report, having served its purpose, was discontinued after 8 weeks' use.

The flexibility both to create and discontinue specific accounting reports is extremely valuable. Once a quirk in the routine statistics is noted, more specific analysis can be quickly undertaken, and the necessary information gathered and monitored while remedial action is being taken. However, once the need for the specific information has passed, the reports can be discontinued, so that management and accounting staff alike cease to be burdened with unnecessary data. Regrettably such flexibility does not appear to be common in computer-based accounting systems, and the above illustration is put forward as an example of what any well-designed accounting information system ought to be capable of allowing with the minimum of programming work.

Summary

This chapter has briefly described the main processes by which management control over colliery managers is exercised in the British Coal Corporation, and the contribution which accounting information makes to these processes. Although British Coal is a public sector organization, its accountability arrangements can parallel those of the private sector, in that it sells its output to customers. Despite having a virtual monopoly over the supply of coal, it operates in the highly competitive energy market and is subject to competition from oil, gas and nuclear power. However, it is also affected by the fact that the majority of its output is sold to a single customer, which is itself the state monopoly supplier of electricity. The result is that British Coal operates systems which would not be out of place in the private sector, but which have to be used with a sensible recognition of the constraints that its public-sector position places on its operations.

The characteristics of an extractive industry also differ from those of manufacturing industry. The environment in which the production activities operate is more hostile and subject to greater uncertainty than that found in a typical factory. In addition, the replacement of production capacity is a regular feature of normal operating activity, with the consequence that a production manager is constantly balancing the need for short-term production against the need to preserve productive capacity in future months and years.

The systems described and the manner in which they are operated thus represent a response to a particular set of circumstances, which are unique to the industry. Nevertheless, it is hoped that the reasons for the choices which have been made can assist others in designing systems which are appropriate to their own particular needs. It is not suggested that the accountability arrangements in British Coal are perfect; however, they have evolved over a considerable period of time and have proved to be robust even when subject to considerable change in the economic and political environment. It is therefore believed that they are a sound example of good management practice.

6 Management accounting in British universities

Graham Keenleside

Evolution of management accounting

There has been increased awareness and use of management accounting techniques within the British university system since the early 1970s, because of its utility in counteracting diminishing financial support from government, and also because of political pressures for accountability. The universities, in common with the industrial sector, encountered serious financial problems after 1973, and the university system, which had enjoyed rapid growth in the post-Robbins era from 1963, suffered a series of cuts in core financial support from government. The decline in funding (Exchequer grant and fees) between 1980–1 and 1983–4 was particularly severe. On average it fell by 17 percent in the total university sector, but differential cuts of between 6 percent to 44 percent were applied to universities during the period. There is every prospect that the rate of financial decline will continue unabated into the 1990s.

As is usual when financial turbulence occurs, management has sought ways and means of making the best use of increasingly scarce resources, and some universities have been quite positive in adopting management accounting techniques to assist with this process. Other universities have been slower to realize the benefits, but fresh impetus has been given through recent efficiency studies of universities and new resource allocation systems introduced by the University Grants Committee (UGC), which will help to accelerate the spread of good management accounting practice. The techniques in use not only include the conventional and narrowly defined application of management accounting data for cost identification, improvement and control, but have also been used in assisting with strategic policy formulation and as a stimulus towards achieving operational objectives. The traditional uses to which management information is applied by industry and commerce – policy formulation, control, decision-taking, disclosure to external and internal interests, and the safeguarding of assets – are all featured in university management accounting. Similarly, management processes – long-term strategic planning, short-term operational plans, financial and management accounting procedures, treasureship and audit – are practised in universities and are described in this chapter.

This represents a considerable advance in university accounting practices in the last 20 years. The state of the art in the late 1960s is neatly summarized by Fielden (1969), who wrote:

> This is a report by an accountant on accountants, but they are not ordinary accountants. The thirty-five I visited administered the expenditure of more than one hundred million pounds in the academic year 1966/67.
>
> It is a world in which commercial and industrial accountancy management techniques have little relevance, so that any external investigator must approach with caution and flexibility.

This was written during the 'halcyon days' of the immediate post-Robbins era, when successive governments aimed to provide student places to all those qualified to benefit from higher education, and investment in university expansion was second only to the development of natural gas. Since the buoyancy of those days, reduced funding and economic uncertainty borne of national economic decline has led to a dilution of the power of universities to influence their own affairs. The 'power of the purse' has been transferred from the universities to the University Grants Committee (UGC), which is inevitably reactive to government policy, particularly when contraction occurs and choice is suppressed.

Universities have responded with a more aggressive attitude to marketing their skills, e.g. research grants and contracts, consultancy advice, industrial units, technology transfer, overseas student recruitment at 'economic' fee levels, etc. These activities all contribute to the academic vitality and financial well-being of the modern university and bring in their train an increased range and complexity to management accounting techniques. Job costing, process costing, overhead apportionment and recovery, marginal and full cost evaluation, investment appraisal, opportunity costs, and cost analysis have all a role to play within the diverse operational framework of a university.

In commenting on the utility of cost analysis, Balderston (1974) said:

> Traditionally, academic leadership has been concerned about ideals, missions and values, to the exclusion of concern about costs except as an unfortunate inhibition. It fell to the business management of academic institutions to account for the funds used and to keep the operation going. Now there is a joining of these two domains of responsibility, and we must talk about cost analysis in the context of what is to be decided and what it is that our universities are trying to accomplish.
>
> Cost analysis is useful for: (1) operating and management; (2) providing critical inputs for planning major changes in capacity, program structure, or institution policies; (3) obtaining comparisons between institutions to help us share insights about what targets to set; (4) justifying to funding services (public and private) what prices we charge for educational and institutional services and what resources are needed (p. 141).

The development of management accounting in the university environment encompasses the preparation of budgets constructed as financial statements of policy; resource allocation procedures geared to performance, which create a market environment to reward achievement; and measurement of indirect costs associated with particular activities.

The financial landscape

There are forty-five universities in the UK system (counting the University of London as one), each receiving Exchequer support via the University Grants Committee (UGC). Table 6.1 shows the growth in the number of universities and the student population since 1950. The percentage of university students reading each of the following subjects in 1983–4 was Science 25, Engineering 13,

Medicine 11, Agriculture 2, Professional and vocational 2, Social studies 23, Languages 12, Arts 8, and Education 4.

Table 6.1

Year	No. of universities	No. of student places
1950	17	85,314
1960	21	107,699
1970	45	228,131
1983	45	301,000

Note: Data supplied by the Department of Education and Science.

The number and disciplinary mix of students has a significant impact on university costs. The course length is between 3 and 5 years (medicine/dentistry) and the total cost per graduate course (at 1982–3 prices), including wastage, ranged from £12,000 per social-studies student to £41,500 per medical student, with an average of £18,500. By international comparisons a UK university degree course is of relatively short duration – 3 years of high quality and with low wastage rates. There is a favourable staff:student ratio of Arts 11.6, Science 9.8, Clinical 6.4, Average 10.2 (1983–4).

The elements of university revenue income and expenditure in 1984–5 are shown in Table 6.2. It will be noticed that a distinction is drawn between revenue support and revenue earning.

It can be seen from Table 6.2 that UGC Exchequer grants in 1984–5 provided nearly 60 percent of university income (77.5 percent in 1974–5). Home student fees are largely a derivative of the student quota approved by the UGC. The UGC does not provide any support for overseas students and, while in theory full economic fees are meant to be charged, the minimum recommended fees are usually adopted, as overseas students would otherwise be dissuaded from applying to the more expensive universities unless they were convinced that expense was commensurate with quality of teaching and research. It will take some time before this correlation exists.

Research grants and contracts are awarded by the research councils, industry, government departments, and other outside agencies in response to submissions from academic staff and after

Table 6.2 *University income and expenditure (recurrent items)*

1974–5 Total UK %		Income and expenditure 1984–5 Total UK £ million	%
	Recurrent income 1984–5		
	Revenue support		
77.5	Exchequer grants	1,310.9	59.8
3.0	Student fees – home	178.7	8.2
1.1	Endowment and donations	22.1	1.0
81.6	Total support	1,511.7	69.0
	Revenue earnings		
1.5	Student fees – overseas	105.1	4.8
12.0	Research grants and contracts	353.6	16.1
2.5	Services rendered	104.7	4.8
2.4	Other income (e.g. investment income)	115.4	5.3
100.0	Total income	2,190.5	100.0
	Recurrent expenditure		
	Academic teaching and research		
	– internally funded	928.0	42.0
	– externally funded	413.4	18.7
	Academic services (library/computers, etc.)	174.9	7.9
	General education expenditure	48.2	2.2
	Staff and student facilities and amenities	49.8	2.3
	Administration and central services	122.8	5.6
	Maintenance of premises	344.0	15.6
	Capital expenditure from recurrent income	50.0	2.3
	Other recurrent expenditure	80.1	3.4
	Total expenditure	2,211.2	100.0

peer-group review in many instances. Government-funded research in universities, particularly that undertaken on behalf of Science Research Council agencies, is based on the dual funding system, in which the research sponsors meet the marginal cost of research, while the universities provide the laboratory and infrastructure costs. This was commented upon in the Merrison Report (Advisory Board for the Research Councils, 1982), which stated:

> The extent of the research infrastructure to be supported from general university funds is not always appreciated. It goes well beyond what is normally referred to as the 'well-found' laboratory, and includes a proportion of salaries of academic, technical, secretarial and administrative staff, of library costs, and of computing and other services, in addition 'to the equipment, recurrent, and maintenance costs more commonly associated with laboratories: there is also the cost of the accommodation itself. In the social sciences administrative costs, and those of secretarial assistance, are of particular significance.

Academics are often tempted to accept a research grant or contracts from industry or other agencies because of its intrinsic academic value, with less importance attached to its contribution to overheads, for fear that heavy overhead loading might dissuade sponsorship. Academic staff are continually exhorted to negotiate a reasonable charge for overheads, and it is important to demonstrate and publicize the true cost of overheads, in addition to the direct costs of performing research. The UGC-advised figure for overhead recovery is 40 percent on direct costs, although going rates vary between 100 percent to zero, depending on the costs to be incurred and what the market will bear.

'Services rendered' in Table 6.2 largely comprises consultancy services and the industrial units which originate and develop from the work of academic staff in departments. Other income includes investment income on working capital deposits and also hire of rooms and facilities.

It is interesting to note the shift from revenue support to revenue earnings which has occurred during the last 10 years. The ratios were approximately 82:18 and 69:31 in the years 1974–5 and 1984–5 respectively. The 'management of change' has been a very real preoccupation of universities during this period.

To complete the picture, it is necessary to note that the UGC also allocates an equipment and furniture grant, which in 1984–5 totalled £92m, and building work funds of £7.3m. In addition, universities are responsible for maintaining halls of residence for some 140,000 students (46 percent of the total full-time student population); and catering services for both their staff and student population, with an estimated turnover of about £100m a year. Conference promotion exploits under-used assets during vacation periods and provides real assistance to keep residence fees and menu prices within the capability of the student purse, as well as contributing to general revenue income. Comparatively recent developments in university financial activity are the creation of science parks, of university-owned companies, and 'spin out' companies created to assist with technology transfer as univerities develop opportunities to contribute to industry on a revenue-earning basis.

Characteristics of management accounting environment

The management accounting needs of universities have to take into account the special characteristics of the operational and financial environment in which universities work. These include:

1 *University objectives*. The Robbins Committee Report (Cmnd 2154, 1963) defined the aims and purposes of higher education to provide instruction in skills, the promotion of the general powers of the mind, the advancement of learning, and the transmission of a common culture and common standards of citizenship. A university's mission is usually described in its charter and statutes and traditionally refers to the advancement of teaching and research. It is now widely understood that universities also have a responsibility for public service, which is pursued through technology transfer, consultancy advice, the promotion of industrial service units and continuing education.

2 *University autonomy*. The autonomy of an academic member of staff and the university institution to conduct research without the interference of government is protected at various levels. At the institutional level the academic enjoys tenure (although the strength of protection varies from university to university) and, unless he is guilty of some moral transgression or suffers from

mental infirmity, he cannot normally be removed. Universities enjoy a measure of autonomy and are governed by their council, which is manned by academics from within the university and also lay people drawn from industry, local government, and the wider community. The importance of lay members to the governance of universities was explained in a passage from the Robbins Committee Report:

> More than 85% of university finance comes from public sources and in our judgement it is in general neither practical nor justifiable that the spending of university funds should be wholly in the hands of the users. Academic autonomy is more likely to be safeguarded where the public has a guarantee that there is independent lay advice and criticism within the university . . . Where men and women of wide experience and high standing in the world of affairs can spare time to associate themselves with university activities, the universities gain from the partnership strength and sagacity in their dealings with the outside world. And, even where academic affairs are concerned, lay arbitration is a valuable resource in case of conflict.

Universities are educational charities and to preserve that independence and status (which as a side benefit has tax implications) a strong lay presence should exist on the council and finance committee (or its equivalent). Financial budgets and accounts are usually the responsibility of the finance committee working on behalf of the council.

3   *University organization.* A university seeks to fulfil a range of objectives and the weight given to specific objectives and their articulation is further confused by the diffusion of authority in a community of scholars. Kerr (1973) states that 'no one has absolute authority within the organisation' and goes on to point out how the organization has to 'operate through overlapping spheres of power and influence'. Moodie and Eustace (1974) state that a university 'is not a simple hierarchical type of organisation. What one finds, on the contrary, is an untidy diffusion of responsibility and a proliferation of centres of initiative and decision-making . . . There is no direct and comprehensive chain of command'.

The organization, responsibilities, and relations of those

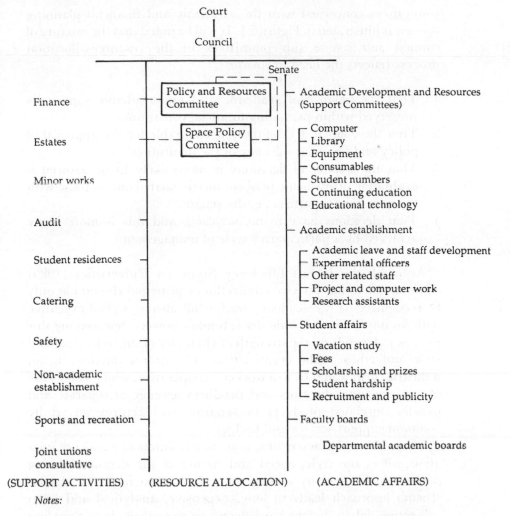

Court

Council

Senate

Policy and Resources Committee

Academic Development and Resources (Support Committees)

Space Policy Committee

Finance

Estates

Minor works

Audit

Student residences

Catering

Safety

Non-academic establishment

Sports and recreation

Joint unions consultative

Computer
Library
Equipment
Consumables
Student numbers
Continuing education
Educational technology

Academic establishment

Academic leave and staff development
Experimental officers
Other related staff
Project and computer work
Research assistants

Student affairs

Vacation study
Fees
Scholarship and prizes
Student hardship
Recruitment and publicity

Faculty boards

Departmental academic boards

(SUPPORT ACTIVITIES)   (RESOURCE ALLOCATION)   (ACADEMIC AFFAIRS)

Notes:

(i) The Policy and Resources Committee will decide the main budgetary parameters, i.e. surplus/deficits, utilization/size of reserves, distribution of budget between academic/non-academic activities, etc.

(ii) The measurement of need, the attainment of academic goals, the review of performance criteria, and the distribution of resource to each academic department are the responsibility of the Academic Development and Resources Committee.

(iii) The resource allocation committees – Policy and Resources and Space Policy – are composed of a mixture of academic and lay representation.

Figure 6.1 *University committee organization*

committees concerned with the academic and financial planning process is illustrated in Figure 6.1. It will be noted that the mixture of council and senate sub-committees in the resource-allocation process reflects the need to ensure:

1   That the balance of academic and non-academic support is preserved within prevailing financial constraints.
2   That the council is essentially accountable for the approval of policy and financial solvency of the institution.
3   That the quality of decisions is more likely to be assured if evaluation of academic performance is carried out by those with the necessary expertise, i.e. the senate.
4   That decisions have to be *acceptable*, and this is more likely achieved by a participative style of management.

Although the Jarratt Efficiency Study on Universities (1985) recommended that the vice-chancellor or principal should not only be recognized as the academic leader but also as a chief executive with an implication of wide discretionary powers, few assume this role, as it depends on the strength of character of the individual and style and ethos of the organization. The nearest analogy to an industrial firm would be to a workers' cooperative, which makes use of non-executive directors and produces a range of separate and usually unrelated products in separate cost centres served by common support service and budget.

These three characteristics, objectivity, autonomy and organization, affect the style, speed and nature of the decision-making processes of university management. The participative and consensual approach leads to long, expensive, analytical and often subjective debate before hard decisions are taken. It is therefore important to enable a university to be responsive to change by ensuring that long-term plans exist, working towards agreed objectives, which contain an element of flexibility to allow for unforeseeable contingencies.

The diffuse objectives and the autonomous structure bring in their train particular problems for the management accountant. Academic and related salaries amount to approximately 44 percent of university expenditure, and when added to the expenditure on local authority rates and the costs of premises, etc., the fixed costs of the university amount to over 60 percent of total revenue costs. Undergraduate students take 3 to 5 years to complete their courses. This means that the ability of universities to adapt to change is severely reduced, and annual perturbations in direct funding present them with great difficulties in maintaining academic balance, preserving financial solvency, and in pursuing longer-term policy objectives.

The translation of input into output also causes problems of accountability. Should the measurement of output be the number of student graduates, the student population, the weight and/or quality of research material, the standards of citizenship adopted by university graduates, the enhancement in their earning potential and hence their benefit to society, or some other unit? The selection of an appropriate unit of output to measure the effectiveness, efficiency and economy with which universities carry out their business has received increasing attention in recent years, although commonly used 'performance indicators' tend to be one-dimensional rather than three, i.e. unit cost is a measure of economy but not of effectiveness or efficiency.

Since the mid-1970s university long-range planning has been frustrated by shorter planning horizons and inconsistency in Exchequer allocations caused by variations in government policies. This criticism of government was highlighted in the Jarratt Report (Committee of Vice-Chancellors and Principals, 1985):

'(i) Government should provide broad policy guidelines within which the UGC and individual universities can undertake strategic and long term planning;
(ii) Government should consider what action can be taken to restore a longer funding horizon for universities in view of the disincentives to strategic planning inherent in the present system;
(iii) Government should avoid thrusting crises on universities by sudden short term changes of course' (p. 35).

Users of management information

The complexity of the environment provides a real challenge to the management accountant if his techniques are to be both meaningful and acceptable, and it is in this environment that management information and processes have been tailored to the needs of those groups accountable for the university system. The primary interests of those concerned can be summarized as follows.

Government

The allocation of funding to universities is a part of the Department of Education and Science's vote, and it is important for government, acting on behalf of the providers and users of the service, to be able to measure the needs and contribution of universities in relation to other competing claims in the context of national economic, social, and political priorities. The government is therefore interested in the universities' contribution to the performance of the economy; the provision of well-motivated, broadly based and highly skilled graduates; the accessibility of universities to prospective students; links with industry; reduced dependence on public finance; and research centres of excellence, etc. These are all themes adopted by government to which university managers have to respond. It is therefore important that management information systems exist to analyse, stimulate and promote the universities' contribution.

The University Grants Committee (UGC)

The UGC has the responsibility for allocating Exchequer funds to each university. The remit of the UGC is to enquire into the financial needs of university education; to advise on the application of grants made by parliament towards meeting them; to collect, examine and publish information relating to university education; and to assist, in consultation with the universities and other bodies concerned, the preparation and execution of such plans for development of the universities as may from time to time be required in order to ensure that they are fully adequate to national needs. In order to accomplish these tasks the UGC has to have the capability, assisted by universities, to record costs, to measure inputs and outputs, to present comparisons according to subject groups in each university, to audit the quality of university departments, and to prescribe student numbers and mix for which support is provided. As cuts have been enforced and the margin for new developments eroded, the UGC has assumed responsibility for allocating money for new developments through earmarked and indicated funds for special initiatives, including 'new blood' appointments and information technology.

The universities

A university is a federation of disparate departments engaged in teaching and research, often with interactive relations with industry and the wider community. Its departments may extend across the broad spectrum of arts, sciences, engineering, and clinical studies, and include the humanities and vocational studies. The balance of teaching and research may vary from one department to another, and from one university to another. All departments within a university, no matter how different they are, provide competing claims on the same budget. It is important that the university deploys its resource efficiently, effectively and economically, notwithstanding that conflicting aims might undermine the objectivity of this process, e.g. teaching v research, applied v pure research, academic investment v non-academic support costs, etc, etc. Policy formulation, implementation and control in a university form an iterative process more fully described later in this chapter. The importance of the budget is emphasized by Balderston (1974):

> The budgets of a university are the surest single indication of what it is committed to do or is stuck with as an institution. This is true partly because, underneath the rhetoric of leadership, there is a hard logic in putting funds where institutional necessity points. It is true even though not all funds of an institution are counted as budgeted funds, causing confusion in the analysis of fiscal patterns; and it is true even though some very important resources are not explicitly dealt with in the budgeting process, while money is (p. 199).

Beyond the three primary groups mentioned, there are the interests of the wider community, prospective students and their parents, and industry, which seeks a supply of suitable graduates and innovative ideas for technology transfer. The management accountant must seek to satisfy the information needs of each of the interested groups and it is helpful if the information is integrated, complementary and capable of audit.

Management accounting practices

Management accounting techniques can be used as an aid to policy formulation, as a means to pursue policy objectives, and to control costs and evaluate performance. This chapter has already referred to the interests of government, the University Grants Committee and the universities, relevant to management of the university system at the national and institutional level. In the paragraphs that follow brief reference will be made to the nature of management information which enables government and the UGC to monitor, appraise and, to some extent, control university performance. Particular reference is made to the UGC resource allocation model, which was introduced in 1986–7. This is followed by a case-study description of budgetary formulation, allocation and control processes found in a British university which is fairly typical of the practices generally adopted.

The government and the University Grants Committee

As the UGC exists, *inter alia*, to enquire into the financial needs of university education, and to assist in the planned development of universities to meet national needs, extensive use is made by government of statistics and management information collected by the UGC, which includes the following:

1 *Students.* Student numbers are analysed according to full-time, sandwich course, part-time, undergraduate, postgraduate, and continuing education students; identified according to subject groups; and expressed as raw numbers and student load. Student performance is monitored via course completion rates, wastage, 'A' level grade scores, and employability according to subject areas. Student funding and support services are analysed by fee-paying status (home or overseas), use of university residences, and sources of finance of undergraduate and post-graduate students, etc.

2 *Staff.* As approximately 72 percent of a university budget meets staff costs, extensive analysis of employment statistics are maintained, including male, female, full-time and part-time staff. Those wholly university financed, and those externally financed are also recorded. Further analysis includes senior:

junior staff ratios, student:staff ratios, deployment of staff to academic and non-academic support services, and classification as academic and academic-related, technical, secretarial and clerical, and other categories.

3 *Income and expenditure analyses.* In addition to analysing financial and statistical inputs and outputs of students and staff, the government and UGC collect detailed information on external funding from research grants and contracts, other services rendered, Computer Board grants and other general recurrent income. Inter-university expenditure patterns are monitored, including internally and externally funded work in academic departments, academic services (including library and computer), general educational expenditure, administration and central services, maintenance and running of premises, staff and student facilities and amenities, and capital expenditure from income. This information is collected annually by the UGC via its Form 3 returns. An analysis of the income and expenditure profiles for 1984–5 is shown in Table 6.2.

4 *Performance indicators.* Performance indicators are used increasingly as a measure of accountability. Classified as internal, external and operating indicators, they encompass government, UGC and university perspectives. The following indicators were those noted by the Jarratt Report (Committee of Vice-Chancellors and Principals, 1985, Appendix G):

'(a) Internal performance indicators include:
 – Market share of undergraduate applications (by subject)
 – Graduation rates and classes of degrees
 – Attraction of Masters' and Doctoral students
 – Success rate of higher degrees (and time taken)
 – Attraction of research funds
 – Teaching quality
(b) External performance indicators include:
 – Acceptability of graduates (postgraduates) in employment
 – First destination of graduates (postgraduates)
 – Reputation judged by external reviews
 – Publications by staff and citations
 – Patents, inventions, consultancies

  – Membership, prizes, medals of learned societies
  – Papers at conferences
(c) Operating performance indicators include:
  – Unit costs
  – Staff:student ratios
  – Class sizes
  – Course options available
  – Staff workload
  – Library stock availability
  – Computing availability'

UGC resource allocation

From 1986–7 the procedure by which the UGC allocated money to universities was recast to incorporate performance criteria. Until the mid-1970s a quinquennial system of financial planning existed. Universities had submitted plans for 5 years ahead and, following consideration and approval by the UGC, a grant was announced for each of those 5 years. Supplementary grants were made towards inflation during the period. This was the block grant allocation, which acknowledged the financial autonomy of universities. The UGC's influence in university planning was largely indirect, although it could influence the shape of a university through earmarked and indicated grants for specific initiatives and by fixing student number quotas, senior:junior staff ratios, capital spending and by various other methods. The UGC also had the right to withhold funds if a university chose to pursue work the UGC did not wish to support.

As financial uncertainty grew, the quinquennial system was eventually replaced by annual allocations, within the context of 3 to 4 year planning horizons. Good intentions were frequently overtaken by financial expediency, and academic and financial plans from 1977, revised in 1980 and again in 1984, were disrupted by stop-go government policies. In 1986–7 the UGC introduced a resource allocation formula which sought to allocate a common unit of resource for teaching within each subject area and reward universities according to the quality of their research and any other special factors.

The UGC exercise introduced selective funding for research in the knowledge that university resources had declined over the years and would continue to do so. It was possible to tune a reduction of resource for teaching with variations in staff:student ratios, but this left residual pressure on the research side. The UGC took the view that if research was to be adequately supported, good research must be distinguished from bad and support given to best effect.

The UGC took as its baseline the expenditures in each subject group during 1984–5, and divided the costs up between teaching and research. Some adjustment was made to restore resource to computer science, which had been regarded as being under-funded, and there was also a shift in resource from physics to engineering. It was also estimated that teaching costs represented 70 percent of total expenditure in each subject group, while approximately 30 percent was applicable to research. It was accepted that excellence in teaching was difficult to measure and therefore it was agreed that equal support costs for teaching should be distributed to universities from 70 percent of the historical expenditure within each of the thirty-seven UGC subject areas. Non-departmental expenditure was split between subjects according to student numbers, and the natural weighting was derived from the differential expenditure per subject area, i.e. grants for laboratory-based technology would be more than those given to arts departments. The teaching component was then distributed between universities in proportion to planned student numbers in the subject at the various universities, again allowing a weighting for undergraduate and postgraduate courses, and postgraduate research.

It can be seen from this description that the allocation of resources on the teaching side lacked selectivity, and was mainly based on historical costs redistributed to provide equal shares to each institution. On the research side the dual support system, which was described in earlier paragraphs, was beginning to falter. Universities were unable to sustain well-found laboratories in the face of declining resource. It was also acknowledged that a Research Council grant imposes an extra cost on the university which undertakes research, and it was estimated that this extra cost averaged at least 40 percent of the value of the grant. The UGC therefore decided to restore a sum equal to 40 percent of all Research Council grant income attracted by each university, out of the 30 percent balance available for research within each UGC subject group area. This had the effect of shifting money towards those universities which did well with Research Council peer-group reviews as opposed to those which did badly. A bonus was also provided to those universities which attracted research grants and contracts from industry. While universities are exhorted to charge full economic costs and overheads to industry, the UGC took the view that further encouragement and reward was necessary through the resource-allocation process.

After the sums allocated for teaching, Research Council over-heads, and industrial bonuses were deducted, a residual sum remained available within each UGC subject-group allocation. This residual sum was divided into two parts: one part to be distributed in an equitable way to ensure that every department had some research base, and the other distributed selectively in accordance with the UGC's judgement of research merit and potential. What became known as the 'egalitarian formula' was based on staff:student ratios, aggregating home and overseas students as part of the equation. The second part – the judgemental factor (or quality factor) – was based on evidence and advice taken by the UGC from research councils, other learned bodies, and from the technological areas of industry. In addition, the UGC took evidence from the universities and laid particular emphasis on the value of research plans and objective evidence of research quality which the universities provided.

The results of this exercise were published by the UGC in the form of a scale, and departments were classified as outstanding (world reputation), above average, average and below average. It was generally accepted that the UGC had got it 'about 80 percent correct' and surprisingly little revision was pressed for or granted. The results of the survey were embodied within the 'research' element contained within the subsequent allocation to each university for 1986–7 and beyond.

Finally, a residual sum was allocated for special factors and took account of extra costs which were not necessarily merit-related. Examples of this would include London weighting, and museums and large scientific installations associated with universities.

After applying these formulae to the historical costs per subject area, suitably inflated to match the following year's total sum available for allocation, the UGC then examined each of the quotients and compared them with the university's allocation in previous years. Any odd results were investigated and, if mistakes were found, the final grant to the university was amended. After completing the exercise, the UGC agreed it would not publish the ingredient allocations to each subject within the block grant, as this might embarrass the university and usurp its right to make its own decisions on resource allocation.

The resource allocation formula can be expressed as follows: $A = T + R + S$, where A = allocation, T = resources to be distributed on teaching-based criteria, R = resources to be distributed on research-based criteria, and S = resources for special factors. T is not broken down any further, but the research is further analysed into four components:

1 SR = resources distributed on criteria related to staff and research student numbers (this is the 'floor' provision for research).
2 DR = resources distributed on the basis of income from research councils and charitable bodies.
3 CR = resources distributed on the basis of contract research income.
4 JR = resources selectively distributed on judgement.

The special factors are further broken down into:

(a) NDS = allowances for non-departmental special factors.
(b) DS = allowances for departmental special factors.

An example of special factors could be London weighting, copyright libraries, museums, galleries and observatories, etc., all of which impose a burden of cost because of their uniqueness or location.

The formula was published in November 1985 and the UGC then carried out an exhaustive peer-group review of research in universities. The results were published in a 'league table' produced against an average 1 percent increase in the level of funding available to UK universities. Some universities received more than 1 percent, a second batch between 0 and 1 percent, and a third 0 to −0.5 percent. It was held that the results of this survey would hold good in allocating annual resources to the end of the year 1989–90. No university was allowed to suffer more than a 0.5 percent cut in the first year, although it was acknowledged that this was purely a transitional arrangement and in due course more severe cuts might be suffered by those universities in the third category.

The allocation of UGC grant to 1989–90 would have the components shown in Table 6.3.

Table 6.3

	Percent
Teaching	61.2
Research	
Grant-related	5.2
Contract income	0.7
'Floor'	14.8
Selective	14.1
Special factors	
Departmental	2.0
Non-departmental	2.0
Total relevant resources for 1989–90	100.0

Source: *Review of UGC* (Croham Report, 1987).

For the first time, the UGC had endeavoured to provide resources on the basis of need and on performance, and, more important, had created an atmosphere in which universities could be seen to be competing one with another for scarce resources. The formula was designed to be both equitable and to spur achievement – to create a market situation in which the strong would survive and be encouraged and the weak would be encouraged to do better if they were to survive.

University management accounting practices

With the demise in 1973 of the quinquennial funding system, which automatically encouraged long-term perspectives, the UGC has since mounted a series of investigative exercises as a precursor to the allocation of Exchequer funds. These exercises have prompted universities to examine their objectives, and to agree long-term policies and the mechanism by which policies should be implemented. The features of the planning, allocation and control process which follow presents a case study largely derived from the processes and approach adopted by the University of Manchester Institute of Science and Technology (UMIST), and while possessing some unique features, i.e. staffing resource allocation through the medium of establishment points quotas (EPQs), it represents a fairly typical example of how a university can develop its rolling budgetary planning process.

Case study

The elements to constructing a financial policy and implementing it are shown in Table 6.4.

Table 6.4

Management function	Management activity	Function/activity consolidated in:
1 Policy formulation	Mission statement of general objectives	Long-term strategic planning
2 Decision-taking	Planning criteria and evaluation of departments	
3 Implementation	Allocation of resources/targets of performance	Short-term operational plans
4 Control	Budgetary mechanisms	Financial and management accounting procedures
5 Review and remedial action	Budget reports	

Policy formulation – mission statement

A policy or mission statement is used to express the aims of the institution in general terms. The possible content of such a statement might be as follows:

The University's overall objective is to remain a specialist institution with emphasis on those key areas of science, engineering, technology and management that will enhance the UK's economic performance. The University will continue to react creatively with both national and regional organisations and institutions. The University will also aim to provide a favourable working environment for staff and students where intellectual enquiry, the exchange of ideas and the enhancement of knowledge is fostered. It will always be alert to develop new areas of teaching, including mid-career training, relevant to national needs and will maintain its emphasis on fundamental and applied research within its traditional disciplines.

While this may appear a rather bland statement, it does indicate the academic emphasis of the university, a close affinity with industry and economic performance, and a readiness to extend its student population to mature entrants.

Decision-taking – planning criteria and evaluation of departments

The resource allocation process must be preceded by an evaluation of departments against appropriate planning criteria. The planning criteria adopted by an Academic Development and Resources Committee (ADRC) would be based on several sources of information, including statistical information gathered by the central administration and agreed with individual departments, and general comparisons with similar departments or subject areas in other universities.

Historical information is complemented by departmental submissions on aims and needs, supplemented by visiting party reports on departmental activity. Visits are considered as just one factor in the procedure, to avoid criticisms of superficiality. The ADRC will then produce concise statements on key points about individual departments and invite feedback from departments during plenary meetings and any subsequent interactions.

General 'environmental' factors taken into account in evaluating departments may include some of the following:

1　A policy of no compulsory redundancy.
2　Adequate time to be given for a department to readjust to a new funding level.
3　Consideration to be given to any residual 'historical' funding patterns.
4　The repercussions of losses in permanent staff which might be the cause of academic imbalance.

5   The age structure in departments and the need to introduce 'new blood' into those departments with predominantly older staff.
6   Comments about subject areas in UGC guidance on policy.
7   The development potential of academic areas and market needs.
8   Matters concerned with academic quality, leadership and success, which are very elusive subjects to define, but nevertheless essential ingredients to planning criteria. At research level, 'success' is linked to the ability and personality of a key individual, or key individuals, able to motivate himself, themselves, a group or a department, to perform above the institutional norm. Teaching quality may be somewhat less dependent on individuals and more related to the ethos of the department. Leadership qualities in organization and administration, leading to optimum departmental development, are usually apparent where it is noted that strong-minded individuals fulfil their individual abilities yet allow themselves to pursue and fulfil a communal goal without constant attendant in-fighting and demarcation disputes. Quality and leadership are what success is all about in any organization, but regrettably their identification and encouragement are possible only to a very limited degree in universities.
9   Equity is to be considered, e.g. in departmental workloads.

Some of the detailed criteria which may be used to examine the appropriateness of the proposed targets imposed on departmental resources may include the following: unit costs, staff in various categories, student numbers, student load/staff ratio (but not as the major planning criterion – workload might be a more appropriate criterion), consumable needs, maintenance of postgraduate schools, research council income, ability to earn other income, standing relative to peers in UK and abroad, intake quality of and output demand for students, national needs and publication records. What is evident is that total costs and unit costs per department will vary widely, and it is difficult to make large adjustments with this in mind, when all the other considerations were being taken into account.

Approximately 65–70 percent of university expenditures are incurred by academic departments. Budgetary submissions are also received and scrutinized, using different criteria for the administration, estates and other supporting services. The budgets are routed to the budget committee via the council subcommittees rather than ADRC.

Implementation

Allocation of resource and targets

Once the planning criteria have been applied and the evaluation of departments has taken place, the allocation of resources to departments can begin. This part of the exercise also relates resource allocation to the establishment of targets for departments. The constituent elements of the planning profiles created for departments are student numbers (home and overseas): staffing quotas; and the sessional resource made available to supplement permanent staff in the form of research assistants, part-time teaching assistants and hourly paid staff. In addition, suggested income-generation contributions are also determined to encourage and reward departments for research overheads, mid-career training and overseas-student recruitment.

Resources to departments are controlled and allocated through an establishment points quota (EPQ). Examples of the EPQ value attached to given levels of staff are as follows:

Professors   1.89 points
Lecturers   1.00 points
Technicians   0.60 points

A correlation exists between the value of the points and total employment costs of each post. The purpose in allocating points rather than cash is that savings can be expressed as points and vary automatically with inflationary trends, and long-term target savings do not need to be recast each year as cash values change. The mixture of staff within the aggregate points allocation to a department – academics, technical staff, clerical staff – is left to the discretion of the head of department, providing a measure of delegated responsibility. Non-salary costs, i.e. consumable allowances and equipment costs, are allocated on a cash limit basis according to a pre-determined formula, which takes account of the number of students, the number of staff, and separate weighting for the discipline concerned, i.e. laboratory-based, classroom-based, etc. Once the departmental establishment points quota (EPQ) is fixed, vacancies will only be filled when the establishment point used (EPU) falls below the EPQ.

Income-generation
As Exchequer resources have contracted during the 1980s, ways and means have been sought to improve income-generation. The search for income can influence university policy, and the university has to be careful that its aims and objectives are not compromised. Income derived from research contract overheads, mid-career training and continuing education overheads, overseas student fees, and other activities are the commonest sources of additional revenue. To stimulate departmental contributions towards revenue activity a university might agree that 50 percent of all additional income should be returned directly to those departments earning it, to augment departmental allocations from the centre. It might be applied by the department to recruit temporary staff, increase departmental allowances or purchase equipment. Then 30 percent might be made available to the ADRC pool for specific purposes, including new research initiatives or the correction of academic imbalance caused by the loss of key staff. The final 20 percent would then be available to the centre to meet fixed costs and administration.

This formula would operate if core government funding met expectations. In the event of a deterioration in Exchequer funding, the constituent allocations would be changed with 10 percent of additional income going to departmental reserve funds, 35 percent contributing to fixed costs and administration, 25 percent only to support permanent staff in the departments concerned, and 30 percent to continue to be credited to the ADRC pool where it might be applied to restore key vacancies. An additional income target should be set against a budgetary timescale. The introduction of income-generation policies helps to provide a measure of financial stability in departments, and also encourages greater interaction with industry.

The ingredients of a departmental planning profile are shown in Table 6.5.

The target year can be 1 to 5 years ahead, depending on the planning horizon. Flexible budgets can also be created to take

Table 6.5 *Example of a departmental planning profile*

	Base year	Target year
Student numbers		
Home and EEC student number ceiling	X	X
Overseas student number target	X	X
Staffing level		
EPQ allowance	X	X
Income-generation contributions		
Overseas students additional to baseline	X	X
Mid-career training overheads	X	X
Research overheads	X	X
Total income contribution – *sub-total*	X	X
Sessional resources		
Research assistants	X	X
Part-time teaching assistants	X	X
Hourly paid staff	X	X

account of perturbations in government funding or unexpected inflation, e.g. wage settlements outside cash limit boundaries. Cuts of 1 and 2 percent per annum can be modelled and agreed in advance of the planning cycle.

Control, review and remedial action – budgetary mechanisms and reports

The budgetary procedure described in this chapter results in the allocation of resources expressed in terms of EPQs (for 72 percent of the salary and wage budget costs) and cash to meet consumables, sessional appointments and other non-pay items. The allocations are made to cost centres identified to specific individuals, usually heads of departments throughout the university. Monthly budgetary statements can be of two types: (1) those which monitor the relation of the establishment points quota and establishment points used for each department and (2) those monitoring the budgetary cash allocation to each cost centre with the expenditure incurred to date plus the commitments within the ordering system. The penalties for overspending result in a freeze on appointments for those departments in excess of their establishment numbers and the carry forward from one year to another of overspending and underspending of the cash allocation. The cash limit procedure thereby ensures that overspending becomes a first charge on the following year's allocation.

Under-performance will be measured in terms of student number shortfall or income generation below target, and will be penalized in the first instance by the ADRC discriminating against those departments below target when the allocation of resource from its income-generation programme is reviewed, and, secondly, less favoured treatment in the allocation of any money available in the future for new developments or to assuage further cuts. Individual staff performance and motivation are largely controlled through the promotions procedure, which focuses on teaching, research, and administrative contributions.

The case-study example is consistent with the recommendations of the Jarratt Report (Committee of Vice-Chancellors and Principals, 1985) on good management accounting practice providing an integrated system which features:

'(i) for cost centre/operating units:
   (a) payments and commitments to date by operating units and projects.
   (b) payments to date by type of expenditure and supplier and discounts obtained.
   (c) uncommitted resources to date.
   (d) other returns to users' requirements.
(ii) for intermediate levels of responsibility:
   (a) summary reports of unit financial operation related to budgets.
   (b) aggregated financial report for the area of responsibility.
(iii)(a) annual first and revised estimates in total and by appropriate sectors of responsibility.
   (b) summary financial reports related to budget in total and by sectors of responsibility.
   (c) cash flow report and forecast.
   (d) performance analyses of relevant indicators such as discounts received, frequency and volume of purchases by type, etc.' (p. 45).

The Jarratt Report also commented on budget centre responsibility:

'(i) Each budget centre should prepare an annual plan including a budget covering all the expenditures for which it is responsible. When this has been approved or amended by the planning and resources committee and Council, the centre should be monitored and held fully accountable for the plan's fulfilment.
(ii) Each budget centre should be given as much delegated authority for administering its plan as is consistent with the procedures and regulations laid down above, and within the requirements of internal audit (see below).
(iii)Where there are intermediate authorities within the budgetary line they should hold the primary budget centres responsible for performance and themselves account to the planning and resources committee' (p. 44).

Conclusions

There are both good and bad examples of management accounting in British universities. Good management accounting practices make a contribution to the determination of objectives, to decision-taking, to the preparation of short-term plans and budgets, and to the evaluation of performance in an environment of complementary and sometimes conflicting objectives. It would be wrong, however, to give the impression that objectives can be achieved on solely quantitative data without a strong qualitative ingredient.

The section dealing with planning criteria places large emphasis on the importance of a detailed examination of departments, according to both objective and subjective criteria. This provides the bedrock for decision-taking – not any formula-induced allocation process.

Given that an awareness of management accounting techniques and their potential is understood, what are the obstacles to the efficient, effective, and economic use of resources? The university system can be criticized as too inflexible. Academic tenure, while originally introduced as a device to avoid interference with academic freedom, is nevertheless from a management accounting viewpoint a stumbling block to change. Although government money was introduced to pay for the Premature Retirement Compensation Scheme (PRCS) during the major run-down period between 1981 and 1984, there were no instances of compulsory redundancy, and as a consequence voluntary retirements often created academic imbalance in departments by their random effect. This was not a cost-efficient way to bring about change, being more concerned with a reduction in the salary and wage bill rather than the deployment of staff.

Many would say that a finance-led strategy is not good for the universities, in that it can be the enemy of originality and creativity, particularly as the units and instruments of measurement are too crude to detect real quality within the system. On the other hand, reduced income has been an instrument of change and has forced universities to reappraise their activities in a radical way. Nationally observed salary scales which do not differentiate between good and bad performance and limit promotion prospects also serve to dampen individual contributions (unlike the American system, where salary levels are usually determined by each university).

Management accounting has sought to provide a means of quantifying performance according to particular criteria, and to stimulate a competitive environment and reward performance. The UGC resource-allocation model is now based on this concept, and it is possible to evaluate research activity within departments according to a scale recording outstanding, above average, average and below average. But it remains to be seen whether a somewhat remote reward system operated by the UGC and not necessarily transmitted by universities to their departments will motivate the creativity and application of individual academics.

As universities move towards the 1990s, the role of the management accountant will assume greater importance. The emphasis on revenue earnings from research grants and contracts, consultancies, industrial units, technology transfer and contract management will require a clear definition of direct costs and overhead recovery. Universities will need to be increasingly equipped to negotiate royalty agreements and participate in joint-venture arrangements with industrial partners. The study of university/industrial liaisons completed by Julian Lowe (1987) describes the growing activity in this area.

Perhaps one should leave the last word to Balderston (1974):

> Universities will survive in the service of a good society, for despite their crankiness and their unsettling qualities, they are essential to it. They operate by internal processes that require high personal motivation on the part of the scholar and student and confer a great deal of individual latitude. This gives them a character that may be a hopeful portent for other kinds of organisations of the post-industrial society (p. 282).

References

Advisory Board for the Research Councils (1982). *Report of a Joint Working Party on the Support of University Science Research* (Merrison Report). HMSO, p. 6.

Balderston, F. E. (1974). *Managing Today's University*. Jossey-Bass.

Committee of Vice-Chancellors and Principals (1985). *Report of the Steering Committee for Efficiency Studies in Universities* (Jarratt Report). CVCP.

Fielden, J. (1969). *University Management Accounting*. University of London, p. 5.

Kerr, C. (1973). *The University as an Organisation*. Carnegie Commission on Higher Education, McGraw-Hill, p. xv.

Lowe, J. (1987). *Management of University Based Companies and Science Parks*. Committee of Vice-Chancellors and Principals.

Moodie, G. L. and Eustace, R. (1974). *Power and Authority in British Universities*. Allen and Unwin, p. 21.

Review of the University Grants Committee (Croham Report). (1987). HMSO (CM 81).

7 Management accounting for recurrent expenditure in the National Health Service

Michael Bourn

The NHS – underfunded or inefficient?

At the time of the foundation of the NHS in 1948 there was a widespread view that, once whatever backlog of illness there was arising through the ravages of war had been cleared up, things would settle down soon into a steady state. The experience has been dramatically different. The population has grown by 7m, or about 14 percent. Nearly half of that growth, about 3.4m, is in the age group 65+, who need far more healthcare per capita than the rest of the population, and within that group the number aged 75 or over has more than doubled. Most of us need in the last year or two of our lives most of the total healthcare provision we ever need, but the need for healthcare clearly increases generally with age. The principal diagnosed reasons for death are changing, as shown in Table 7.1. New technologies for diagnosis and treatment have been introduced. There has been a political willingness, and even desire, through much of the period to improve the level of service given, and the demand for treatment has grown steadily to take up that service.

The effect of all of these considerations has been that, in money terms, public expenditure on the NHS has increased from £437m in 1949 to about £21 billion in 1987, almost fifty times as much in total, and around forty times as much per capita. Much of this is of course price inflation. Even so, when the figures are adjusted by the GDP deflator, total spending in 'real' terms in 1979 was three times the amount in 1949, and by 1987 was four times as much. As a

Table 7.1 *Percentage distributions of deaths (all ages), by cause (Great Britain)*

	1970	1979	1985
Diseases of the circulatory system	51	51	49
Neoplasms	20	22	24
Diseases of the respiratory system	15	14	11
Accidents, suicide, murder and other violence	4	4	3
Diseases of the digestive system	2	3	3
Infectious and parasitic diseases	1	0	0
Diseases of the nervous system	1	1	2
Mental disorders	0	1	2
Other	6	4	6
	100	100	100

Based on OHE (1987), Table 1.6 and Figure 1.3.

proportion of the Gross National Product, expenditure on the NHS increased from 3.92 percent in 1949 to 5.37 percent in 1979, and 6.17 percent (est.) in 1987 (OHE, 1987, Table 2.3).

Despite this massive commitment and growth the NHS is in the centre of political controversy about its funding. In particular, it is argued that pay awards agreed nationally are not being fully funded. The underfunding in 1987–8 has been calculated to be 1.21 percent of the total revenue cash limit, with a further 0.54 percent deficiency arising from DHSS under-allowance for other forms of price inflation. The annual cost of these shortfalls is about £160m (NAHA, 1987). Senior consultants have petitioned the Prime Minister, there are numerous reports of hospital beds being closed and yet more reports of increasingly long waiting lists, and a general public air of malaise and crisis in the service. As this is written (December 1987) the newspaper headlines are yet again about this crisis of confidence, but this time about the government's response – essentially to require greater accountability for 'productivity' in return for additional funding provided in the face of the apparent 'crisis'. On the one side there is the claim that underfunding is causing the problems of waiting lists and closures. On the other side there is the response that if the apparently less productive units were as active as the better ones, there would be no 'crisis', because sufficient funding has been provided.

There are clearly many tangled threads in such a contentious situation. In relation to the hospital in-patient service what seems to have happened is this, during the period from 1970 to 1985 (the statistical data are derived from OHE, 1987, Section 3):

1 The number of hospitals has fallen by nearly one-fifth, from 2,931 in 1970 to 2,603 in 1979 and 2,423 in 1985. Similarly, there has been a fall in the number of available beds in all the main groupings except geriatrics, the total fall being about 20 percent over the whole 15-year period.

2 The average number of beds available per hospital has stayed about the same, but the number of large (1000+ beds) hospitals has declined, with proportionately more beds now being in hospitals within the range 500–999 beds.

3 There has bee a slight tendency for the percentage of available beds occupied (on average) to fall.

4 The total number of deaths and discharges has increased in every main grouping, in all by about 25 percent. Similarly, the deaths and discharges per available bed have increased by a little over 50 percent.

5 This great increase in the productivity of the fixed assets has been achieved by two principal means. The first of these was a massive increase in the numbers of staff between 1970 and 1985 – 60 percent more medical and dental staff, 50 percent more nurses and midwives and over twice as many in both the professional/ technical and administrative/clerical categories, counter-balanced by a slight (3 percent) reduction in domestic and ancillary staff, and all adding up to a 43 percent increase in total staff from 699,000 in 1970 to 998,000 in 1985. These staff increases are further reflected in the data for the number of staff per available bed: for both medical and nursing staffs this number approximately doubled between 1970 and 1985.

The second means of effecting the increased productivity per bed has been a reduction in the average length of stay in hospital per patient. This fell by just over one-third overall, and exactly one-third in acute specialties. Work previously undertaken has been found to be either unnecessary or transferable to the patients and their families, relatives or friends and their GPs.

The net effect of all of these changes – the increased productivity per available bed through increased staffing and reduced length of stay –is that the productivity of staff has fallen in terms of deaths and discharges per doctor (228 in 1970, 170 in 1979 and 180 in 1985, a net fall of 21 percent) and per nurse (18 in 1970, 15 in 1979 and 15 in 1985, a net fall of 17 percent), let alone per administrator or professional (although *not* per ancillary staff member).

Cannot management accounting information supply a coherent and objective analysis to show the full underlying 'truth' about all of this? The answer is 'probably not' at present, and probably not for the foreseeable future. In trying to say something about why this is so, this chapter will, first, outline the organization and spending patterns of the NHS; second, indicate the basic nature of resource allocation practices in the NHS; and, third, consider recent changes in management accounting and related practices in the NHS. The chapter will concentrate on the hospital service. It will be descriptive, but some evaluation is inevitable, implicitly as well as explicitly.

NHS funding and accounting in outline

Total funds

The sources and applications of funds in the NHS are shown in Figure 7.1. This applies only to England, but the pattern is similar in Scotland, Wales and Northern Ireland, for which there are separate parliamentary votes, and separate administrative arrangements under the Scottish, Welsh and Northern Ireland Offices instead of the DHSS.

The main sources of income are general taxation and national-insurance contributions. Expenditure is channelled in two principal directions. These are the Hospital and Community Health Services (HCHS) and the Family Practitioner Services (FPS). The Central Administration of the DHSS takes 4.4 percent out in what most HCHS and FPS staff will see as sheer unmitigated overhead!

The Family Practitioner Services (FPS)

The FPS is intended to be demand-led. It is therefore not as yet

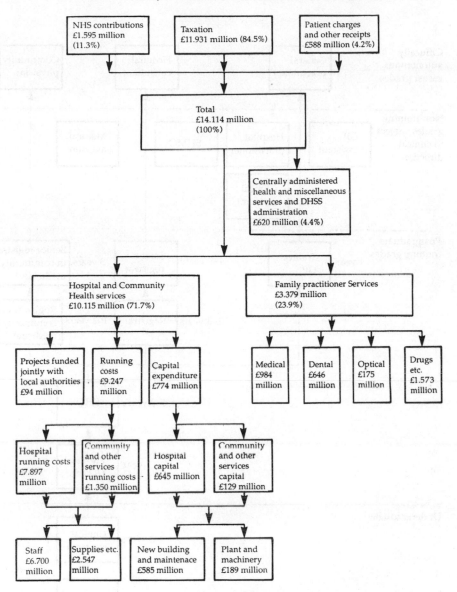

Figure 7.1 *NHS funding and expenditure* c *1984–5*

Source: *NHS in England*: Annual Report 1985–6, DHSS, 1986

cash-limited as the HCHS is, although there are putative government proposals to change this. Nevertheless, the FPS is the relatively

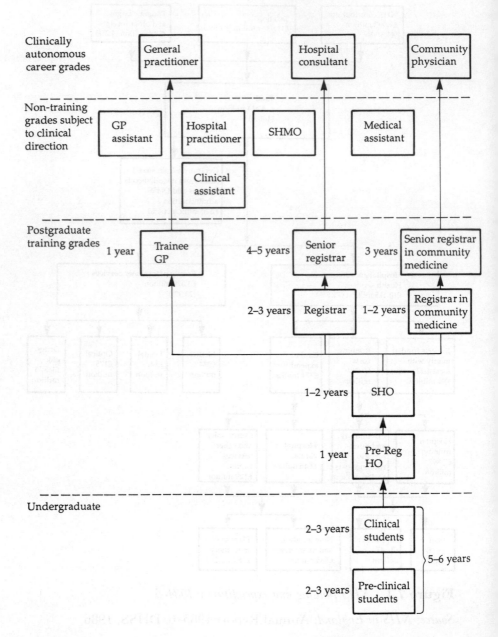

Figure 7.2 *Medical career structure within the NHS*
Source: OHE, 1987, Figure 4.6

poor relation. OHE (1987) gives data that detail this.

Although the cost of the FPS in 'real' terms, i.e. expenditure adjusted by the GDP deflator, nearly trebled between 1949 and 1987, this is markedly less than the fourfold increase for the NHS as a whole. Correspondingly, the FPS took under 23 percent of total NHS funding in 1987, as opposed to 33 percent in 1949. It was about £73 per head of the population in most of the Regions of the NHS in 1987.

Administratively, there are family practitioner committees which run in parallel to, but are distinct from, the regional and district health authorities of the HCHS.

The number of general practitioners increased by around 20 percent between 1975 and 1987 to nearly 33,000, including about 2,000 in training grades. The medical career structure within the NHS is shown in Figure 7.2. There were about fifty-eight general practitioners per 100,000 population in most parts of the country in 1987, giving an average patient list size of about 2,000.

The Pharmaceutical Service is also part of the FPS. Its 12,190 chemists and appliance contractors dispensed almost 400m prescriptions in 1986 (over four times as many as in 1949), of which 82 percent were dispensed without charge. About 40 percent of prescriptions are for people of retirement age. The total cost of prescriptions was over £2 billion in 1986. The gross cost of the pharmaceutical service has always fluctuated around 10 percent of total NHS costs since 1949. Since 1980 diuretics and heart preparations have displaced minor analgesics, hypnotics and particularly sedatives and tranquillizers, in the list of the most frequently prescribed groups of preparations.

The cost of the General Dental Service has fallen slightly in 'real' terms since 1974–5, when adjusted by a price index specific to the FPS, even though the number of dental practitioners has risen rapidly from 13,000 to 18,000 in that time, and the number of dental cases from 30 million to 40 million. This apparent contradiction is at least partly explained by significant reductions in the numbers of teeth filled or extracted and the proportion of dentures, bridges, etc., and by increased charges to patients. It probably remains the case that the proportion of the population with no natural teeth increases as one moves from south to north and from Social Class I to V, a measure identified by the Royal Commission (1979) as indicative of the general health of a community.

The Hospital and Community Health Services (HCHS)

The HCHS is organised into Health Boards (in Scotland, Wales and Northern Ireland) and fourteen Regional Health Authorities (RHAs) (in England), the latter operating through 192 District Health Authorities (DHAs), which in turn operate through around 1,000 units (hospitals, or groups of hospitals).

The Wessex RHA provides an example. It serves an area from Bath to Basingstoke, subdivided as the map (Figure 7.3) shows into ten DHAs, with a population of nearly 3m people. In 1985–6 its net expenditure on both capital and recurrent items (excluding patients' charges, direct credits and income) was £779m ranking it eleventh of the fourteen RHAs. On the other hand, its growth in net expenditure from 1974 to 1984 was 19 percent in 'real' terms (adjusted by an average specific NHS pay and price deflator), making it the fastest growing region over that period (along with East Anglia).

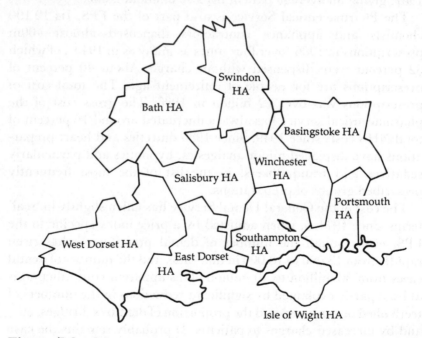

Figure 7.3 *Wessex region*

Regional Health authorities

The role of the RHA comprises resource allocation to districts and monitoring their activities. However, the lines of responsibility are not entirely clear, as each district is a separate legal entity with its own lay authority, to which the officers such as the general manager, the treasurer and so on report. On the other hand, clinical contracts are held with the region.

The ten DHAs in Wessex operate through forty-eight units: Salisbury and Winchester have three each and Bath has nine, the rest having four, five or six. Southampton, which has a teaching hospital associated with the University's Medical School, has five units: between them they operate through thirty-seven hospitals, homes and health centres, although the Southampton General Hospital dominates by its size.

The nature of the subdivision into units varies somewhat from district to district, being influenced by the distribution of the population and the inherited provision of hospitals, etc. All have in some guise at least one acute unit, a psychiatric unit and a community services unit, and add others such as maternity, mental handicap or geriatric according to need. Some major intra-regional, but inter-district, changes are planned, an example being the move of psychiatry from Basingstoke to Winchester. There are also around twenty regional services, financed by the region but located in a particular district (many in Southampton), for such special needs as cardio-thoracic surgery, neurosurgery, radiotherapy and oncology.

Recurrent expenditure patterns

Separate cash limits for revenue, capital and joint funding are applied to the HCHS. The joint funding provision enables authorities to undertake ventures jointly with local authorities. This is particularly important in respect of residentially based community services.

The typical recurrent expenditure patterns within the HCHS may also be illustrated by reference to Wessex RHA. Figure 7.4 gives expenditure percentages for salaries and wages (74 percent), medical expenses (9 percent) and other expenditure (19 percent). Within the salaries and wages component the expenditure on medical and nursing staff is tending to increase and by now is probably around 45 percent of total expenditure. It is perhaps surprising that the expenditure on maintenance and fuel/water is only about 7 percent of the total spend, given the number, variety and age of the many properties!

1 *Salaries and wages*	%	
1A Medical – consultants	4.29	
– other	5.03	
		9.32
1B Dental – community health, etc.	0.39	
– other	0.23	
		0.62
1C Nurses and midwives – other trained staff	21.03	
nursing assistants and auxiliaries	7.59	
other	5.78	
		34.40
1D Professional and technical PTA professions		
supplementary to Medicine	3.06	
other	0.38	
		3.44
1E Professional and Technical PTB: MLSO	1.34	
other	1.53	
		2.87
1F,G Opticians and pharmacists: opticians	0.02	
pharmacists	0.36	
		0.38
1H Administrative and clerical		8.15
1I Ancillary staff: Whitley-negotiated	10.88	
other	0.06	
		10.94
1J Maintenance staff: Engineering trades	0.99	
other	0.91	
		1.90
1K Ambulance staff		1.92
TOTAL 1A–1K		73.94
1L Non-NHS staff (incl. nursing)		0.31
1M Chairman's remuneration		0.02
TOTAL 1A–1M		74.27

2 *Medical expenses*	
2S1 Drugs	3.25
2S2–4 MSSE, gases, dressings	3.80
2S5 X-ray	0.57
2S6 Patients' appliances	0.91
2S7 Laboratory equipment and services	0.56

2S8 O and IT equipment & materials	0.05	
2S9 Fluoridation	0.00	
		9.14

3 Other expenditure

3T10–11 Provisions	2.00	
3T12–13 Staff and patients' clothing	0.43	
3T14–15 Fuel and water	3.46	
3T16–20 Laundry, cleaning F&F, hardware and		
crockery, bedding and linen	1.48	
3T21–22 Eng. and bldg. maintenance, gardens	1.94	
3T23–24 Computers and office equipment	0.58	
3T25–29 PPS, phone, advertising	1.86	
3T30 Transport	0.81	
3T31 Travel and subsistence	1.87	
3T35 Rates	1.24	
3T32–34, 36–41 all other	3.19	
		18.86
		102.27

4 Other authorities

Services received	1.22		
Services rendered	(1.36)	(0.14)	
5 Direct credits		(2.12)	(2.26)
			100.01

Figure 7.4 *Wessex RHA Districts' expenditure patterns (based on 1983–4)*

This expenditure analysis is given in the main form adopted within the hospital service for recurrent grant accounting. It is known as a 'subjective analysis', i.e. analysis of 'subject' of expenditure (the different categories of staff or materials).

'Functional' analysis

This subjective analysis is then disaggregated into a primary 'functional' analysis. That for hospitals is given in Figure 7.5, showing the subdivision into direct and indirect expenditures, the direct patient service expenditures being further subdivided into (i) direct treatment services and supplies and (ii) medical and para-medical supporting services, the latter being yet further subdivided into diagnostic and other services. The precise analysis may vary according to which of the nineteen types of hospital recognized for costing purposes is under consideration. This level of analysis produces the annual accounts which are presented to parliament.

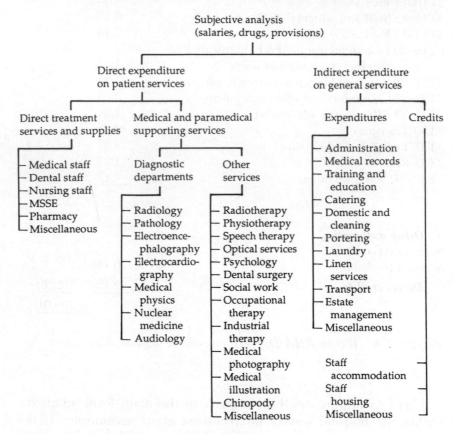

Figure 7.5 *Primary functional analysis*

Source: Developed from Rigden (1983)

There is a further level of 'secondary' functional analysis, which produces cost information about broad service groups. For the community service there is a fifteen-part analysis. For hospitals the analysis recognizes four main patient groups: inpatients (IP), out-patients (OP), day-patients (DP) and accident and emergency patients (A+E). The main thrust of this analysis for costing purposes is to calculate figures of average total cost per patient–day and per patient–case, in order to permit comparisons between regions, districts, units or other groupings. Such measures are now complemented by a growing battery of performance indicators (PIs), and it is these which have prompted the Treasury pressures for 'productivity' noted above.

Limitations of the accounting analyses

Even so brief a sketch of the NHS recurrent expenditure accounting system as this indicates some of its major limitations for management accounting purposes. Bourn and Ezzamel (1986a) raise a number of such issues. Costs are not related to workload, which is itself merely a substitute for a satisfactory definition and measure of outputs, of which there are none. Utilizing proxies for output, such as workload, may prompt people to bend their actions in marginal situations so that they achieve a good 'score' on the proxy; but in this case, as Williams (1985) points out clearly, reducing the length of stay in order to reduce the average cost per patient–*case* may increase the average cost per patient–*day* and have other dysfunctional effects. Other limitations are the absence of worthwhile standard costs and only limited 'decision relevance' and 'reliability'. Furthermore, the system does not produce the multi-layered analysis needed for an organization in which some costs are attracted by individual patients, some by groups of more-or-less similar patients, some by beds and some by wards, some by operating theatres and some by other groupings.

The functional analysis reflects the simple functional structure which essentially still shapes the NHS as an organization; it tells little about the commitment of resources by specialist consultants working in 'firms' or teams and provided with ward and theatre space, nursing and other direct-support staff, and the range of service departments. In such a context the idea of an informed 'doctor-manager' seems often rather remote, a finding reflected also by Coombs (1987) in his case study in two Swedish hospitals.

The core systems

The many detailed sub-systems necessary to maintain the accounts and records of a district can be grouped for convenience into five principal core systems. Those developed within the Wessex RHA, for implementation eventually through the Region's Information System Plan (RISP), are as follows:

1 *Hospital information*, incorporating the patient master index, clinical support (including decision support), order communication and results reporting, theatre scheduling, diagnostic test requests and results, and paramedical service (physical, occupation, speech and industrial therapies).
2 *Community healthcare*, incorporating community care (client register, workload scheduling, and performance recording), prevention via health surveillance and screening, and workload and resource budgets.
3 *Manpower and personnel system (MAPS)*, incorporating personnel records, manpower budget modelling, medical staff availability and scheduling, nursing-practice data maintenance, nurse scheduling, facility data, and theatre staff scheduling;
4 *Accounting*, incorporating financial accounts, patient account maintenance, audit procedures, patient costing, standard costs, budgets, and the analysis of options;
5 *Estates Management*, incorporating capital developments, maintenance management and stores control, estate register, and estate-usage analysis.

These core systems resemble closely those set out in IHSM (1986).

Not all of these requirements have been fully available within the region in the past. In order to move towards the integrated core systems a number of 'interim systems' are under development; they will not necessarily be integral to the core systems but are intended at least to be compatible with them. They include systems for supplies, pharmacy and pharmacy manufacture, sterile supplies, catering, support services (housekeeping, laundry, portering, equipment maintenance), ambulances, payroll and payroll sub-systems, and payments (RISP II, 1984, pp. 69–71).

Resource allocation

Equity

Resource allocation within the politically determined budget of the NHS may be undertaken in a variety of ways. Not all have been, or are likely to be, considered suitable for use within the NHS.

On a world scale perhaps one of the most widely spread types of system of resource allocation has been some form of patronage, i.e. systems in which the exercise of a high degree of personal choice by the resource distributor is subjected to only modest accountability controls. To the extent that such systems tend to be subject to, at the best, significant elements of unpredictability and inconsistency, and, at the worst, bribery and corruption, they are not likely to be widely and openly acceptable within a formally bureaucratic organization such as the NHS in the UK.

A more likely future candidate is the use of more or less open markets to allocate resources within the system. This has been done already in some segments of the NHS, particularly in putting out contracts for cleaning and catering. There is also the use of supply services for nurses, and the beginnings of some elements of buying and selling medical services between separate NHS organizational groupings or between the NHS and the still relatively small private sector. Such transactions might particularly smooth out peaks and troughs in demand. However, the most radical variant of this is to provide for the sale of a service to the patient–customer, who pays at the point of use (probably based on privately purchased health-insurance schemes). Health is then no longer available free of charge to all in need at the time of need, within the capacity of the system.

Pricing is of course a classic way of controlling a demand which appears to be burgeoning when a good or service is free. The 'payment' might also come through some kind of voucher system, apparently rather like wartime ration books, enabling the sick person to use up his entitlement at the hospital (or GP) of his choice: a similar kind of idea has also been ventilated in respect of schools. The problems of matching the demand with the supply in such a half-way house system may well be such as to produce dysfunctional effects which outweigh any sought-for benefits. Possible examples of disbenefits are self-confirming rankings of providers, which relegate some of them to ghetto positions at the bottom of the list; and increasing inequity in the accessibility of resources to disadvantaged groups, particularly anyone who is old and poor, or unemployed and poor.

The final step along this line is of course the transfer of functions elsewhere, (e.g. local authorities), as part of the general thrust towards caring for the elderly and the mentally ill in the community. Alternatively, it could be to the private sector, in a variety of forms, of which private hospitals are one obvious example, but, say private warden-assisted sheltered housing for the elderly (such as the McCarthy and Stone developments) is another. These again raise important issues of equity relating to the accessibility of resources, a potential reflection of Galbraith's depiction of public squalor amidst private plenty in an affluent society.

These questions of equity are crucially important in relation to the ethos of the NHS. The professed aim is equal opportunity of free access to healthcare for people at equal risk. That may not be fully achievable, but so long as it remains the aim, it sets the direction of change in the pattern of resource distribution. Since the mid-1970s it has been the guiding consideration in the application of the RAWP system, developed by the Resource Allocation Working Party.

RAWP

The RAWP scheme allocates financial resources, not 'real' resources, to regions. It calculates for each region an equitable allocation of funds from the global amount available, so as to distribute funds equally across the population according to their health risk, a factor which varies geographically around the country. The scheme is thus concerned with means and not ends. It does not consider how the funds allocated are actually deployed; that is left to the RHAs, subject to proper review and accountability procedures which are outside the RAWP system.

The starting point for the RAWP estimates is the nearest midyear estimate of the crude population figures for each region, provided by the Office of Population Censuses and Surveys. These estimates are then weighted in various ways to reflect the potential demands on the various kinds of services offered by the NHS, and the weighted populations thus calculated are summed. The revenue available is then allocated to the various regions in proportion to the weighted populations.

The weightings used are, in effect, proxy measures of need. They are of two main kinds. The first kind is a weighting for age and gender, more weight being given to groups which are relatively heavy users of healthcare services, particularly infants, the very elderly, and women during child-bearing years.

The second kind is a weighting for susceptibility to illness, i.e. for morbidity. This is a difficult area. Possible indicators are generally either not coherently measurable (e.g. workload) or inherently unreliable (e.g. sickness certification). It seems likely that a wide mix of social, occupational, genetic and environmental factors influence morbidity. However, there is quite good evidence that mortality experience correlates positively and quite highly with a range of possible indicators of morbidity, when broad geographic regions are considered. In particular, when standardized for the age and gender composition of the population, standardized mortality ratios (SMRs) appear to match quite well similarly standardized measures of self-reported chronic illness and self-reported acute illness. In the North-West mortality experience is higher than these morbidity measures; East Anglia's chronic illness experience exceeds its mortality measure; and Outer London's acute illness experience exceeds its mortality measure. Otherwise they match broadly, with the East and West Midlands having a 'medium' mortality measure, everywhere North and/or West of there being 'high', and everywhere South or South-West being 'low' (except the area of the old GLC, which was also 'medium'). SMRs are therefore used as proxies for morbidity data.

Three other possible adjustments should be mentioned. First, technology and costs are assumed to be the same everywhere, except in respect of the London weighting for salaries, so that apart from this there is no cost weighting included to distinguish between regions. Second, there is a Special Increment for Teaching Hospitals (SIFT) allocated to regions with one or more such hospitals in recognition of the higher levels of staffing they need. The costs of university medical schools are met by the University Grants Committee and the research councils, but because university clinical staff also practise within the NHS, and NHS staff may also teach and/or research in the universities, there are possibilities of cross-subsidization; it is generally accepted that these cancel out, and so an uncosted 'knock-for-knock' arrangement exists in order to encourage flexibility. SIFT makes this workable from the NHS side. Third, adjustments are made for cross-regional boundary patient flows, costed at national average costs.

The weighted populations produced by these methods are then combined in proportion to the revenue expenditure on each type of

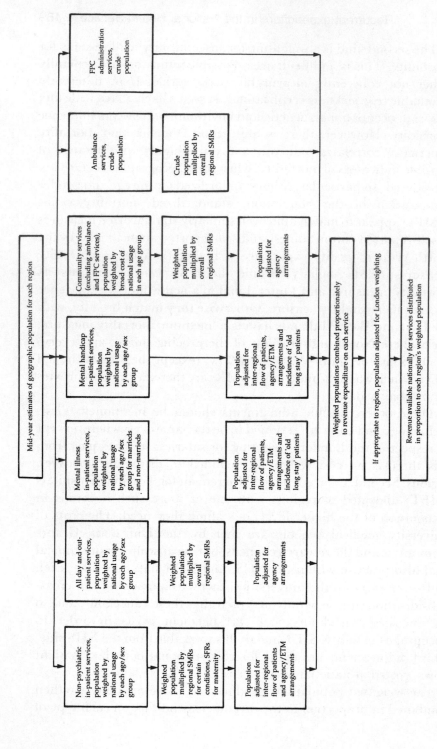

Figure 7.6 *RAWP: The build-up of a revenue target*

service. After the London weighting adjustment, the funding available is allocated to regions in proportion to the weighted populations. The whole system is summarized in Figure 7.6. There is a related scheme for capital allocations.

The allocations produced are target allocations. When the scheme started, regions were receiving funding over a range of 90–115 percent of their targets. RAWP was therefore planned to move regions towards the targets over a number of years. Progress in doing this has been slow, frustrating the hopes and plans of both the underfunded and the overfunded. Even after 8 years of RAWP, Wessex RHA was still 8 percent below target funding.

Sub-regional allocation

The application of RAWP at the district level is much more tendentious, since the acceptability of the SMRs as the basis for distinguishing at this finer and more localized level is much less. There may be a much bigger cross-boundary flow problem, and regional services raise a number of issues (such as the parent–district element, in essence another aspect of cross-boundary flows). There may be pragmatic inexpedience – the failure, say, to open a new hospital because of staff shortages – requiring more flexibility than a mechanistic funding formula can provide. Nevertheless, as part of their 10-year planning strategies, regions normally show targeted moves towards some notion of normalized district allocations, and, as at the inter-regional level, may move slowly towards them.

Within districts it is even clearer that allocation is essentially incremental. Present activities are recosted to allow for inflation, specific adjustments to the range of service and for technological changes (including staffing) are made, workloads confirmed or renegotiated, and other factors allowed for. The result is a series of targets which must be reduced to match the funding available. Within the units similar methods apply, in more detail.

Planning

One of the more patent absurdities among the constraints on the resource-allocation system is the inability, even with creative accounting, to carry balances across accounting year-ends. Allocations must be spent or lost. Shortfalls cannot be financed by past surpluses or by mortgaging future allocations. The tightness with which this restriction is applied is damaging and indefensible from a managerial point of view, and an inhibition on sensible planning, particularly in the short term.

In essence, regions are required to produce annual rolling long-term plans covering the next decade. Any annual allocation is the first step towards that longer-term plan – or away from it, on occasion! The essence of long-term planning is to determine service requirements by care groups (e.g. Maternity, Physically Disabled), mode of care (IP, OP, DP, A+E), and location (e.g. hospital, health centre). The service requirement for each such category is based on catchment population (recognizing age and gender balance), cross-boundary adjustments, the apportionment of beds to clinical specialities in proportions bearing some known relation to the national distribution and future change factors. However, these are not simple measurements; for example, it is well established that

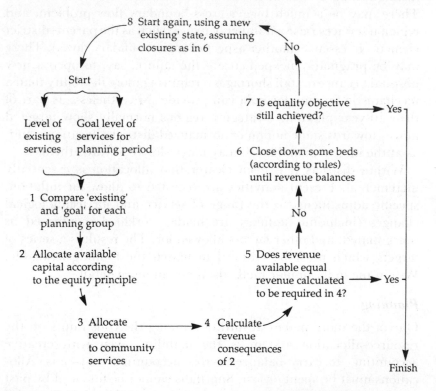

Figure 7.7 *Wessex Regional Health Authority – planning model*

demand follows bed provision to some to a considerable extent, and *not* just the other way round (IHSM, 1986).

This goal or target service level is then compared with the level of exceeding services, and an iterative planning cycle undertaken, as shown in Figure 7.7 (taken from Stephens, 1986). It seeks to pay particular attention to the calculation of the revenue consequences of capital schemes, one of the important practical constraints in producing a workable plan which recognizes in a dynamic way the predicted future availability of resources, the analysis of alternative options, and the possibility of 'policy'-based choices of priorities. (For a description of the concept of option appraisal in the NHS see Mooney and Henderson (1986)). The Wessex Plan has three important characteristics, according to Stephens (1986):

'(a) It only produces Regional spending programmes which can be afforded according to the prediction of future resource availability.

(b) It can be made to follow national and regional policies, for example, that positive discrimination be afforded to community services in the Districts.

(c) It shares out resources in an "equitable" way' (i.e. in the event of resource limitations "equal proportionate misery" is applied).'

Some recent developments in management accounting

Specialty costing

Specialty costing has been applied relatively widely in the NHS in the last 10 years. It seeks to allocate costs to the forty or so medical and surgical specialties, thus disaggregating the functional analyses noted above (p. 184).

The original work at Bridgend (Magee, 1981) was extended in a seven-hospital study funded by DHSS (Hillman and Nix, 1982). Other examples are reported from St Thomas's Hospital (Carter, 1983a) and three hospitals in Preston DHA, with special reference to neurology, neurosurgery, and plastic surgery (Edwards *et al.* 1981). The general aim of such work is to permit comparisons between units, or between budget and actual performance, in terms of average total costs per IP day, IP case, and OP attendance, *by clinical specialty*. This is clearly an advance on the broad all-hospital averages calculable under the secondary functional analysis.

However, the validity of both the calculations and the comparisons may be open to question on numerous grounds. Thus, although in principle direct costs should easily be traceable to specialties, that may not always be the actuality. The bases for allocating overheads may be 'reasonable' but nonetheless crude and arbitrary; Edwards *et al* (1981) allocated such indirect expenses as catering, laundry and cleaning proportionately to meals served, articles laundered and floor area respectively; and other overhead costs (e.g. central administration) proportionately to IP days. The units compared may vary in many ways, say in the range of service provided (e.g. are children included, or treated in a separate group?), the case-mix, and the success of treatments as evidenced by the proportion of deaths to discharges.

A further study of this kind, made under the general supervision of the author, is reported in Bourn and Ezzamel (1986a).

Clinical budgeting

Clinical budgeting attempts to allot budgets to clinical teams by negotiated consensual agreement. A well-known, though limited, example is the PACT system of 'planning agreements with clinical teams' (Camp, 1981). These restricted the agreements essentially to non-staff matters, thus reducing their scope and effectiveness.

Another example along slightly different lines is reported by Wickings *et al.* (1983), working at Brent Health Authority in London. All consultants were given monthly reports of their demands on all diagnostic and some other departments (with the related cost), and of the number of patients treated by them. Wickings *et al.* could find no evidence that, after 3 years of these reports, 'any consultant's pattern of work or expenditure had changed markedly . . . nor was there any evidence to suggest that the district's overall performance had altered compared with other districts'.

This failure to interest consultants effectively was reported also in the West Midlands (Davis and Miles, 1984) and at St Thomas's (Carter, 1983b). Wickings *et al.* (1983) attribute it to the absence of any regular or new operational systems that depended on the use of the new cost data. All these studies indicate that a system concerned with budgeting rather than merely ex-post costing reports *might* be more successful. This idea was one of the central features of the NHS Management Inquiry (Griffiths, 1983), which made one of its main recommendations the introduction of what is called 'management budgeting'.

Management budgeting

The basic view underlying the thrust of the Griffiths Report was that the NHS and commercial organizations are more alike than is usually accepted. The report states:

> We have been told that the NHS is different from business in management terms, not least because the NHS is not concerned with the profit motive and must be judged by wider social standards which cannot be measured. These differences can be greatly overstated. The clear similarities between NHS management and business management are much more important. In many organisations in the private sector, profit does not immediately impinge on large numbers of managers below Board level. They are concerned with levels of service, quality of product, meeting budgets, cost improvement, productivity, motivating and rewarding staff, research and development, and the long term viability of the undertaking. All things that Parliament has been wishing on the NHS.

The report identified five elements, in what it termed the 'institutional stagnation' of the NHS, in which the 'devolution of responsibility is far too slow because the necessary direction and dynamic to achieve this is lacking'. The five elements were the following: lack of real continuous assessment of performance against established criteria, poor measurement of health output, lack of clinical evaluation of particular practices, lack of economic evaluation of particular practices, and lack of any means of assessing the effectiveness with which the healthcare needs and expectations of the population were being met.

In order to overcome these deficiencies Griffiths made several recommendations. In particular, he urged the appointment in each region, district and unit of management of a general manager to 'be the final decision taker for decisions normally delegated to the consensus (management) team, especially where decisions cross professional boundaries or cause disagreements and delay at present'.

Great emphasis was placed on day-to-day management at the unit level, the aim being to bring in the clinicians, 'consistent with clinical freedom for clinical practice'. It would be necessary to develop budgets to monitor performance at all levels, to create rules for virement of expenditure between and within units across heads of expenditure, and to determine expenditure-authorization limits. General managers should be rewarded by the carrot of an additional element of pay related to performance and the stick of fixed-term, but renewable, contracts.

The appointment of so many general managers at more or less the same time was obviously something of an adventure. In the event, the majority of those appointed were former administrators; few were doctors, and few were from outside the NHS.

The second main recommendation of the Griffiths Report was 'that each Unit develops management budgets which involve clinicians, and which relate workload and service objectives to financial and manpower allocations, so as to sharpen up the questioning of overhead costs'. The involvement of clinicians was emphasized because 'their decisions largely dictate the use of all resources and they must accept the management responsibility which goes with clinical freedom'.

Griffiths recognized that these proposals 'will require major changes in the stance and style of management at the centre and in the public and parliamentary requirements of the NHS management process'. He also recognized, but significantly underestimated, the problem of reconciling the vocational nature of the organizational culture within medicine with the new managerialist ethos of the report's recommendations. This same culture clash can be seen in other cases, where practitioners believe the service needed by the individual in need at the time to be important over and beyond mere financial constraints, which may well be perceived as quite arbitrary in their particular incidence. Not only doctors, but teachers and clergymen also, live within a clan culture in which precise objectives are ill-defined and there is great ambiguity over performance measurement (Bourn and Ezzamel, 1986b). Furthermore, they share the view that their work is ultimately worth doing for its own sake and as a contribution to social welfare, and that economic considerations should not be allowed to intrude into the making of judgements about how to carry out their crucial activities.

Even before the Griffiths Report was published, the DHSS set up four experimental management budgeting schemes. Two were to be developed by the management consultants Arthur Young (at Southmead and North Tees DHAs) and two by Coopers and Lybrand (Basingstoke and Ealing).

Davies and Prowle (1984) set out the intended structure of the Basingstoke and Ealing schemes. There would be four classes of budget-holder: (i) support service budget-holders (catering, cleaning, laundry, etc.); (ii) facility budget-holders (nurses in charge of wards, theatres and clinics); (iii) diagnostic and treatment budget-holders (e.g. radiology, pathology, pharmacy); and (iv) consultant budget-holders (by 'firm' within specialty). The system would work by recharging costs from budget-holders supplying services to other budget-holders who use them, on the basis of agreed price lists.

Unfortunately the systems did not work. Indeed there was a very early moratorium in respect of consultant cooperation and participation at one site (Ross, 1985). All the schemes fell rapidly behind schedule. Finally, in November 1986 the DHSS formally accepted that all four pilot studies had failed, and that 'no worthwhile contributions to the planning and costing of patient care had been achieved' (DHSS, Circular HN(86)34).

What went wrong?

Such schemes might be thought from the start to be too complex in their arrangements for recharging. They might also be thought to utilize budgetary groupings too small to gain any significant benefit from virement in relation to savings achieved (Bourn and Ezzamel, 1987). The finance director of the NHS recognized that the systems were being seen 'as an end in themselves, instead of being integral and producing the patient care and case mix information that doctors (are) interested in'. He also perceived that 'an increasing number of consultants now see general management as "anti-patient" and using finance for an attack on spending levels', thus connecting the dysfunctional aspects of the two principal innovations deriving from the Griffiths Report (Mills, 1986).

There were other evident problems. The original timescale (6 months to implementation) was patently absurd. In coping with time slippage it was decided to concentrate first and foremost on technical developments to improve accountability. However, in concentrating within this on the development of the information base, while deferring consideration of management and reporting issues, the developers neglected the opinions of the users, leaving them largely unconsulted and uninformed about what was going on. Even financial staff were unclear as to how the new management budgets were supposed to relate to the old functional budgets, and how everything was to be integrated to maintain control within cash limits; from this point of view the devil known was perhaps better than the devil unknown, and priority should thus be given to the functional budgets. Clinicians expressed doubts about the extent of their real capacity to control costs, on the grounds that the provision of healthcare is demand-dependent. Attempts to explain the systems had been found to be too theoretical and too time-consuming, and at one district a 2-month training scheme had to be cancelled because of a complete lack of support. Clinicians could not relate what they had earlier been told about the potential of management budgeting with what seemed to be going on.

The crux of all this seems to have been a fatal attempt to segregate the technical and organizational behavioural issues, and to overrate the former relative to the latter, not recognizing the depth of the opposition and the great length of time necessary to allow it to change.

This is a familiar problem in systems development. It is one face of the long-running battle between designers and users about whose views shall prevail. In the context of the NHS this boils down to the primacy given to patient care. The various groupings of staff in a hospital negotiate between them a division of labour which enables the integration of patient care functions with non-patient ones. Malvey (1981) has written a very shrewd and perceptive account of a relatively small, though important, system development in two North American hospitals. She is well worth quoting at length. As she expresses it, this process of integration is done

. . . so that whatever other values rise to the surface of the organisation's attention, such as efficiency or economy, the process of negotiation acts to restore patient care values to the ascendancy . . . Many hospital information systems fail to take into consideration the relationships between information and behaviour in the hospital, or to pay attention to the enormously complex responses that constitute routines, standard operating procedures, and the like. MIS frequently fail because they are not embedded in the organisation's complexity. They fail also because they offer no inducements to co-operation, or alternatives to the sensitive and effective mechanisms of exchange, which make the organisation work.

This might make a suitable inscription for the tomb of management budgeting. However, 'The King is dead, Long live the King!' Management budgeting was relaunched in a small number of pilot districts late in 1986, to a more measured timescale, and under the new name of 'resource management'. Have enough of the lessons been learned?

Other developments

There are several other development areas of potential relevance to management accounting for recurrent expenditure in the NHS.

Standard costing is at the root of the American idea of Diagnosis Related Groups (DRGs) (Fetter *et al.* 1980). This classifies the many thousands of definable health conditions into 467 diagnosis-related groups, according to their principal diagnoses, the presence of a surgical procedure, age, the presence or absence of significant complications, and discharge status. The DRGs are further combined into twenty-three diagnostic categories. The DRG may be used as the basis of a standard costing system in establishing a resource allocation system, once workloads have been negotiated for a particular specialty. In the USA they are used as the basis of reimbursements to hospitals by the major health insurance schemes. In the UK there has been work, based particularly in a children's hospital, to develop 'case-mix costing', using a variant of DRGs (Scott and Sherwood, 1984). Other work suggests that variation in medical practices between countries may require corresponding variety in the DRG schemes of classification (Jenkins and Coles, 1984).

A growing range of performance indicators (PIs) has been developed and published by the DHSS. These compare regions or districts along a variety of dimensions, rather in the manner of a scheme of inter-firm comparison. Their utility depends on the

significance of the measures adopted as representative of performance, the reliability of the data collated in the measurements
themselves, their accessibility to a wide-ranging managerial group,
and their interpretability into managerial actions conducive to social
welfare (as well as the inevitable personal alibis and defensive
apologia!). There are considerable doubts on each of these grounds
about all of the sets of PIs so far produced. However, they do prompt
questions about performance, even if they cannot offer many
answers. Experimentation will undoubtedly continue in this area.

It is becoming widely accepted that there is an emerging gap
between expected demands on the NHS and its capacity to deliver
healthcare, despite the 'real terms' growth in its resourcing (see e.g.
Thwaites, 1987). This implies increasing need to ration patient care.
One approach, associated particularly with Maynard, a professor of
economics, is the selection of patients for treatment according to the
number of Quality-Adjusted Life Years (QALYs) which treatment
might be expected to give. Seen by some commentators as practical
euthanasia, and by others as only an identification of what happens
in practice anyhow, the idea has created some heated discussion. A
more formal presentation of much the same approach can be found
in Ramanathan (1985).

Another aspect of development in the NHS is of course database
development. The various reports of the Steering Group on Health
Services Information (Koerner, 1981–4) develop the idea of
'minimum data sets' in relation to a variety of aspects of NHS work,
including patients and staffing as well as financial information. A
deadline of April 1987 was set by DHSS for the creation of the
minimum data sets by all health authorities. This was not achieved,
but the exercise will continue. It is a criticism of the Koerner Group's
approach that to stockpile data with little clear indication of how
they might be used is a costly and perhaps ultimately unproductive
approach. Time will tell.

A 'National Strategic Framework for Information Management'
was published in 1987. Bourn (1987) provides a summary and
evaluation. The 'Framework' advocates better information to be
developed through regional information strategies, in order to
support 'clinicians, nurses and staff in their day-to-day work; and
the supply of valid and flexible management information, wherever
possible, as a by-product of these operations'. Doubtless the pun was

unintentional! The 'Framework' avoids the issues raised above in relation to management budgeting, and the further complication and hesitation likely to be induced by the prospective use of any information collected 'to challenge health authorities' (in the words of Sir Kenneth Stowe, the Permanent Secretary to the DHSS, before the Public Accounts Committee).

Comparisons over time show considerable improvements in health during this century. For example, the traditional infectious diseases have almost disappeared, life-expectancy continues to rise, and so on. The reasons might include changes in working conditions, diet, housing, employment prospects and other social developments. Medicine's contribution is likely to be important, but it is not entirely clear just *how* important. Within the broad spectrum of medicine it is similarly not easy to distinguish the particular contributions of hospital, community, general practitioner, dental, and social services, and indeed of the electronics and pharmaceutical industries. In addressing one important current problem Wistow and Hardy (1985) show the difficulties in the way of achieving cooperation between municipal and health authorities in developing policies for 'care in the community' for the elderly, the mentally ill, and the mentally handicapped. If management accounting is to contribute to such services being offered in a coordinated manner, it must be able to extend beyond just the NHS itself.

Conclusion

In an epigrammatic phrase Higgins (1987) suggests that 'The Conservative reaction in the 1980s in many areas of domestic policy has been to throw managers at problems'. She suggests that this is 'especially true in the NHS', following Griffiths. If the managerial ethos is to flourish in the NHS, then NHS managers, whether doctors or not, will need good management accounts. The present state of the art is rudimentary, and the predictable (and predicted) collapse of the management budgeting experiments sounds a warning against a naive rush to change things too dramatically too quickly. But change *is* needed, and will have to be undertaken successfully as one contribution to the NHS moving forward, and not backwards, into the 1990s. It will be readily apparent that present systems contribute little to resolving the current debate

Pendlebury (1989)

about whether the service is underfunded or inefficient, both or neither.

References

Bourn, A. J. H. (1987). Fighting truth decay in the NHS. *Accountancy*, 100, No. 1129, September, 120–1.

Bourn, A. M. and Ezzamel, M. A. (1986a). Costing and budgeting in the National Health Service. *Financial Accountability and Management*, 2, No. 1, Spring, 53–71.

Bourn, A. M. and Ezzamel, M. A. (1986b). Organisational culture in hospitals in the National Health Service. *Financial Accountability and Management*, 2, No. 3, Autumn, 203–26.

Bourn, A. M. and Ezzamel, M. A. (1987). Budgetary devolution in the National Health Service and Universities in the United Kingdom. *Financial Accountability and Management*, 3, No. 1, Spring, 29–46.

Camp, E. (1981). Maximising resources. *Health and Social Science Journal*, XCI, 12 November, 1385–7.

Carter, J. (1983a). Thoughts on the development of financial information for health services: a case study based on West Lambeth Health Authority. *Warwick Papers on Industry, Business, and Administration*, No. 10.

Carter, J. (1983b). Recent developments in financial information for health services. *Warwick Papers on Industry, Business, and Administration*, No. 11.

Chawner, J. (1983). The consultant's role in NHS management. *British Medical Journal*, 287, 10 December, 1916–18.

Coombs, R. (1987). Accounting for the control of doctors: management information in hospitals. *Accounting, Organisations, and Society*, 12, 389–404.

Davies, P. and Prowle, M. (1984). Management budgets in the NHS. *British Medical Journal*, 289, 1 December, 1552–4.

Davis, W. A. and Miles, A. J. (1984). *A survey of consultants to determine their financial and workload information needs*. West Midlands RHA.

DHSS (1986). *The NHS in England: Annual Report, 1985/86*. DHSS.

Edwards, M., Strudwick, B. G. and Thompson, M. A. (1981). Specialty budgeting in the new District Health Authorities. *British Medical Journal*, 283, 12 September, 741–3.

Fetter, R. B., Shin, Y. and Freeman, J. L. (1980). Case mix definition by diagnosis-related groups. *Medical Care*, 18, No. 2, February, 1–53.

Griffiths, R. (1983). *NHS management inquiry* (Griffiths Report). DHSS.

Higgins, J. (1987). The National Health Service. In *Inside British Society* (Causer, G. A., ed.). Wheatsheaf.

Hillman, R. L. and Nix, G. R. (1982). *Specialty costing report: DHSS funded research into specialty costing*. DHSS.

IHSM (1986). Information Technology in Health Care. Kluwer.

Jenkins, L. and Coles, J. (1984). Information tools for the future. *Health and Social Services Journal*, 94, No. 4909, 9 August, 948–9.

Koerner, E. (1981–4). *Reports of the NHS/DHS steering group on Health Services information.* HMSO.

Magee, C. C. (1981). The potential for specialty costing in the NHS. *Public Finance and Accountancy*, March.

Malvey, M. (1981). *Simple systems, complex environments.* Sage.

Mills, I. (1986). Reported in the *Health and Social Service Journal*, XCVI, 13 March, 3.

Mooney, G. and Henderson, J. (1986). Option appraisal in the UK National Health Service. *Financial Accountability and Management*, 2, No. 3, Autumn, 187–202.

NAHA (1987). *Autumn Survey, 1987.* National Association of Health Authorities.

OHE (1987). Compendium of health statistics. Office of Health Economics, 6th ed.

Ramanathan, K. V. (1985). A proposed framework for designing management control systems in not-for-profit organisations. *Financial Accountability and Management*, 1, No. 1, Spring, 75–92.

Rigden, M. S. (1983). *Health Service finance and accounting.* Heinemann.

RISP II (1984), *Regional Information Systems Plan*, vol. II, *Implementation.* Wessex RHA.

Ross, A. P. J. (1985). Reported in *British Medical Journal*, 290, 23 February, 652.

Royal Commission (1979). *Report of the Royal Commission on the National Health Service.* HMSO.

Scott, T. and Sherwood, D. (1984). DRG treatment profiles. *Public Finance and Accountancy*, 11, No. 11, December, 34–6.

Stephens, A. (1986). The information requirements of the Regional planning model at Wessex RHA. Wessex RHA, Management Research Programme, Research Note no. 6, July.

Thwaites, B. (1987). *The NHS – the end of the rainbow?* Institute of Health Policy Studies, University of Southampton.

Wickings, I., Coles, J. M., Flux, R. and Howard, L. (1983). Review of clinical budgeting and costing experiments. *British Medical Journal*, 286, 12 February, 575–8.

Williams, A. (1985). Performance measurement in the public sector: paving the road to Hell? University of Glasgow, Arthur Young Lecture no. 7.

Wislow, G. and Hardy, B. (1985). Transferring Care: Can Financial Incentives Work? *Public Money*, 5, No. 3, December, 31–6.

8 Capital accounting in the National Health Service

Anthony Cook

Introduction

In the NHS, funds for revenue and capital items are provided for under separate cash limits and are accounted for separately in the financial accounts. There is no balance sheet, no statement of the historic or current cost of NHS fixed assets and no depreciation or other charge for the use of assets in the income and expenditure account.

That this is a limitation has been recognized since the Guillebaud Report of 1956. The extent to which it is a limitation on the efficient use of resources in the NHS has been debated from time to time since then, and is currently again under consideration. We shall discuss the probable direction of moves towards enhanced capital and asset accounting in the future later in this chapter. However, any such moves would require changes in the way the NHS is funded. Accordingly these issues are different from those concerning capital accounting which arise within the *present* funding structure.

The statutory responsibility for capital expenditure rests with the regional health authorities (RHAs). However, it is traditional for the funds for, and the management of, smaller capital schemes to be delegated to district health authorities (DHAs), with the larger schemes being handled by regions. Recently (since HC(85)26 – DHSS, 1985) there has been pressure for the planning of even larger schemes to be delegated to districts, but there has been no change in the statutory responsibilities of RHAs.

It is normal for an RHA to contain a 'works' department employing architects, engineers and quantity surveyors on the planning and design of major hospital building schemes. However, the size of the regional works department varies considerably from one region to another and not all schemes are designed 'in-house'. Indeed, as part of the government's privatization programme, there has been increasing pressure both to 'contract out' such design work and, to demonstrate that 'in-house' design functions are cost-efficient.

The development of capital accounting in the NHS

There is an evoluntionary nature to management accounting in the NHS. Until the mid-1970s the continuing growth in real terms in the level of NHS resources served to ameliorate financial pressures, so that the issues of financial management were only gradually emergent. Since the mid-1970s there has been a change in NHS resourcing – to declining growth, then to level funding and even to declining funding (relative to the increasing demands being placed upon it). This factor – together with increasing pressures of public accountability which require that the NHS demonstrates that it is delivering Value for Money (VFM) from the resources at its disposal – has accelerated change, and brought further recognition of management accounting issues. Nevertheless, it remains an evolutionary process and it is possible to anticipate further developments 'in the pipeline'. In order therefore to have an understanding of the current 'state of the art' and of the likely direction of future developments, it is appropriate to examine the development of capital accounting in the NHS and the points at which current issues of financial management did emerge.

The early years

In 1948 the newly created National Health Service inherited some 2,800 hospitals and in excess of half a million hospital beds. Add to that the very limited capital building which had taken place during the first decade or so of the life of the NHS, and by 1960 it was inevitable that there should be pressure for a major programme of hospital building. The programme was doubly significant in that, firstly, it represented a *government* commitment and, secondly, it embodied a central role for the Ministry of Health in defining the physical standards to which hospitals were to be built.

The hospital building notes[1]

These notes stemmed from this recognition. The first note was issued in 1961, when the ministry also indicated its intention to publish cost limits for building departments within which boards[2] would work.

A hospital plan for England and Wales (Ministry of Health, 1962)

The 'Plan', published in May 1962 as a White Paper, was the formal issue of the programme. It purported to take a comprehensive view for building, remodelling and improving large numbers of hospitals. The quantitative standards of provision were designated by taking population projections by district and applying to them ratios of hospital beds per 1,000 population. The plan was also significant in that it formally established and incorporated the concept of the district general hospital (DGH).

Perhaps the first hint that there might be financial and economic problems lying within the plan came when Abel-Smith (1962) wrote: 'The economic principles used in this programme do not have the firm empirical foundations they should have'. Those financial and economic problems were confirmed when it became necessary to revise the plan in 1966 (Ministry of Health, 1966). Retitled *The Hospital Building Programme*, this document within its opening paragraph restated the validity of the principles of the plan but noted that many of the schemes then anticipated were 'inadequately defined and imprecisely costed'. Hence a review was necessary in order to relate more closely the proposed schemes to the resources likely to be available.

So here we have the emergence of a major issue of financial management for the NHS – namely how to plan and retain financial control over a substantial programme of capital expenditure.

The hospital building procedure notes – 'Capricode'[3]

The first hospital *building* note was issued in January 1961. Others followed, supported by hospital building bulletins, technical memoranda, design notes, etc. This material was concerned essentially with the functional planning, design and operation of buildings. Parallel to this advice the DHSS prescribed in 1962 a *procedure* for the preparation of individual building schemes. Subsequently the 1962 procedure was revised in five hospital building *procedure* notes (issued between 1967 and 1972) and collectively referred to as '*Capricode*'. HBPN1 was itself reissued in 1974 in the light of the Cruickshank Report (1973).

The 1974 reorganization

The reorganization, the first since the creation of the National Health Service in 1948, established a new structure of regional health authorities (RHAs), area health authorities (AHAs) and health districts. Its general aims were to create a fully integrated health service in which every aspect of healthcare could be provided by members of the healthcare professions, and to provide that care as far as possible locally.

Before 1974 there was no formal comprehensive planning system, although of course there were ad-hoc plans for development. The 1974 reorganization led to the introduction of a formal planning system in which the identification of 'service need' meant that capital projects would in future be firmly grounded in the context of the development of health services, in contrast to the philosophy of the hospital plan, which had proposed a 'capital-led' development of the NHS.

The introduction of RAWP (Resource Allocation Working Party) also stemmed from the 1974 reorganization. The distribution of capital funds from 1977–8 onwards is significant in that it gives each RHA a capital allocation within which it must work, rather than the previous 'bottom-up' approach based on existing capital commitments, priorities, and bids for specific schemes.

NHS capital expenditure was first *cash limited* in 1977–8, causing different problems to arise compared with revenue. Each individual payment is a 'one-off' whose precise timing is difficult to anticipate. While the cash-limit system was primarily designed to prevent overspending, it also creates problems for health authorities who are facing underspendings. There is limited scope for virement and in principle a health authority which does not spend up to its cash limit in one year simply loses the funds. Thus the impact of the introduction of RAWP and of cash limits together has been to exacerbate the problems of controlling a capital-expenditure programme.

The Public Accounts Committee

During the 1960s and 1970s the Public Accounts Committee (PAC) of the House of Commons examined aspects of several NHS hospital-building schemes. It devoted considerable attention to the need for a logical project-management procedure and whether this need was satisfactorily met by the introduction of Capricode. Several detailed changes were made as a result of its recommendations.

Royal Commission on the NHS (1978) – Research Paper No. 2

The paper was the product of an extensive research programme conducted by a team led by Professor John Perrin of the University of Warwick. It examined the management of financial resources in the health services of the UK, with particular reference to the relevant information, planning and control systems. Predominatly, its attention was devoted to aspects of accounting for NHS revenue resources. However, with regard to capital the report particularly noted that there was a need for an improved form of *investment appraisal* in the NHS. So it is at this point that we have the emergence of the second of the current major issues of management accounting, namely what is the appropriate form of investment appraisal in a public service which does not charge for its products and cannot put a price on them.

Review of Health Capital (DHSS, 1979)

This was a major report, much of which was indeed a review of the nature of capital expenditure in the past and did not contain any radical recommendations. However the *Review* did consider the process of investment appraisal, thus picking up the discussion from the Royal Commission and taking it a stage further.

The appraisal of options procedure

The formal process of investment appraisal was incorporated into the procedure for hospital planning with the issue of Health Notice (81)30 (DHSS, 1982a).

The 1982 reorganization

District health authorities (DHAs) were substituted for area health authorities and health districts. Each DHA would in turn be split into units, and there was to be considerable emphasis on the devolution of managerial responsibility to them.

The Griffiths Report (DHSS, 1983a)

Not officially a reorganization, this report still brought about the introduction of the concept of 'general management' (in place of consensus management) and the appointment of general managers at regional, district and unit level, together with new management structures. On the revenue side Griffiths gave a considerable impetus to improved management accounting with the introduction of 'management budgeting' – subsequently revised as 'resource management'.

The Ceri Davies Report (DHSS, 1983b)

The committee of inquiry was established primarily 'to consider means which will ensure that Health Authorities identify underused and surplus land and property, and when appropriate dispose of it in ways which will create maximum benefit for the service'. The report raised issues of capital and asset accounting, and among its recommendations was one advocating the use of notional rents for NHS property as part of the annual accountability reviews of health authorities.

Managing Capital Assets in the NHS (AIIST, 1985)

This report came from the Association of Health Service Treasurers, which continued the debate on asset accounting and, in particular, whether health authorities should bear some form of charge for the use of capital assets in their income and expenditure accounts.

1986 'Capricode' reissued (DHSS, 1986b)

The detailed changes made to the health building procedure notes since 1974 were consolidated.

From this chronological development of NHS capital accounting it is evident that three management accounting issues have emerged:

1 How to retain financial control over the cost of individual capital schemes and of a capital programme as a whole.
2 What should be the form of investment appraisal in the NHS?
3 Should the structure of NHS funding be modified to incorporate some form of charge for the use of capital in the income and expenditure account and in the management accounts of a DHA?

We shall look at each of those issues in more detail, with, in respect of 1 and 2, specific case studies.

Controlling the cost of hospital schemes

Before considering examples of hospital schemes it is necessary to outline in more detail some aspects of the system. Planning, designing and building a new hospital can take several years, the time may be broken down into two distinct periods – the 'planning period' and the 'construction period'.

The planning period

Capricode sets out a logical sequence of events which lead from the original project policy through to the evaluation of the completed building. During the planning period (and prior to HN(81)30 – DHSS, 1982a) there were three *cost estimates* (stages I, II and III) produced in accord with Capricode. However, there would usually also be a cost estimate produced at a pre-Capricode stage. For example, in the South Western Region that estimate is known as a CAP 1. This is prepared by the DHA for submission to the RHA and serves as a vehicle for taking a scheme out of the appropriate strategic plan (where the 'service need' will already have been identified) and putting it into the capital programme. Cost estimates produced at the CAP 1 stage can vary enormously in detail. Usually, however, they are no more than broad brush estimates which may represent the views of the DHA on what funds it would choose to allocate to a scheme rather than what it would cost. In contrast, when we move on to cost estimates produced in accord with Capricode, we see a logical sequence whereby each estimate is a refinement of its predecessor as the planning of the hospital progresses.

Expenditure on hospital building can be allocated to the following elements of cost:

1 *Works cost*. This includes the cost of all the items which physically form the main hospital structure, such as building and engineering elements. In most estimates works costs will be further divided into *departmental costs* and *on-costs*. Departmental costs are the costs of providing only the main departments in a building. On-costs cover the provision of communication space between departments (corridors, stairways, etc.) and 'below the ground' items (such as supply of mains services, car parks, etc.).
2 *Equipment costs*. These cover the furniture and equipment necessary to fit out the building.
3 *Professional fees*. These fees cover the employment of consultant architects, engineers and quantity surveyors, etc.

Land can of course be a major item of expenditure. The NHS has formal procedures for both the acquisition and disposal of land, which fall outside the scope of Capricode, although land costs are required to be taken into account in the investment appraisal procedure.

Capricode is supported by the *hospital building notes*. Each note relates to a hospital department of a particular type (operating theatres, x-ray departments, etc.) and sets out the accommodation and equipment required for the provision of a given service from that department. The original notes are now being replaced by a new series. Whereas the original notes did express *areas* of accommodation which could be provided, the new notes do not give department areas, but give critical dimensions in respect of certain activity spaces.

The hospital building notes are, in turn, supported by a series of *departmental cost allowance guidelines* (DCAGs), which give cost allowances in respect of each building note and in respect of a range of sizes for each department. There are two sets of DCAG allowances, one for the 'mainstream' of hospital building and a second covering residential accommodation and mental handicap units, etc. The DHSS view is that it is possible to build hospital accommodation within the DCAG allowances, but the history of the allowances has been one of imposing an ever-tightening squeeze on

RHAs, which stems from two sources. Firstly, new legislation from time to time has specified improvements in the standard of accommodation provided, but given no corresponding increase in allowances and, secondly, allowances have simply failed to keep pace with inflation.

This may be due to the more straitened economic circumstances of the late 1970s and 1980s and to recognition that some of the 1960s standards were unnecessarily lavish. Inevitably this squeeze could only be accommodated by some reduction in provision, so it became the practice to design departmental accommodation to reduced areas from those shown in the original notes. Thus, when a hospital scheme was planned in accordance with the original notes, the basic departmental areas might be taken initially as nominal areas. When, however, the room layouts were finalized and the plans drawn up, it became the expectation that the actual areas would be some 20 percent less.

There is a significant *engineering element* in hospital building schemes. However, its cost is not shown separately in the cost estimates but is included in both the departmental costs and the on-costs.

In some regions an anomaly exists in respect of professional fees. When outside consultants are employed, their fees will be charged direct to a scheme under 'professional fees'. However, when the work is done internally, the cost is not directly charged. Instead, the cost is part of the 'technical staff salaries', which are shown in the capital programme, and not itemized by scheme.

Cost estimates for an 'old' Capricode Stage I Submission are calculated by taking the appropriate DCAG figure and then adding estimates for on-costs, equipment and fees – each calculated as a fairly arbitrary percentage of the departmental cost. Thus at Stage I it is the departmental accommodation which is crucial and two schemes providing the same departmental accommodation will show the same Stage I cost regardless of the fact that one may be destined to become a square building on a hilly site and the other may be a rectangular building on a flat site. In particular, if professional fees are accounted for as described above, the percentage shown will reflect an average weighting of work which is done 'in-house' and outside. Inevitably therefore the final figure will differ in that it will increase if the professional work is done outside and it will reduce if it is done 'in-house'.

By the time a Stage II submission is prepared, each of the cost elements can be calculated independently. Outline plans will have been prepared by the architects to show the general shape and size of the building. The nature of the communication space between departments will be known. The site will have been surveyed and bore holes drilled to reveal the underlying rock strata. At Stage II therefore the departmental cost will have been calculated, as at Stage I, but the on-costs will be calculated independently, having regard to the shape of the building and the nature of the site, and will be reasonably accurate. Equipment costs can be calculated by reference to the ECAG (*equipment cost allowance guidelines*) allowances, which similarly give a standard allowance for equipment for hospital accommodation. Finally professional fees can be calculated more accurately, having regard to whether the work is being done by outside consultants or in-house.

At the Stage III submission the process has moved on even further. Detailed plans now show the structure of the building and the layout of each department. A bill of quantities has been prepared and it is this 'bill' which forms the basis in due course of contractors' tenders. Accordingly the works cost is calculated not by reference to standard allowances but by reference to physical quantities of concrete and steel, etc. It also follows that the distinction between departmental cost and on-cost disappears. Equipment costs are no longer calculated on the ECAG allowances but on detailed costed schedules. The process has therefore been one of continuing refinement of information.

The construction period

Once a pre-tender estimate has been prepared, tenders are invited for the main building contract and the sub-contracts for mechanical and electrical engineering, and perhaps major items such as lifts. The tender will have estimated amounts for materials or services from nominated suppliers, sub-contractors or statutory authorities)'prime cost' items) and the successful tender, as adjusted by the substitution of some actual sub-tenders for those estimated amounts, establishes the new 'project approved sum', against which cost control is exercised.

However, the provisions of the standard form of contract can lead to a higher final cost for a number of reasons, including:

1 Further substitutions of actual costs for prime costs and other provisional sums.
2 The architect may issue design changes (variations), whose direct cost may be recovered under the contract.
3 The contractor may be reimbursed for certain items of loss of expense incurred by him and not otherwise covered.
4 If the contract is scheduled to run for more than 2 years, it will provide for adjustment for fluctuations in wages and prices compared with those on which the tender was based.

When the Public Accounts Committee (PAC) examined the post-contract control on six hospital schemes, it concluded that effective control of contract variations began with the pre-contract preparation of a scheme. As a result of these inquiries, the DHSS made it mandatory for authorities to certify that they were ready to proceed to tender and that the procedures had been followed.

The capital programme

An RHA monthly capital programme report shows projected expenditure on individual projects and the resource assumptions derived from the capital cash limits. As a control document, its key function is that it relates the two and shows projected under-/over-commitments.

The figures presented in the capital programme are at constant prices. However, there are two sets of 'constant price figures', derived from two sources. The capital cash limit for the current financial year and the resource assumptions for subsequent years are at 'forecast outturn prices' for the current financial year. Project costs in the capital programme are based on the current departmental cost allowances, which are derived independently.

There is a range of index numbers relating to the cost of new construction, most of which are produced by the Property Services Agency of the Department of the Environment. Indices fall into three categories:

1 *Construction input cost indices*. There will be a 'labour cost index' and a 'materials price index' for several different categories of construction and engineering. These are indices of costs which will be borne by building and engineering contractors.

2 *Tender price indices*. These are indices of the prices of successful tenders for public-sector building schemes. Again there are several such indices for different categories of scheme, and the two series of DCAG allowances used in health buildings are based on different tender indices. The mainstream DCAG allowances are reviewed in the light of movements in the Directorate of Quantity Surveying Services (DQSS) Tender Price Index. A 5 per cent movement in the indices initiates a review, but not an automatic movement, of the DCAG allowances.

3 *Construction output price indexes*. These are indices of the prices actually paid by public authorities for construction schemes. The cash limits are calculated by reference to anticipated readings of these indexes.

The three types of index therefore represent a progression through the process of building a hospital. Obviously the level of construction input costs has a considerable bearing on the level of tender prices. Similarly the level of tender prices has a considerable bearing on the level of construction output prices. However, there is not a direct mathematical link from one category of index to the next, nor for several reasons can there be.

Thus the NHS has different price bases for calculation of the funds available, on the one hand, and for the calculation of the cost of schemes, on the other. In these circumstances an inconsistency between the capital programme and resource assumptions can arise, particularly when the two sets of prices can change independently, thus disrupting the balance of, and making it impossible to retain tight control over, the capital programme. In the short term a purely fortuitous change in one factor can mean that a capital programme which shows an over-commitment in one period can show an under-commitment in the next. At times of high inflation these price movements have created many dramatic problems of financial control for at least one RHA. One improvement would be to review the DCAG allowances at the same time as the setting of the coming year's cash limit.

We do therefore have in Capricode what is apparently a highly structured approach to the planning and processing of hospital schemes. Nevertheless, there are areas where problems can arise, as the following case studies illustrate.

Case Study 1 – a residential unit for the mentally handicapped

The 1971 White Paper 'Better Services for the Mentally Handicapped' stressed the modern philosophy for providing residential facilities for the mentally handicapped in small units in a community setting. It invited health authorities to design and plan purpose-built residential units for up to twenty-four beds.

In accordance with the White Paper one RHA developed its own design for a twenty-four-place residential unit. By the late 1970s proposals to build six such units in one district in the region were well advanced. A second district was recognized as being deficient in its provision of facilities for the mentally handicapped, and agreed to the provision of five standard residential units. The sites were not specifically identified but – on the basis of a unit cost of £400,000 (shown below) – £2m was specifically allocated in the regional capital programme.

Residential units for the mentally handicapped: breakdown of capital programme estimate of cost

	£
Departmental cost as per HN(80)21 (January 1980 prices)	197,400
May 1980 increase in cost allowances – 12½%	24,675
Departmental cost at May 1980 prices	222,075
On-cost at 50% departmental cost	111,038
Total works cost	333,113
Fees at 10% of works cost	33,300
Equipment at 17% departmental cost	37,750
Total capital cost	404,163

Estimate as per capital programme, say £400,000

Significantly, although the need for supporting educational and therapeutic facilities was clearly identified, and the possibility that they too would have to be built from scratch was realized, no specific provision for them was made in the capital programme.

The detailed planning of a capital project is undertaken by a project team, which contains medical, nursing, works and administrative representatives from the appropriate DHA and from the RHA. In this case a project team was set up to process schemes for units at two different hospitals. We will consider one of the schemes.

In 1980 the DHSS published formal cost allowances for the units, which had the effect of bringing the cost-control aspect of providing this accommodation within the 'mainstream' of hospital building. When the RHA first made provision for these units at a capital cost of £400,000, they were consistent with DHSS advice as far as the departmental cost was concerned, although they provided for on-costs at 50 per cent rather than 33 percent, as recommended. This estimate also provided for the equipment cost to be 17 percent of the departmental cost and for fees to be 10 percent of the works cost. In November 1980 the cost allowances were further increased by $7\frac{1}{2}$ percent. If this is applied to the original capital programme figure of £400,000, we arrive at a total cost figure of £434,000. Although the figure of £434,000 could be regarded as a first estimate (i.e. before the project team had started investigating the detailed factors affecting each site) of each project, it never appeared as such in the capital programme. Instead for some time, the blanket figure of £2 million (which, originated from 5 × £400,000) for mental-handicap developments was used.

Table 8.1 shows the development of the estimated capital costs at the site. It has five vertical columns, one each for 'Departmental cost', 'On-cost', 'Equipment cost', 'Fees' and 'Total'. It starts with the estimated total cost of £400,000 and its analysis to the four main elements. It then shows the increase in allowances to give an adjusted total of £434,000.

We now move to the work of the project team in identifying specific features appropriate to this development. Between its first meeting and the preparation of Capricode Stage I cost submission the project team identified a number of minor changes in the detailed requirements, the departmental costs of which were estimated by the project team's quantity surveyor. To these are applied the originally

Table 8.1 *Development for the mentally handicapped. Reconciliation of capital-cost estimates at the Capricode planning stage*

	Departmental cost £000	On-cost £000	Equipment £000	Fees £000	Total £000
Original estimate as per capital programme (Std 24-place residential unit at May 1980 cost allowances)	222	111	38	33	404
Increase in cost allowances, Nov. 1980 + 7½%	17	8	3	2	30
Original estimate @ Nov. 1980 cost allowances	239	119	41	35	434
Detail changes in functional content	–	8	–	1	9
Provision of activity centre	75	37	12	11	135
Sub-total	314	164	53	47	578
Changes in bases of assessment					
Professional fees not required				–47	–47
On-costs – first site assessment		–69			–69
Equipment costs – first estimate			–13		–13
Stage I submission	314	95	40	–	449
Changes in functional content					
Treatment room provided	4	1	1		6
Minibus			8		8
Changes in bases of assessment					
Professional fees (site investigation and structural engineers)				3	3
equipment costs			–9		–9
Stage II submission	318	96	40	3	457
No further changes					
Stage III submission	414		40	3	457

estimated percentages for on-costs, equipment and fees. This would keep these changes on a consistent basis with the original estimated cost. On this basis the impact of these detail changes is small; collectively they increased the cost of the project by some £9,000.

However, the next item appearing in Table 8.1 is the provision of an activity centre. We have already shown that it was considered essential to ensure that appropriate educational and therapeutic facilities would be available to residents at these units. A working party of the project team, established to define the 'operational policies', i.e. the daily working arrangements, of the units, found that suitable local authority provision of educational and thera-peutic facilities would *not* be forthcoming, so that it would be necessary to provide an activity centre in which this training could take place.

The activity centre takes the form of a separate building, providing rooms in which various educational and therapeutic activities can be pursued. It was designed by the project team architect, and the departmental cost was estimated at £75,000. If the same percentages for on-cost, equipment and fees are applied, then the total cost of the centre would be £135,000.

The provision of this activity centre was therefore a major increase in the cost of the developments. On the same basis, the sub-total in Table 8.1 shows us that the total cost of the project had now risen from £434,000 to £578,000.

The physical changes identified above were all that occurred before the Stage 1 submission was prepared, and the departmental cost was unchanged at £314,000. However, there were significant changes in the bases of assessment of the remaining items (on-costs, equipment and fees). Firstly, the total provision for fees was deleted from the Stage I submission, as all the architectural, engineering and quantity-surveying work was being done 'in-house'. Secondly, an initial appraisal of the sites showed that on-costs would be considerably less than the 50 percent allowance used previously, thus bringing savings of £69,000. Thirdly, a preliminary look at the equipment requirements showed that a figure of £40,000 (which is less than 12 percent of the departmental costs, rather than the 17 percent originally used) would be adequate. These changes collectively *reduced* the total cost by £129,000, and were therefore of the same order as the additional costs incurred by the decision to build the activity centres. Accordingly the Stage I submission showed a total cost of £449,000.

A similar process could be followed in reconciling from Stage I to the Stage II submission. However, the changes which occurred were much less dramatic and the Stage II submission (at £457,000) showed an increase of only £8,000 over Stage I.

The Stage III Submission – the 'pre-tender estimate', which is accompanied by fully detailed building plans and bills of quantities – appeared later. In total it agreed with the earlier Stage II and does not therefore affect the analysis shown in Table 8.1.

Table 8.2 *Development for the mentally handicapped*
Comparison of 'control' totals

	Departmental cost £000	Total works cost £000	Total direct cost £000	Total cost £000
1 Original capital programme, estimate adjusted to Nov. 1980 cost allowances	239	358	399	434
2 Stage I submission	314	409	449	449
3 Stage II submission	318	414	454	457
Percentages	%	%	%	%
Stage I/original estimate	131	114	113	103
Stage II/Stage I	101	101	101	102
Stage II/original estimate	133	116	114	105

Table 8.2 demonstrates the misleading picture which can be obtained by concentrating simply on one 'control' total. It shows four possible 'control' totals: Departmental cost, Total works cost (i.e. including on-costs), Total direct cost (including equipment) and Total cost (including fees). The four totals are shown at the three stages of development, i.e. as per the original programme (adjusted for the November 1980 increase in cost allowances), as at Stage I, and as at Stage II. It then shows percentages relating Stage I to the original estimate, Stage II to Stage I and Stage II to the original estimate.

With the addition of the activity centre the scheme increased considerably in size. Yet that is only shown clearly by the percentages in the 'departmental-cost' schemes. On all the other columns the impact of the changed bases of assessment of on-costs, equipment and fees has been to hide the real increase in costs incurred by the activity centre. What the departmental-cost column shows to be a real increase of 30 per cent the total cost column shows as a reduction of 2 percent.

Subsequent to the preparation of the Stage III submissions the schemes moved on from the planning stage to the construction stage and the scheme is now complete and in use.

This project illustrates a number of problems that can arise in practice.

1   The blanket provision for this programme in the monthly capital programme reports and the failure to identify sites sufficiently early and with adequate background research.

2   The project team began its work without a clear brief as to whether or not it was to provide supporting facilities, and whether funds were available for such a development or not.

3   The provision of fees in the capital cost estimates. For a sizeable sum of money to be provided and then not be required, even though the services of architects, engineers and quantity surveyors *are* required, is an anomaly of the accounting for the RHAs and outside works professionals.

4   The assessment of on-costs. For standard twenty-four-place residential units on-costs are assessed – on the same price base – at 48, 53, 65, 69 or 120 thousand pounds. As it was the higher figure – which is 2½ times the lower – which was first estimated, a considerable 'slack' was built into the programme.

5   The problems with control totals. Where there have been changes in the bases of assessment of on-costs and fees, a misleading picture arises if one looks only at the total cost. A more detailed analysis is necessary to reveal the full picture.

What this relatively small scheme also demonstrates is the tendency for NHS schemes to increase in size in real terms *after* the point where they have first been approved in principle.

Case Study 2 – a new general hospital

A very different project, now also completed and in operation, was the scheme to build a major new General Hospital in a West Country seaside town. The history of this particular project dates back many years (the requirement was identified in the wartime Survey of Hospital Services) and has progressed through several phases. In the mid-1970s detailed plans had been produced for a full 420-bed district general hospital before *that* scheme was abandoned. Planning for the current 252-bed hospital began in the late 1970s with the acceptance by the then area health authority of four key principles:

1 There would be replacement-bed provision only, rather than an expansion of numbers.
2 There would be sufficient beds to justify the appointment of two consultants in each specialty.
3 There would be a comprehensive accident and emergency department.
4 Reference would continue to be made to Bristol for the most highly specialized services.

Within these principles considerable attention was devoted to 'defining the brief' before a project team was established and detailed planning began. Once established, the project team was successful, both in adhering to a very tight timetable and in keeping the capital and the anticipated revenue costs under control. However, in the preliminary planning of the hospital its size increased by approximately one-third *after* the four key principles had been defined.

This is confirmed by Table 8.3, which shows various capital cost estimates prepared during its planning stages and then adjusts them to a common price basis. This shows an increase in total capital cost from £12.275m to £16.767m on the same price basis – an increase of 36.6 percent. So here we have a major scheme – generally regarded as being well managed – which nevertheless demonstrates precisely the same substantial increase in cost during the crucial early planning stages.

Table 8.3 *New general hospital – comparison of main capital cost submissions*

	1	2	3	4	5
					Increase over previous stage (at May 1981 prices)
Price base	Oct. 1977	July 1979	April 1980	May 1981	
Percentage uplift to May 1981	67.0%	24.7%	−0.8%	–	
	£000	£000	£000	£000	
AHA Papers Jan. 1978					
Departmental cost	3,665			6,121	
On-cost	2,185			3,649	
Total works cost	5,850			9,770	
Equipment	623			1,040	
Total direct cost	6,473			10,810	
Fees	877			1,465	
Total capital cost	7,350			12,275	
Stage I cost Aug. 1979					
Departmental cost		6,280		7,831	1,710
On-cost		3,768		4,699	1,050
Total works cost		10,048		12,530	2,760
Equipment		1,099		1,371	331
Total direct cost		11,147		13,901	3,091
Fees		1,507		1,879	414
Total capital cost		12,654		15,780	3,505
Stage II cost Aug. 1980					
Departmental cost			8,135	8,070	239
On-cost			5,015	4,975	276
Total works cost			13,150	13,045	515
Equipment			1,426	1,415	44
Total direct cost			14,576	14,460	559
Fees			2,292	2,273	394
Total capital cost			16,868	16,733	953
Stage III cost Jan. 1982					
Total works cost				12,900	−145
Equipment				1,619	204
Total direct cost				14,519	59
Fees				2,248	−25
Total capital cost				16,767	34

A survey of a capital programme

The two projects above were studies in some depth as part of the South Western RHA/University of Bath Joint Research Study (Cook, 1983) into the problems of capital expenditure planning and control in the NHS. In order to confirm that they were not simply isolated examples but were typical of the NHS a survey of capital projects in the region was conducted.

The survey embraced the whole capital expenditure programme between 1974–5 and 1981–2, i.e. the lifetime of the old AHAs, when expenditure for the period was some £200m. Within that programme sixty individual schemes – selected on the basis of having a capital cost of greater than £100,000 – were examined in more detail. For each a table similar to Table 8.3 was completed, so that all cost estimates for all the schemes could be compared at May 1981 prices.

Unfortunately much of the data was incomplete so that its interpretation was a process of the application of subjective judgement rather than mathematical precision. Nevertheless, the following conclusions, in descending order of certainty, could be drawn from the survey:

1 Schemes usually do increase in cost in real terms during the planning stage, confirming the findings of the case studies.
2 That increase is probably in the order of 23–33 percent. It is not possible to quantify it to a higher degree of probability.
3 In an analysis by type of scheme no real conclusions are to be drawn. In our survey the 'general' schemes showed increases well above average but only five schemes fall into this group. All the other categories showed similar profiles.
4 In an analysis by employment of architect, those schemes in which consultant architects were commissioned show above-average increases, whereas in those schemes where regional architects were employed the increases were well below average.
5 In an analysis into the old single- and multi-district areas, the highest increases occurred in multi-district areas.

There is overwhelming evidence therefore to indicate, notwithstanding the structure provided by Capricode, that schemes do increase in cost substantially as they progress through the system.

One way to overcome that would be to insert a more formal

'decision point' into each region's procedure. This would reduce the 'snowball' effect, whereby schemes, once in the programme, increase in size as they progress. In my view the most appropriate stage at which to insert such a decision point would be the Stage II or budget cost submission.

Investment appraisal

A formal investment-appraisal procedure was introduced within the requirements of Health Notice (81)30 (DHSS, 1982a), when the 'old' Capricode Stage I, II and III submissions were replaced by 'approval in principle submissions', 'budget cost submissions' and 'pre-tender estimates' respectively.

The most significant of these is the requirement for an 'approval in principle submission' (APS), an essential component of which is the explicit identification and *appraisal of options* and justification of the preferred option. This requirement takes Capricode beyond being a procedure for controlling the building of a given hospital on a given site to ask 'Why that particular hospital and why that site?' However, it does not take Capricode into the business of establishing (or questioning) the service need which leads to the decision to build something. That is, and remains, the task of the NHS Planning System. Clearly there is a very significant difference between the previous procedure and the requirements of HN(81)30. Previously the selection of the preferred option had been done (usually implicitly) at the 'pre-Capricode' stage. Now it is to be done explicitly (indeed the information should be made public) and – given that there will continue to be a need for a Cap 1 or something similar – at the *second stage*.

In addition there is a recognition that this can be a lengthy procedure. A considerable amount of information needs to be assembled about each option before a proper appraisal can be carried out. It follows also that it is not possible to make a meaningful estimate of the capital cost of the chosen option until this process is complete.

HN(81)30 gave no information as to what degree of detail would be required at the approval in principle stage. There was, however, the proviso that should the budget cost estimate in respect of the preferred option differ significantly from the estimate shown in the appraisal of options, then that exercise must be reviewed. That requirement was formally set out with the issue of HN(82)34 (DHSS, 1982b), which stated that should 'the cost' of the preferred option at the budget cost submission exceed that of the APS by more than 10 percent, then approval in principle would lapse. Thus the appraisal of options procedure created pressures suggesting that Capricode cost estimates should be produced to a greater degree of accuracy early in the planning process than had previously been the case.

The wording of the structure of an Appraisal of Options has been revised (and improved) in the 1986 reissue of Capricode and new guidance has been issued (DHSS, 1987). An option appraisal framework should now contain the following steps:

1   Place the scheme in its strategic planning context.
2   Define objectives, constraints and performance criteria.
3   The formulation of options.
4   The evaluation of options:
    (a) Identifying and assessing the extent and timing of costs and quantifiable financial benefits (if any) occurring over the functional life of options, using discounted values to assist comparisons.
    (b) Identifying and describing all service benefits and outputs over the functional life of options, using measured assessments where possible.
    (c) Test for uncertainty.
5   The selection of the preferred option.

Thus we have the introduction of a DCF-based form of investment appraisal but, to the management accountant, only in a very limited form, in that the discounting is essentially applied to the capital and revenue costs of each option (4a above). This is on the assumption that it is not possible to put a financial price on the benefits (in the form of improved healthcare) accruing from each option. They have to be assessed separately under 4b above. (The economist would describe the procedure as a 'cost-effectiveness analysis' rather than a 'cost-benefit analysis'. Cost-benefit analysis *is* employed elsewhere in the public sector. However, while it might be possible to apply cost-benefit analysis to lives saved as a result of NHS care, it would be very difficult to do so for schemes designed say to improve the quality of care for long-stay patients.) The operation of the procedure therefore still relies on a considerable element of subjective judgement, particularly in assessing relative service benefits.

An appraisal of options

A key principle of healthcare planning, particularly in rural health authorities, is that the district general hospital will be supported by smaller community hospitals in outlying towns.

One market town, identified by the DHA as requiring a medium-sized community hospital, in fact contained two smaller hospitals. One (Hospital A) consisted of 1960s-type accommodation on a site with spare land at the rear; the other (Hospital B) was a late nineteenth-century building which was very much overcrowded and outdated and which occupied a valuable town centre site.

A joint RHA/DHA project team was established to identify options and to make recommendations for the replacement of this second hospital. They quickly identified the following options:

Option A   Provide new accommodation on available land at Hospital A.
Option B   Redevelop and upgrade Hospital B on its present site.)
Option C   Buy a third site on which to build a new replacement hospital for B.
Option D   Buy a larger new site on which to build a new replacement hospital for both Hospitals A and B.

As we noted earlier, there are key aspects to the evaluation of options: assessing the costs of the scheme and assessing the benefits.

Table 8.4

	Land[1]* £000	Estimated building costs[2] £000	Annual revenue costs[3] £000	Net present costs[4] £000
Option A	600	4,521	2,250	45,843
Option B	900	1,500	2,293	41,733
Option C	900	4,487	2,275	44,338
Option D	1,000	6,623	2,235	44,834

*see notes on page 228.

It is sensible to approach these separately. The costs can be summarized as in Table 8.4.

1 Capricode requires that the value (estimated at opportunity cost) of all land occupied should be included in each option, even where land is already owned by the NHS. Most commercial management accountants would adopt the 'cash flow' approach of including a figure only where there is actually a transaction for the purchase or sale of land. The outcome, however, is the same.
2 Estimated building costs calculated as per Capricode *except* for Option B – which is a notional figure for upgrading the present hospital. Options A, B and C postulate a 2-year building period, Option D 3 years.
3 Annual revenue costs estimated for the hospital(s) once complete.
4 Discounted at 5 percent (the Treasury recommended test discount rate) over 62 years – i.e. allowing a 60-year working life for options A, B and C, and 59 years for D.

Clearly on the basis of the net present costs Option B (as would be expected) is the cheapest, while Option D (as would also be expected) is the most expensive. However, equally clearly, it would be a mistake to assume without further analysis that Option B is to be selected. Such a decision would be to conclude that the benefits from each option are the same, which obviously they are not.

In fact in this case there are very substantial differences between the benefits accruing from each option. For example, Options B and C will still call for split site working, while A and D give the benefits of single-site operation. Options A, C and D give new accommodation which will be to building note standards, Option B does not *and* would probably cause the closure of Hospital B while it was being redeveloped. Options A, B and C could be completed inside 2 years, whereas D will take 3. Option D, however, will provide the required new accommodation and modern facilities to replace the 1960s' accommodation of Hospital A, which is already becoming dated.

Clearly a further analysis is required in order to assess the relative benefits of each option. Note that it is sensible to assess them as benefits rather than as advantages and disadvantages. For example,

Table 8.5

Criteria	Weights	Option A	Option B	Option C	Option D
1 Provision of replacement accommodation for Hospital B	10	10	5	10	10
2 Provision of replacement accommodation for Hospital A	1	–	–	–	10
3 Early provision of new accommodation	3	7	7	7	4
4 Lack of disruption to present hospitals	10	8	4	10	10
5 Single-site working	5	10	–	–	10
6 Provision of car parking	5	7	1	8	10
7 Accessibility to public transport	5	8	10	6	6
Total assessment of benefits		326	166	291	352

Summary of costs and benefits.

	Net present cost £000	Assessment of benefits
Option A	43,642	326
Option B	41,733	166
Option C	44,330	291
Option D	45,843	352

it would be very easy to assess the lack of car parking which would apply in Option B as a disadvantage. However, it makes more sense to regard the provision of car parking as a criterion against which each option should be assessed. It is then possible to give Option B a low mark against this criterion and Options A, C and D higher marks.

One approach which would achieve this is to follow a four-stage process of:

(a) Identifying the criteria which would be met by the 'ideal' scheme.
(b) Assessing the relative importance of those criteria by 'weighting' them.

(c) Assessing the extent to which each option meets each criterion by awarding marks out of 10.
(d) Multiplying the marks awarded under 'C' by the weights identified under 'B' to give a total score of benefits for each option.

Applying this system to this example can give the assessment of benefits shown in Table 8.5. Table 8.5 also provides a summary of the costs and benefits of each option and from this it is clear that while Option B is the cheapest, it also scores very badly on our assessment of benefits and should therefore be eliminated. Option C is both more expensive than A and gives a lower score of benefits and can also be eliminated. Option D gives a marginally higher score of benefits than A but is very much more expensive and probably does not represent value for money. Which leaves us with the choice of A as the preferred option.

The final element of the appraisal of options procedure is sensitivity testing. This will of course be familiar to management accountants as a process of changing the assumptions built into the model by asking a number of 'What happens if?' questions. This process will test the robustness of the original assumptions and will assist in identifying what are the key variables in the whole equation. It is a crucial part in recognizing the uncertainty of investment appraisal.

One can speculate that the requirement for an appraisal of options – which has been inserted into the Capricode procedure at a point at which capital costs are very much less than certain – will cause difficulties, particularly if the rate of inflation were to increase significantly. In my view RHAs should refrain from committing themselves *in principle* to a scheme until the budget cost submission has been prepared. At that stage, and only at that stage, can they be satisfied that the correct choice of options has been made and that they have a reasonably reliable estimate of the capital cost.

Further developments in capital and asset accounting

In the short term, further developments in capital and asset accounting in the NHS are likely to centre around the 1985 report of the AHST (AHST, 1985). Some of the recommendations of that report, such as the need to establish comprehensive asset registers, are straightforward. Somewhat more radical are the recommendations that there should be the introduction of a full balance sheet and that there should be revenue cash charges to DHAs for the use of capital assets. Such charges would then be returned to RHAs to fund future capital expenditure.

Three variants of this system have been suggested:

(a) With asset depreciation charges.
(b) With leasing charges.
(c) With leasing charges for land and buildings and depreciation charges for equipment.

Pilot studies are now being established in Calderdale, Peterborough and Chester Health Authorities, and a report is expected in 1988. However, there is as yet no evidence as to the practicalities of such a system and certainly no evidence to demonstrate that its introduction brings about a more efficient use of NHS fixed assets.

Looking even further ahead, one can see a greater integration of capital and asset accounting with improvements in the NHS systems of budgetary control. The latest developments are being referred to as 'resource management' and are incorporating trials in case-mix accounting. In these what are, in essence, standard product costs are being created for resource-homogeneous categories of patients referred to as diagnosis-related groups (DRGs). There are several detailed variants to this approach, but for the moment they include only revenue costs. The management accountant will readily recognize, however, that if a comparison is to be made of the costs of two alternative treatment regimes (one of which is, say, 'high tech' and capital intensive, and the other is, say 'low tech' but perhaps nursing intensive), then the only way it can be done is by introducing some capital element into the DRG calculations. For the moment there are other considerable problems to be overcome with DRGs and such refinements are something for the future.

Conclusion

We have a National Health Service which in capital accounting as in so many other areas is evolving. Three main issues have emerged:

how to control the cost of capital schemes, what form of investment appraisal to adopt, and what form, if any, of capital and asset accounting to adopt. In all three cases there are still lessons to be learned. Several RHAs still have difficulty in controlling the cost of their capital programme. The appraisal of options procedure is still new to many health authorities, and the NHS is just tentatively experimenting with a new system of capital and asset accounting.

It will continue to be a changing picture.

Notes

1 Hospital building notes are issued by the DHSS. They are updated from time to time and published by HMSO.
2 'Boards' refers to the regional hospital boards, which were the predecessors of regional health authorities.
3 Hospital building procedure notes (Capricode) are issued by the DHSS and published by HMSO. The notes that have been issued include the following:

HBPN.1 (1967) Revised 1974) Procedure for Planning and Processing of Individual Building Projects.
HBPN.2 (1969) Planning Policies.
HBPN.3 (1969) The Assessment of Functional Content.
HBPN.5 (1970) The Development Control Plan.
HBPN.6 (1972) Cost Control.

In 1986 Capricode was reissued (DHSS, 1986b), and this publication consolidated all the detailed changes that had been made to the above hospital building procedure notes since 1974.

References

Abel-Smith, B. (1962). Hospital Planning in Great Britain. *Hospitals*, 36, 1 May, 30–5.
AHST (1985). *Managing Capital Assets in the NHS*. London: CIPFA.
Cook, A. N. (1983). *Capital Expenditure Control in Health Authorities*. Bristol: South Western Regional Health Authority.
Cruickshank, H. J. (1973). *Planning, Design and Construction of Hospital Buildings for the National Health Service*. London: DHSS.
DHSS (1979). *Review of Health Capital*. London: DHSS.
DHSS (1982a). *Health Notice HN(81)30*. London: DHSS.

DHSS (1982b). *Health Notice HN(82)34*. London: DHSS.

DHSS (1983a). *Report of the Committee of NHS Management Inquiry*. London: DHSS.

DHSS (1983b). *Underused and Surplus Property in the NHS*. London: HMSO.

DHSS (1985). *Health Circular HC(85)26*. London: DHSS.

DHSS (1986a) *The NHS in England – Annual Report 1985/86*. London: DHSS.

DHSS (1986b). *Capricode – Health Building Procedures*. London, HMSO.

DHSS (1987). *Option Appraisal – A Guide for the National Health Service*. London: HMSO.

Ministry of Health (1962). *A Hospital Plan for England and Wales (Cmnd 1604)*. London: HMSO.

Ministry of Health (1966). *The Hospital Building Programme (Cmnd 3000)*. London: HMSO.

The Royal Commission on the NHS (1978). *Research Paper No. 2 – The Management of Financial Resources in the NHS*. London: HMSO.

9 Management accounting developments in the Customs and Excise Department

Tony Killikelly

Introduction

The Commissioners of Customs and Excise, who are appointed by Her Majesty under the Great Seal of the United Kingdom, constitute the Board. Each commissioner (director) is responsible for a directorate consisting of a number of divisions headed by assistant secretaries (Grade 5). The Customs, Internal Taxation and VAT Control Directorates formulate policy and are responsible for seeing that it is applied consistently in regional offices throughout the country (known as the outfield). The Personnel, Organization

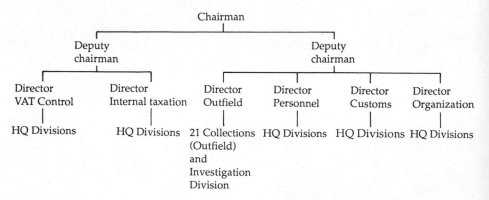

Figure 9.1 *The Board of Customs and Excise*

and Outfield Directorates are responsible for staffing and training, organization and other management matters. An organization chart is shown in Figure 9.1.

The board is advised on legal matters by the solicitor and on accounting issues by the accountant and comptroller general. They may be invited to attend meetings of the board but are not appointed as commissioners. The outfield is divided into twenty-one geographical areas known as collections. Each is headed by a collector (equivalent to assistant secretary Grade 5). Each collection (with the exception of London Airports Collection) is split geographically and by function into VAT, excise and customs offices. A typical organization chart is shown in Figure 9.2.

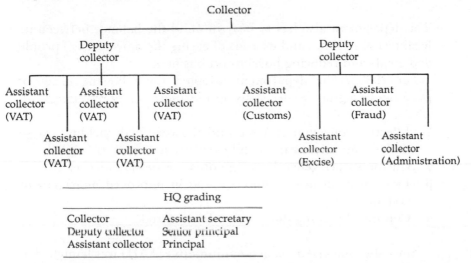

Each assistant collector (VAT) manages a Local VAT Office (LVO) of about 80–100 staff

Each collection about 1000 staff

Figure 9.2 *Typical collection structure*

The department's main responsibilities are:

1 Collection of VAT and excise duties.
2 Collection of customs duties and agricultural levies for the European Community.
3 Enforcement of prohibitions and restrictions on imports and exports.

4   Tasks connected with foreign trade, e.g. trade statistics, on behalf of other government departments.

The department needs an order of priorities among its wide range of responsibilities in order to help in the allocation of resources. A balance has to be struck between the following:

(a) Collection of revenue.
(b) Protection of society (from drugs, weapons, diseased animals etc).
(c) Collection of customs duties and levies on behalf of the EC and protection of the UK and EC economies (import quotas, etc.).

The department also has to bear in mind the balance between its legal responsibilities and its aims of easing the movement of people and goods and reducing burdens on business.

For 1986–7 the department adopted the following order of priorities as a guide to decisions on the allocation of resources:

1   Effective collection of VAT and the very high yielding excise duties; and investigation and prevention of drug-smuggling.
2   Customs work generally (preventive, trade statistics, etc.).
3   Investment in new technology and in improved management systems.
4   Continued investigation of significant fraud.

Since the financial management initiative (FMI) was launched in 1982, the department has looked critically at all its management systems. It has geared them firmly to improved value for money and results. It was considered vital that the board should show the way, and so the department decided quite deliberately to publish a management plan each year and to state publicly the targets it hoped to achieve. The plan leaves the staff in no doubt of what the board considers important. The management plan for 1986–7 was the fourth in the series. It is endorsed by Ministers and published at the start of each financial year. The plan sets out the priorities, aims and objectives and the resources for each work area. It is developed at lower management levels into specific objectives and targets.

In particular the plan sets quite specific targets for the twenty-one senior operational managers in the regions – the collectors, who manage four-fifths of the department's 25,000 staff. They each have a block budget covering nearly all their running costs and averaging £10m. Each collector knows what results are expected of him and this has made his position much more exposed and accountable. In HQ a smaller range of budgets is delegated through directors to assistant secretaries, but from 1 April 1987 each director had a manpower budget delegated to him.

In the autumn and at the end of each financial year the board reviews progress against the plan. Also in the autumn it reviews future plans and the allocation of resources for the next public expenditure survey period (PES) during an intensive series of formal review meetings.

The department has set value for money targets against a background of continued growth – on the customs side in the form of freight traffic and passengers, and on the VAT side in the number of registered traders. For example, since 1979–80 import entries have increased by 36 percent, the number of passengers arriving from abroad by 26 percent and the number of VAT-registered traders by 11 percent. In the same period the department's staff has fallen by 7 percent, and it has sought to make good the difference through improvements in efficiency. The department has also shifted resources from administration into frontline areas like VAT-control visiting and customs preventive work. About 11,000 staff work on VAT (in HQ and the outfield) and the major emphasis in this chapter will be on how the management accounting practices of the department affect performance in VAT collection and investigation.

VAT is a self-assessed tax which in general falls on final consumer expenditure. It is administered by the trader, and its collection is scrutinized and checked by customs and excise officials. In the outfield there are about ninety main local VAT offices (LVOs) covering the whole of the United Kingdom and each office has between ninety and 100 staff. The offices are responsible for the local administration of VAT, for advising registered persons whose principal places of business are in their areas, and for visiting registered persons to check that their tax returns are correct and their tax accounts adequate. These visits absorb approximately 50 percent of LVO manpower. The offices are also engaged in enforcement measures in respect of unpaid tax and failure to furnish returns of tax. All work connected with the collection of tax on normal returns is, however, dealt with at Southend by means of large mainframe computers.

VAT is a very big revenue earner. In 1980–1 £10.9 billion was collected and by 1986–7 this had risen to £21.4 billion (the rate of VAT has not changed during this period). It is also cheap to collect, the cost as a percentage of revenue having fallen over the same period from 1.2p per £1 to 1p per £1. The total take of course is much affected by the level of consumer expenditure and by price levels, but the yield also depends directly on the department's efficiency, first in identifying all the tax that is properly payable and then in ensuring that that amount of tax is paid on time.

The main objective of the FMI since 1982–3 has been to change the attitude of managers and introduce management systems, emphasizing:

(a) The need for well structured and coordinated planning and budgeting.
(b) The inclusion of expected productivity and outputs (target-setting) as well as resource estimates (inputs) in the planning and budgeting processes, i.e. consideration of all aspects of the organization and not just financial resources.
(c) The need for a formal in-year achievement review procedure, so that senior management can assess progress against the planned objectives and make more informed decisions on any necessary action, taking into account the relative priorities.

What follows is a description of what these management systems are and what they are already achieving, using the VAT area for specific examples.

Budgetary control and the planning system

The department's method of financing is through the PES system. The Finance and Manpower Division (FMD) is responsible within the department for commissioning forecasts for PES and supply estimates, scrutinizing and challenging these where necessary and advising the board on the bids to be submitted to Treasury. Negotiations with Treasury fall in the first instance to FMD. The division is also responsible for monitoring expenditure during the year and for advising the board on any measures needed to ensure that the cash limit is fully utilized but not breached. FMD is itself the budget centre for salaries and wages.

HQ budget centres, of which there are twenty-two, are the repositories of expertise on individual budgets. They are responsible, in conjunction with budget-holders, for providing PES and estimate bids to FMD, advising FMD on trends and policies affecting particular budgets, monitoring expenditure during the year, forecasting the likely outturn, and, if necessary, taking steps to ensure that the outturn on a particular budget is achieved.

Budget-holders are line managers who hold delegated budgets and responsibility for specific types of expenditure related to their operational area. They take part in forecasting for PES and estimates and have a critical role in controlling expenditure during the year and providing accurate projections of the outturn.

The whole of the department is divided into cost centres for budgetary purposes. The cost centre generally represents an identifiable part of the organizational structure, e.g. a division or branch of the department. The use of cost centres allows budget-holders to build up their budget and to receive cost reports at a greater level of detail. This enables each cost centre's performance to be measured against a plan. Cost-centre managers can compare forecasts with outturn, relate these to their targets and begin to find out whether or not they are achieving value for money.

The budget-centre system has been successful in that it provides an effective means of keeping expenditure within cash limits. However, the ability to make value for money judgements is compromised to some degree when the budget centre is remote from the point where expenditure decisions take place. Since 1983 therefore control of cash limits has been progressively delegated by budget centres to local budget-holders. This has meant that by 1 April 1986 all collectors in the outfield had been delegated budgets representing some 96 percent of their total running cost expenditure. These budgets include salaries, accommodation, overtime, travel and subsistence, micro-computers and so on. The collector is given these budgets in the form of a single block budget worth on average

£10 million per annum, and has the ability to switch expenditure from one cost element to another. Where it is practical and beneficial to do so, collectors sub-delegate these budgets to those managers at lower levels whose decisions incur expenditure. The important questions in determining the level of budgetary control is to what degree the level of delegation is commensurate with:

(a) Accurate information about costs on an attributable basis.
(b) The manager's ability to exercise a meaningful degree of influence over his costs.
(c) Balancing the time and effort in calculating a particular element of cost and the likely benefits of such cost control.
(d) Meaningful influence over output and activity.
(e) Relating budgets to management plans and measures of output.

As part of the improvement to its management information systems the department realized that on the budgetary side a modern accounting system was essential. It therefore installed, at its computer centre at Shoeburyness, a general ledger package to provide both financial and management accounting information. The new system, known as the departmental accounting system (DAS) became operational on 2 January 1987, and replaced mechanized accounting – the department's twenty-year-old bespoke central financial accounting system, and F-micro, a two-year-old interim stand-alone micro-based management accounting system (again based on bespoke software), which was used in the outfield.

DAS is based on GL Plus, a package marketed and maintained by McCormack and Dodge and installed on the department's 39/80 computer. The system supports 58, soon to rise to 64, accounting centres, which input on line to a batch update to the system by means of an existing communications network to Harmondsworth and a new X.25 network from Harmondsworth to Shoeburyness. On-line access for output will be available to both these accounting centres, using intelligent Merlin terminals and approximately thirty head-office users employing either Ferranti dumb terminals or, in the case of low-volume users, Tontos on a dial back basis. Data input to the system will be by means of interfaces from, for example, payroll or as specified above. Outputs from the system will be by hard copy reports or on-line access to either pre-defined 'query shells' or ad hoc account code access. Plans are in hand to supplement and partly replace these outputs by distributed reporting as an output across the communications network.

The scope of the DAS and its planned use mean that all areas of the department's operations will be affected:

1 All budget-holders, present or planned, will receive reports from the system, so that significant training/familiarization will be needed for all affected personnel, apart from changes arising out of delegation of budgets.
2 HQ Divisions will see considerable changes in (a) the type of information produced, and (b) the frequency of and access to information.
3 The accountant and comptroller general's office will take a more active role in the control of the DAS, permitted by the interrogation and exception reporting facilities of a package system. Changes will be required in input and reporting procedures to obtain maximum benefit.
4 Collections will be affected in respect of data input and will require preparation for new code structures, or detailed analysis and changes in revenue-recording procedures.

The planned outputs of the DAS may be simply categorized as:

(a) Financial accounts, incorporating statutory annual accounts, period revenue accounts and vote accounts.
(b) Management accounts, incorporating cost-centre analysis, varying levels of management reports tailored to the recipient's needs, and budgets – actual comparisons and similar control-oriented reports.
(c) Budget reports, at varying levels of consolidation, for use in connection with PES, and for management control purposes.
(d) Audit/control reports, incorporating a large number of the existing system outputs.
(e) Exception reports on user-defined parameters.
(f) On-line enquiries.
(g) In due course, cost-allocation reports.

Turning specifically to local VAT offices (see Figure 9.3 for typical structure), each assistant collector has a small number of budgets sub-delegated to him and each of his subordinate managers at district level is a cost centre. Because the delegation of the salaries budget to collectors is only in its second year, that has not yet been sub-delegated to assistant collectors. However, this is being tried in one collection as an experiment on a pilot basis.

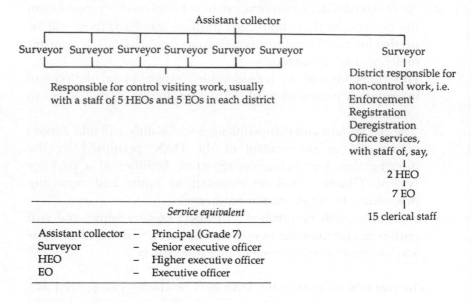

Figure 9.3 *Typical local VAT office (LVO) structure*

Now that the DAS system has been installed, a study has begun on the potential use of functional activity costing in the local VAT offices (LVOs), using decision support system software in conjunction with information from DAS. The department believes that this approach, together with the more detailed planning system that has been created, will have an additional favourable impact on results. With the development of the management-planning system and the delegation to collectors of nearly all their running costs, the department is now well on the way to establishing the position where managers at all levels work to agreed plans and budgets and are accountable for the results they achieve. But how does this actually come about?

At the top level of the department the chairman, supported by the two deputy chairmen (Corporate Management Group – CMG) and the remainder of the board, consider and decide upon the submission to Treasury ministers for departmental resources in PES in relation to targeted outputs, taking account of efficiency and productivity improvements. In the light of decisions in PES they challenge and approve the plans and budgets for the following year for each area of the department, and review past and current performance. They focus on the resources required for each of the three main functional areas of the department (customs, excise and VAT) in relation to a business strategy for each, and specific output targets and efficiency indicators. The functional plans incorporate the following elements:

1   A forward look over the PES period (and beyond if appropriate). This identifies the main developments and direction and any significant trends and assumptions, e.g. traffic/trader growth and mix, resource implications, etc.
2   The year ahead, focusing on the main operational activities and setting out the key effectiveness targets/standards to be achieved, relating these closely to the changes in manpower proposed in the PES submissions; and specific objectives for the outfield/HQ.
3   Resources – the manpower assumptions on which the plan is based, including the principal changes envisaged by the PES submission, productivity and/or efficiency savings. Where possible, the plans also indicate, in qualitative/narrative terms, the implications for manpower-related costs, especially travel and subsistence and overtime, e.g. more VAT control visits mean more travel and subsistence expenditure. It is envisaged that the relationship between functional plans and cash requirements will be further developed as the PES and budgeting processes increasingly show cash items on a functional basis.
4   Activity/output or performance indicators – the broad relationships assumed by the plan between input/outputs, workloads/resources, etc. for the main operational activities.

The functional plans are supported by service plans, individually tailored to fit the nature of the activities undertaken and the resources used, i.e. cash and manpower, largely cash, etc. Some, such as those for investigation, training and legal services, follow the functional plan format; others which are largely cash-driven (e.g. research and development, general supplies, accommodation, etc.), are presented in schedule form (expected expenditure analysed by project, programme or activity). Service plans in general concentrate on the year ahead and aim to relate planned activities to the resource assumptions (cash, manpower or both) underlying the PES submission. There is also a forward look over the PES period (or longer), outlining expected developments and changes in the service areas. This is particularly relevant in the context of the information technology service plan.

To sum up therefore, arrangements whereby budgets are clearly associated with plans for outputs and activities are now firmly in place. Budgets at the highest level are associated with functional and service plans. Below that level budgets are associated with collection plans. In HQ, budgets can be related to directorate and divisional plans. The department is continuing the drive towards enhancing the amount of output and performance indicators contained within these plans/budgets, and the next part shows how this is being done specifically in the VAT functional area.

VAT operational planning systems and results

To ensure that collection-planning is consistent with the board's priorities and objectives, the VAT Directorate has identified a number of key result areas and national targets in the board's plan for collectors to meet. These in turn are reflected in collection plans and finally in the operational unit plan, which in the example of VAT is the local VAT office (LVO) plan. There are five major targets for the outfield in the board's management plan for 1986–7, which relate to:

(a) A quantified proportion of VAT resources devoted to control visiting.
(b) An 18 percent increase in productive time spent on visits by LVO staff (over 2 years).
(c) Specific visiting targets designed to give priority to those traders who produce the highest revenue yield.

(d) A national target to increase the value of additional tax discovered in real terms compared with the previous year.
(e) A 5 percent reduction in the average VAT debt owed by traders in the LVOs.

Before FMI was instituted, the department had an extensive quarterly management information system (MIS), but it was not geared towards serving the needs of individual managers. In particular, it provided information only on actuals (e.g. resources used, cases completed, revenue recovered) and made no comparisons with plans, thus giving very little guidance to achievement of objectives. In addition, each operational unit manager received the results of every other operational unit and tended to concentrate on comparisons with them rather than concentrating attention on information relevant to his own area of responsibility. The consequence was an attempt to design and develop an improved management reporting system which would support the new planning and budgetary process by helping managers to evaluate achievement against their own explicitly agreed plans. The aim was to identify performance indicators which reflected achievement of agreed management objectives in the plans so as to sharpen a manager's concept of what he or she is expected to achieve and at what cost. The indicators take the form of:

(a) Economy indicators, showing the amount of resource a manager is prepared to invest in a planned level of activity.
(b) Effectiveness indicators, showing what has been achieved compared with what was expected.
(c) Efficiency indicators, showing the relation between inputs and outputs (productivity).

It was decided to develop these new management reporting systems for each of the three main functional work areas, and to start with one for VAT.

The major inputs to the system are the profiled plans for the financial year for operational units (LVOs) and then the records of resources used and results achieved in each reporting period throughout the year. For 1986–7 all LVO assistant collectors were asked to indicate in their plans the resources (by grade) allocated to

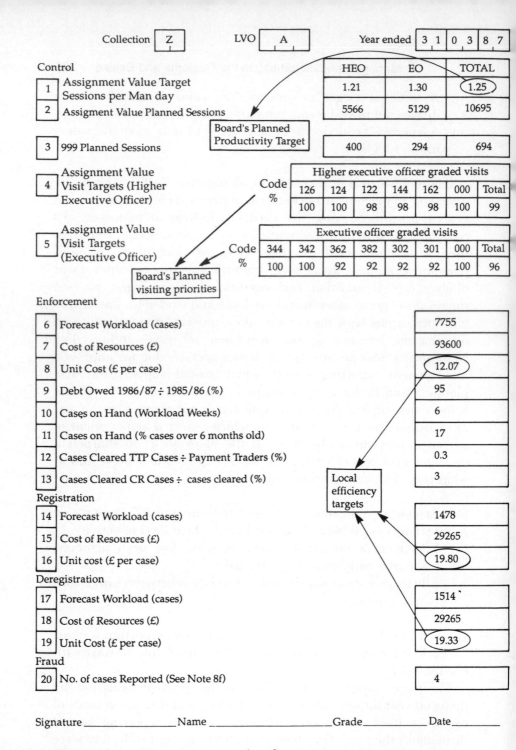

Figure 9.4 *Planned outputs and performance*

Table 9.1 *Management information system*
Period: April to September 1986   Allocation of net effective strength to activity

£000s	AV control		999 Traders		Fraud		Enforcement		Registration		Deregistration		Other		Total	
	Actual	% Plan	Actual	% Plan	Actual	% Plan	Actual	% Plan	Actual	% Plan	Actual	% Plan	Actual	% Plan	Actual	% Plan
	1	2	3	4	5	6	7	8	9	10	11	12	13	14	15	16
Newtown collection – last quarter	828	100	91	59	29	91	177	96	61	110	64	94	239	101	1489	95
LVO A	245	104	29	46	9	72	51	92	22	108	20	104	91	104	467	94
LVO B	228	105	23	53	7	70	68	108	13	115	21	76	48	102	409	97
LVO C	237	105	30	61	13	149	48	96	16	113	15	111	59	92	419	98
LVO D	247	98	18	56	1	19	52	102	25	103	25	97	67	108	440	96
LVO E	246	93	32	80	13	146	46	100	17	112	21	96	69	108	445	96
LVO F	240	94	23	62	9	120	45	92	11	97	10	84	72	100	411	92
LVO G	226	107	24	55	13	138	49	103	16	109	17	106	70	92	414	99
Newtown collection – year to date	1670	100	179	58	65	101	365	99	121	108	130	95	476	101	3005	96
All High		172		141		195		123		235		181		161		113
Mid		95		63		82		96		112		95		106		95
LVOs Low		55		17		6		71		74		19		36		43

each major operational activity (e.g. control, enforcement, registration) and set productivity and output targets so as to provide a basis for evaluating the achievement of objectives. An example of the form for planned outputs and performance targets is given at Figure 9.4. One of the output reports then compares actual with planned use of resources, which provides a basis for the interpretation of the reports showing actual outputs against plan for each activity (see Table 9.1).

The major outputs from the system are quarterly report packs which show achievement for the last quarter and the cumulative financial year to date. Information is aggregated and reported at three management levels: operational unit (LVO), collection and national. A typical report shows a manager the performance of his command and the cumulative figures for the management units at the next lower level. For example, a collector report will give quarterly and cumulative information for the collection and cumulative information for each LVO in the collection. In this way the manager's attention is focused on his unit's performance and its first level of disaggregation. To help each manager put his achievement into a departmental context, high, mid and low values of achievement against the plan for each indicator across all LVOs nationally are included.

Relating the report to the major targets, the first target specified that collectors should aim to organize the work of LVOs so that by the 30 June 1986 each office had at least 77 percent of HEO available man-days and 61 percent EO available man-days on control work. The report at Table 9.2 shows whether this was being achieved for one of the LVOs (LVO A) in a collection (see columns 1–4 for AV control) and, in addition, gives the resource devoted to the other major activities of the LVO. The report also expresses the actual allocation of resources to activity as a percentage of the planned allocation. Column 11 shows the total allocation for the whole collection and column 12 reveals the average of actual against plan for the whole collection, thus permitting the comparison of an individual LVO with the collection average.

The second target calls for an 18 percent increase in productive time spent on visits by LVO staff. VAT control visits vary in length and frequency according to the size and risk of trader. The aim is to maximize cost-effectiveness within a control programme by allo-

Table 9.2 *Management information system*
Period: April to September 1986   Allocation of net effective strength to activity   *MIS303*

Man-days	HEO		EO		CO		CA		Total		Collection total	
	Actual 1	% Plan 2	Actual 3	% Plan 4	Actual 5	% Plan 6	Actual 7	% Plan 8	Actual 9	% Plan 10	Actual 11	% Plan 12
LVO A												
AV Control	1,825	102	2,329	106	0	*	0	*	4,154	104	27,992	101
999 Traders	380	45	61	53	0	*	0	*	441	46	2,713	58
Fraud	77	62	63	100	0	*	0	*	140	75	1,065	102
Enforcement	130	74	371	103	479	89	223	100	1,203	93	8,542	99
Registration	57	114	145	122	207	96	113	102	522	105	2,971	107
Deregistration	49	132	109	92	227	106	110	99	495	102	3,060	95
Other	406	195	689	77	335	104	568	102	1,998	101	10,947	99
Net effective strength	2,924	90	3,767	98	1,248	97	1,014	101	8,953	95	57,290	97

cating attention to traders in relation to their apparent revenue risk, while seeking to sustain preventive and deterrent effects. The department sets a productivity target which is designed to encourage this.

The third target for 1986–7 was to achieve 100 percent of the target visits to traders in assignment value (AV) bands 126, 124, 344 and 342 and a minimum of 90 percent of target visits for each of the other AV bands. Each trader who is visited is allocated on the computer system a notional time for completion of the visit, based on certain risk characteristics such as trade, turnover, etc. Those traders known to be of a kind where, historically, significant amounts of additional tax have been recovered are allowed more resource time than for other visits. The notional time is measured in half-day sessions and ranges from one session (half-day) to several days. The AV also shows whether the trader should normally be visited by an HEO or an EO. Table 9.3 shows the achievement of HEO-graded control visiting work broken down to the various assignment value priorities (columns 5–11). A separate report shows achievement of EO-graded control visits against the assignment value priorities.

The fourth indicator, which is targeted *nationally*, was to achieve an increase of between 12 percent and 15 percent in the amount of additional tax discovered on visits compared with 1985–6. This is tax which has not been declared by the trader on returns for perhaps up to 6 years before the VAT control visit, and is an output measure of effectiveness which can be related directly to the application of the efficiency indicator for productivity. Table 9.4 shows in column 7 the amount of underdeclaration per sessions (half-day) being achieved by each LVO and thus its contribution to the national target. Although this is not a local target, it is an important indicator of effectiveness, and local offices compare the figures with their own figures for past periods. The 'projected underdeclaration' at column 8 is not a target either. It is calculated centrally and compares the ratio of local to national performance in the current year against the same ratio established last year, and is for management information only.

In order to determine productivity the notional time allowed for completion of a series of visits is compared to the time available in the periods to make them. The target set in 1985–6 was to achieve

Table 9.3 *Management information system*
Period: April to September 1986   *HEO-graded visits by AV (excluding AV 999)*   *MIS308*

	% of planned cost	No. of visits			% of planned visits to traders of assignment value							AV sessions per man-day	
		Completed	Deferred	% Plan	126	124	122	144	142	162	000	Actual	Plan
	1	2	3	4	5	6	7	8	9	10	11	12	13
Newtown collection – last quarter	97	2,434	87	99	99	92	102	119	122	106	78	1.10	1.20
LVO A	102	681	20	93	92	89	88	146	147	114	58	1.12	1.15
LVO B	106	681	61	105	106	94	112	56	130	141	81	1.03	1.17
LVO C	94	522	49	88	78	83	89	157	107	97	76	0.92	1.20
LVO D	98	639	7	100	85	90	101	148	166	162	51	1.07	1.20
LVO E	94	690	8	90	94	93	89	100	101	97	63	1.06	1.25
LVO F	88	571	8	84	77	82	81	88	111	87	73	0.91	1.20
LVO G	103	789	13	92	92	92	92	129	88	144	67	1.11	1.24
Newtown collection – year to date	98	4,573	166	93	90	89	93	117	119	118	67	1.03	1.20
All High				123									
LVOs Mid				92									
Low				58									

Table 9.4 *Management information system*
Period: April to September 1986   *AV Control visit performance (excluding AV 999)*

	% of planned cost	No. of visits			AV Sessions per man-day		Underdec. per AV sessions		Overdecs £000s
		Completed	Deferred	% plan	Actual	Plan	Actual £	% projected	
	1	*2*	*3*	*4*	*5*	*6*	*7*	*8*	*9*
Newtown collection – last quarter	100	8,285	121	109	1.30	1.25			
Year to date									
LVO A	104	2,215	21	101	1.17	1.26			
LVO B	105	1,988	71	103	1.17	1.22			
LVO C	105	2,305	105	108	1.18	1.25			
LVO D	98	2,370	12	95	1.21	1.26			
LVO E	93	2,422	16	121	1.31	1.25			
LVO F	94	2,117	9	89	1.11	1.28			
LVO G	107	2,108	19	108	1.30	1.25			
Newtown collection – year to date	100	15,525	253	103	1.21	1.25			
All LVOs High				179					
Mid				99					
Low				45					

over a 2–year period a visiting rate equivalent to 1.25 half-day visit sessions per man-day available. This measure of efficiency is set as a basic target for VAT offices to plan their examination of traders' accounts to coincide with the notional time allocated although more time may be given if there are valid reasons for this. Since the notional times set are related to the perceived revenue risk, they are geared to achieve optimum cost-effectiveness. This will also improve the cost/yield ratio of the activity and lead to an improvement in the revenue yield.

Table 9.4 reports achievement of this target in columns 5 and 6, an aggregate of HEO and EO work.

The final VAT target relates to a 5 percent reduction in the average VAT debt owed by traders in the LVOs, i.e. improving the speed with which the tax properly due actually comes in. This is known as 'enforcement' in the LVOs, and Table 9.5 shows not only performance against the 5 percent target (see columns 10 and 11 noting that in this case percentage of plan greater than 100 indicates *under-achievement*) but the other aspects of enforcement work, such as average cost per case against a pre-set local target.

The efficiency and effectiveness indicators are thus applied to all LVOs to set targets and to monitor performance. At the national level they help to indicate areas where more resource is needed, to identify extremes of performance in LVOs and to focus effort on visiting traders who are likely to yield the most additional tax. At the LVO level the targets have given managers a clear guidance as to what their objectives should be. They are used by LVO managers to help diagnose the reasons why their particular office might be under-performing and to identify the possible causes of under-performance. The local managers can then take the appropriate action either by switching more effort into the potentially high yield visits or by trying to encourage and motivate staff. But has the development of the planning, budgeting and management reporting system actually achieved anything and can it be quantified? The answer to both questions is a resounding 'yes'.

In 1985–6 the yield from control activities amounted to £496m, an increase of about 20 percent in real terms (£104m over 1984–5). This was accompanied in 1985–6 by a 17 percent increase in productive time spent on visits compared to 1984–5, and it is estimated that

Table 9.5 *Management information system*
Period: April to September 1986   *Enforcement work*   MIS

	% of planned cost	Average cost per case (£)	% plan	No. of cases received per 100 pay trads	No. of cases completed	Civil recovery No.	% plan	Weeks' work	% plan	Cases on hand Value £000s	% plan	Older than 6 months	% plan	No./100 pay trads	% plan	Value % prev. yr
	1	2	3	4	5	6	7	8	9	10	11	12	13	14	15	16
Newtown collection— last quarter	96	13	103	13	13,738	157	130	5.6	84	15,934	74	855	86	0.21	82	80
LVO A	92	12	98	16	4,428	94	142	3.0	57	1,132	52	8	53	0.18	92	70
LVO B	108	16	105	15	4,308	20	79	7.7	72	4,349	81	317	97	0.40	360	71
LVO C	96	14	101	14	3,468	22	95	5.6	109	1,555	73	35	75	0.27	135	109
LVO D	102	14	103	12	4,190	38	118	6.3	106	1,967	56	204	111	0.21	131	146
LVO E	100	11	108	14	4,165	27	95	3.6	68	1,620	87	28	31	0.05	11	63
LVO F	92	11	93	13	3,918	64	163	6.7	89	2,646	83	171	97	0.11	76	139
LVO G	103	13	117	16	3,739	55	167	6.0	91	2,978	88	166	89	0.28	56	33
Newtown collection— year to date	99	13	104	14	28,216	320	129	5.5	84	16,247	75	927	90	0.21	81	82
All High			167				321		246		127		295		550	
Mid			107				95		96		88		114		79	
LVOs Low			74				4		56		44		8		11	

£16m of additional tax was recovered from VAT control visits due solely to increased productivity.

With experience the department is getting better at assessing and targeting the various factors that contribute to such an increase:

(a) Central planning of visits.
(b) Greater productivity from control staff.
(c) Greater expertise among control staff.

On the last point, for example, the department has in the last few years invested in more specialist training for key staff who visit the largest and most complex traders. Since 1983 the department has nearly trebled the additional tax resulting from these control visits to large traders, with a current return of over £15 for every £1 spent by the department.

One further important point is that research within the department shows that VAT control visiting also has a preventive value. This means that after a visit a trader is likely to behave in a more conscientious manner about the tax he declares. This effect the department calculates to be at least equal to the amount of additional tax discovered.

In VAT the department's strategy for the period to 1991 is to improve trader compliance and control and to counter tax avoidance so that the proper yield from the tax is achieved. In its control visiting the department will aim for the time being to continue the upward trend in the real level of underdeclarations of tax discovered and in cost yield ratios by targeting control resources at the areas of greatest risk and potential revenue yield. There are many uncertain factors, but in broad terms the department expects the total underdeclaration discovered over the period to 1991 to be in the range of £2 billion to £3 billion, excluding the preventive effect (estimated to be at least an equivalent sum).

In seeking to improve the speed with which the tax properly due actually comes in, in 1985–6 the local VAT offices secured a 17 percent real reduction in their share of the debt (worth £46m in total value). In 1986–7 the department is on course for at least a further £60m reduction in the VAT debt.

The new systems have thus begun to demonstrate how the use of key output and performance indicators as part of a comprehensive planning system can produce significant improvements in the productive use of resources. This means that the department is obtaining better value for the expenditure of public money. These systems are the first steps in a staged development. Work is in progress on the detail, design and development of an even more sophisticated VAT management reporting system, based on the same principles but with a more comprehensive range of indicators, which will be reported monthly. It is also planned to introduce pilot management reporting systems for the other two main functional work areas (customs and excise) in 1987–8.

Conclusion

When the department embarked on its management-accounting activity back in 1983 it was of course not starting with a blank sheet of paper. Collectors and assistant secretaries had already some budgets delegated to them, and collectors had in addition a great deal of staff complementing delegation. Initial thinking on the basic shape of a Board's Management Plan had already taken place; operational management information existed for VAT, customs and excise; and the department had a computerized financial accounting system, though an old one. What has happened since is that the new systems introduced (refined by experience) have made the approach to managing the department more modern, systematic and disciplined.

Inevitably, at this stage, staff are still digesting a massive diet of change, and the change at its core is attitudinal. Not surprisingly therefore changes are evolutionary, and some staff have adapted more quickly than others. Work continues on improving communication, which enables managers and staff to see the rationale of management change of this kind in relation to their local pre-occupations and concerns. For example, it has to be clearly demonstrated that those whose main task is to prevent drug-smuggling see that the department's management systems enable them to improve their operational capability.

Targetting undoubtedly has influenced behaviour, e.g. in the productivity increase achieved over the past 2 years by VAT control staff. On the other hand, the department has become more experienced in the setting of targets and is becoming more subtle and sophisticated in their use. Certainly there is a danger that if targets are seen as one-dimensional and crude they could demotivate staff. The department therefore is proceeding on the basis that:

1 Much of the work of the department cannot be measured in any scientific way, and that the department has a vital preventive role which must always be taken into account.
2 Individual assessment of performance by local managers must always pay due regard to quality as well as quantity, and take account of all relevant contributory factors.
3 The setting of targets does not mean that their achievement can be guaranteed or that not completely achieving them should be regarded as failure.

The board wants all managers to use the new systems with discretion and sensitivity and to use management information as a systematic way of asking questions in the search for improvement in the way the work is done but no apology is made for the emphasis on results.

Some staff also see financial management techniques as being all about cutting costs and having the same or larger workload to cope with fewer resources. Again the board is trying to make clear to staff that of course in any large organization of over 25,000, with a running cost budget of some £400m, there must be areas where the spending of money is not always producing the best value. That is why, in delegating budgets to the manager whose decisions incur the expenditure, the department is expecting those in the best position to make value for money decisions to have the budget responsibility and the accountability.

However, because of the new planning and budgeting arrangements, the department is now in a better position to transfer any savings made to other expenditure within the department on the priority activities, which will give the department and hence the public better value for money. In addition, because of the department's highly cost-effective work in VAT, extra resources have been given in this area for the past 3 years and in 1987–8 an additional 330 staff will be put into this work. On customs work too, especially in the prevention of drug-smuggling, resources have been increased at an even greater rate, and this has prompted the department to provide better additional training for all staff on drugs, to invest £10m on technical aids for its staff and to set up experimental work on drugs' targeting to influence staff behaviour and direct activity to the risk areas likely to give better results and improved value for money.

In trying to practise financial management in these ways the department is faced with many constraints not met with in the private sector. For example, the department must carry out a number of statutory duties even though they do not necessarily give value for money from an accounting viewpoint. However, they are services considered necessary from a wider perspective: for example, manning very small airports to help business users, and allowing smaller traders whose turnover is below the registrable minimum (at present £20,500 a year) to be registered for VAT.

It is becoming increasingly apparent that arguments about the allocation of resources across Whitehall are related more and more to the ability of departments to establish a relation between workloads/outputs and a given level of resource. In other words, what can departments give by way of increased performance from increased resources? The department sees this process as very much a continuing one, carrying with it certain logical consequences. The essence of the management reforms is to sharpen authority and accountability for getting results all the way down the management chain. It follows that as more experience and confidence are gained in judging performance, the greater will be the pressure from line managers to remove constraints on their ability to use resources in the way they consider gives optimum value for money.

Already, as we have seen, managers within the department have block budgets and a wide degree of flexibility in how they use them. There are moves within the Treasury towards putting the emphasis on single cash control over departments rather than a staff in post limit. The department is getting greater authority over common services formerly supplied on a tied basis, e.g. stationery supplies and increasingly accommodation. In the same fashion there are similar pressures now pointing to a greater degree of departmental discretion in the treatment of pay and allowances, which are the most important aspects of a manager's budget – over 70 per cent in customs and excise.

The financial management system which customs and excise has introduced can be looked on as a form of 'seamless web'. This connects the department's ability to secure resources for its functions and activities with the ability of people all down the management chain, using the planning, budgeting and performance systems, to account for the resources used and the results obtained. The extent to which the department can continue to improve this accountability will establish the degree to which it is likely to get the resources necessary to do its work.

Index